Learn to create practical programs right away

.No previous knowledge of Java
 is required
. Step-by-step skill acquiring
 through programs & solutions
. Every chapter focuses on an important
 aspect of Java
. Many programs and their outputs in
 order to demonstrate the application of
 programming concepts
. A complete self-contained course for
 individual learning and a workshop
 companion for practical work in Java
. Creating your own Java applets for
 the Internet

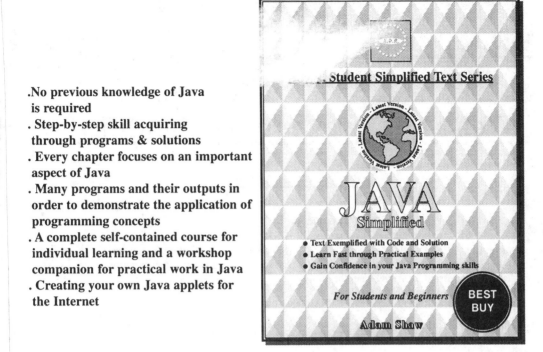

Student Simplified Text Series

JAVA
Simplified

● Text Exemplified with Code and Solution
● Learn Fast through Practical Examples
● Gain Confidence in your Java Programming skills

For Students and Beginners

BEST BUY

Adam Shaw

ISBN: 190 1197 883 Paperback £15.99 1999 Size: 249x190 mm Pages: 325 (Total)

. No previous knowledge of C++
 is required
. Step-by-step skill acquiring
 through programs & solutions
. Every chapter focuses on an important
 aspect of C++
. Many programs and their outputs in
 order to demonstrate the application of
 programming concepts
. A complete self-contained course for
 individual learning and a workshop
 companion for practical work in C++

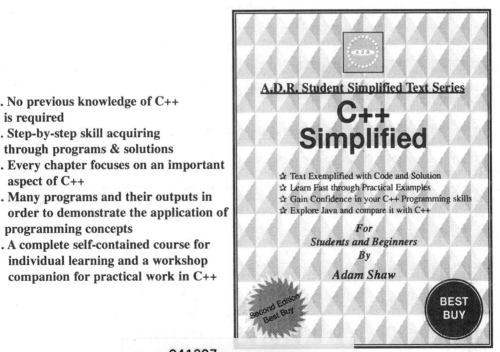

A.D.R. Student Simplified Text Series

C++
Simplified

☆ Text Exemplified with Code and Solution
☆ Learn Fast through Practical Examples
☆ Gain Confidence in your C++ Programming skills
☆ Explore Java and compare it with C++

For
Students and Beginners
By
Adam Shaw

Second Edition
Best Buy

BEST BUY

041207

ISBN: 190 1197 999 Paperba____ ___0x190 mm Pages: 309 (Total)

A.D.R. Student Simplified Text Series

Web Site Development Simplified

Latest Version

© A . D . R . (London) Limited 2000

British Library Cataloguing in Publication Data

A catalogue record for this book is available from the British Library

ISBN 190 1197 808

Trademarks and registered Trademarks & Acknowledgements

Computer hardware and software brand names mentioned in this book are protected by their respective trademarks and are acknowledged as being the property of their owners. ADR cannot guarantee the accuracy of information.

Warning and Disclaimer

Every effort has been made to make this book as complete and as accurate as possible, but no warranty or fitness is implied. The information given in this book, is on an "as is " basis. The author and the publisher shall have neither liability or responsibility to any person or entity with respect to any loss or damages arising from the information contained in this book or from the use of the Web site or programs in it. Readers are advised to check the current position with the appropriate organisations before entering into any arrangements whatsoever.

Direct Order

In case of difficulty, you can obtain this copy from the publisher.

A . D . R . (London) Limited
24 St. Alban Road
Bridlington
YO16 7SS
England

Tel: 01262 400323/605538
Fax: 01262 605538
E-mail: sales@ adrlondon.ltd.uk
Web site: http:// www.adrlondon.ltd.uk

Printed in Great Britain.

A.D.R. Student Simplified Text Series

A person who searches for knowledge is a student

WEB SITE DEVELOPMENT
Simplified

. Build a cost-effective Web Site yourself
. Manage your own Web Site yourself with least cost
. Use it with confidence to achieve your aims on the Internet

By

Daniel Lancser

A.D.R.(London)Limited

Preface

Why should you buy this book?

ADR Student Simplified Text Series is comprised of practical programming and Web books for you to acquire new knowledge and skills and apply them in order to improve your chances of success in this increasingly competitive world. The amount of positive feedback we have received from our readers confirms that self-motivated people have undoubtedly benefited from our books.

In accordance with our approach to the subject matter and readership, a person who searches for knowledge is a student. Therefore, if you buy this book with a view to learning and, applying this knowledge in order to develop your own Web site or contribute towards the development of a Web site at work, as a member of a team, you are a student. Indeed, you will find this book worth possessing.

Irrespective of your current economic activity, this book is intended to guide you through scores of worked and fully illustrated examples of the application of HTML 4.0 version for the development of a Web site. It also provides you with some relevant invaluable information and additional sources of practical information on how to go about doing business on the Internet.

Chapters 2-11 are filled with numerous practical examples and their solutions, which are coded in HTML 4.0 version and explained. For testing each worked example, the HTML document is written for previewing it in the Internet Explorer. The screen captures for all worked examples are included so that you can see the outcome of each one. You can preview your HTML documents in another browser. For instance, you can preview documents in the Netscape Navigator. The solved practical examples which may appear to be simple at first but they demonstrate the development of the Web site. The output of the document developed is an important part of an example as it will enable you to learn the features of the" markup language" introduced. You are advised to try these out on your computer as you progress through the book. A practical skill is best learnt by a hands-on approach; therefore, it is recommended that you work through these examples. The other parts of the book include concise and precise up to-date practical information on marketing your business on the Internet.

It is a practical book and thus covers those topics for which space was available to demonstrate their application. I believe that the contents of this book without the inclusion of some other HTML 4.0 topics, is sufficient for the development and working of a Web site. For any specific need, you have to obtain some reference books which include worked examples and solutions to meet your practical requirements. There are a large number of reference books, but you must select a book, which provides full proof of the working of the solved examples, not just a skeleton of the solution.

The emphasis is on learning from experience and applying it. The book will enable you to achieve your objective to develop a Web site either individually or as a member of a group at work or on a programme of Web site development learning. It will lay the foundation for advancing your practical skills in this comparatively new technology.

I hope you derive as much pleasure and satisfaction from it as I enjoyed in its writing. Good luck!

Daniel Lancaster
England

June 2000

Contents

****

Preface

Chapter 4 Including lists in your Web page 61

Chapter 5 Colours & style sheets 81

Chapter 6 Including tables in your Web page 110

Chapter 7 Including complex tables in your Web page 133

Chapter 8 Creating documents with links 146

Chapter 9 Frames in your documents (1) 180

Chapter 10 Dynamic frames in your documents (2) 200

Chapter 11 Forms for on-line application 225

Chapter 12 Thinking about E-commerce 246

X

Chapter 13

Your Web pages for public viewing 253

References 264

Index 277

Chapter 1

Introduction

The chapter introduces you to some essential ideas necessary to understand the World Wide Web, the Internet and related services required to be on-line. It lays the foundation towards the understanding of the next chapter and beyond.

. Introduction

The **World Wide Web or WWW** or **Web or W3** is a distributed information service. It was developed, in the early 1990s, at CERN, the European Centre for Practical Physics, Geneva. In short, the **Web** is the most exciting and popular part of the **Internet**, that is a computer communications network system. It was developed during the 1970s in the USA. It is now a huge collection of computer networks linked together world wide. You can even link loosely your own PC system to the Internet.

. What is a network?

The word network features in this chapter and elsewhere in this book. It is essential to establish its meaning in the context of the Internet, prior to discussing the Internet. It will help you to understand the Internet and the Web.

In its simplest terms, the network means computers linked to each other by cables in order to share and exchange data or information. The network also enables its users to share other devices such as printers, and other resources. Historically, there were just two types of networks namely, **Local Area Network (LAN)** and **Wide Area Network (WAN)**. A local area network exists in many organisations in both the private and public sectors of the economy. For instance, you can find **LAN** in schools and companies. Some commercial firms have local area networks if they do not have to cover a large geographical area, to exchange and share data and other computing resources with colleagues.

The diagram 1 exemplifies a local area network. You can see a number of devices are linked together.

This interconnection of computers and peripherals, such as different kinds of printers, scanners, storage devices (hard disks) enables four persons working at the same time on their PC's, to share computing resources. In a network system, a PC or a computer is called the **client**. In this diagram, you can see a PC labelled as the **server**. The prime function of this computer (**server**) is to administer the network by means of software called the server. This is why this particular computer is known by this name. The server co-ordinates the activities of all equipment and the network as a whole. Thus, it is more powerful than other PC's in the LAN. It has its own large storage device (hard disc) and fast printer. It has to be faster than the other PC's linked to it. It must also have faster peripherals attached to it, so that it can serve, if necessary, all users/clients simultaneously.

An example of a network

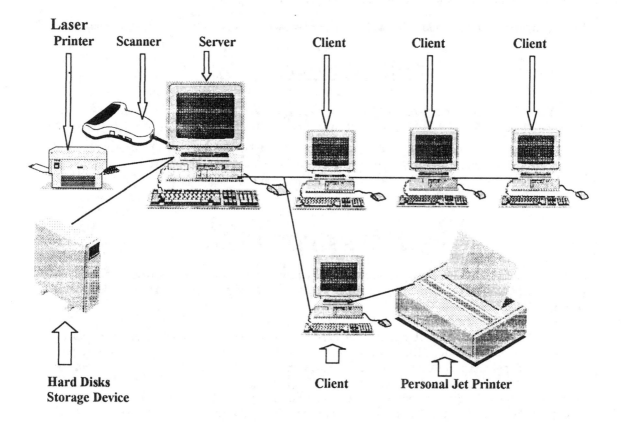

Laser Printer   **Scanner**   **Server**   **Client**   **Client**   **Client**

Hard Disks Storage Device   **Client**   **Personal Jet Printer**

Diagram 1

A LAN is connected by dedicated electrical cables. These cables are shown by simple lines in the above diagram.

The **Wide Area Network (WAN)** exists mainly in large organisations, as they can handle a large volume of data and cover a large geographical area at a very fast speed. Since it covers a wide area, it can have a number of LAN's at different places within the organisation at remote locations.   Thus, a WAN comprises of several LAN's at different places. A WAN is connected by high speed and high volume cables (optical fibre cables). In order to operate the WAN over a wide geographical area, radio or satellite links are required. WANs are rather complicated and expensive, and require the services of specialist telecommunication organisations. In the UK, BT, Mercury , AT & T are three such WAN connections service providers.

The invention of the network has led to the development of the Internet. Now, it is the right time and place in this book to discuss the Internet.

The Internet (Net)

Since the Web is the most exciting and popular part of the Internet, it is desirable to know the answer to the question:

. What is the Internet?

In order to answer this question, firstly, I must briefly trace the history below that has led to the development of today's Internet.

Yes, indeed, it is a computer communications network system. Its historical development goes back to the year 1969, when in the USA, the Advanced Research Projects Agency, abbreviated as **ARPA**, was established by the United States Department of Defence. The ARPA established a network known as Advanced Research Projects Agency Network, abbreviated as **ARPAnet**. The ARPAnet connected a number of military and research sites, developed a communication protocol, and methods for routing data through communication paths. In the 1970s, still in the USA, some other networks developed, using the technology developed by **ARPAnet**. These networks were used by universities and some commercial enterprises.

Again, in the USA, in the 1980s, some more networks developed. Among these networks, the National Science Foundation **(NSF)** developed **NSFNET**, which was used by universities. The NSFNET provided very high speed connections, and thus became popular.

Some more networks developed and interconnected, and were used by universities, researchers and some commercial enterprises. In Britain, in 1984, the Joint Academic Network (Janet) developed from a number of separate networks. Similar developments took place in some other parts of the world. Thus, the beginning of ARPANET and its various developments led to the growth of a number of other networks world wide.

This growth of **inter**connected **net**works collectively is known as the Internet (or **Net** for short). With the aid of diagram 2, you can visualise the Internet as a huge (over 70,000 networks) network of networks of interconnected computers world wide. At the beginning of the third millennium, the Internet is not just a network of computers for some universities or government agencies. On the contrary, it is increasingly used by all kinds of small and large organisations in both private and public sectors. It is also increasingly used by people from all walks of life all over the world through services provided by commercial organisations. These commercial organisations have made it possible for personal computer users to loosely link their PC's to the Internet by means of the modem and telephone line. It can bring a vast amount of information into your home or office in the form of words, numbers, pictures, visual, and audio. Its major features are that it:

- **connects a myriad of computers all over the world** - tens of thousands of computers, which are known as servers are connected to the Net to make up the Net itself. Each year, the Net is getting bigger and bigger.

- **has databases** - information held within a computer system. There are an enormous number of databases on the Net for all kinds of purposes, one can imagine. For instance, databases for library resources, travel information, entertainment information, and weather information. You can think of any other topic, and it is highly likely that you will find some information on it on the Net.

- **facilitates e-commerce -** the new buzz word invented in the late 1990's. It is another way of doing business which relies on the Net. You can do all kinds of business on the Net. For instance, a shopkeeper can place an order for goods. A housewife can buy groceries from a store, and so on. You can set up your own shop, accountancy, estate agency or any other type of business on the Internet, and hope to sell your products or services to your prospective customer/clients anywhere in the world.

- **is a means of e-mail -** you can send and receive post or messages instantly anywhere in the world by means of the Net.

- **has newsgroups -** There are very many newsgroups for topical discussion with like-minded people across the world. It is highly likely that on the Internet you will find more than one news group dedicated to the subject area of your interest on which you wish to exchange, information, views or whatever. It could be baking bread, or looking for a brain surgeon for a friend. Newsgroups are often used for 'chat' . If you are interested in entertaining yourself , or debating a topic and the like, you can try newsgroup.

- **has FTP - File Transfer Protocol -** On the Internet, you can transfer a file across the Internet from one computer to another. It is often used by companies for things such as software delivery instantly and directly to the computer where it is needed.

. Internet is not a single entity

It does not exist as an entity in its own right. Therefore, it is not owned by any one organisation or a group of companies. Thus, there is no single centre or an organisation to manage the Internet world wide. It is managed and owned by thousands of individual organisations who own and manage these individual networks throughout the world, which constitute the Internet.

Some writers show the Internet by an uneven circle or by a cloud form figure surrounded by computers, which are linked to it making a network together. These representations give the wrong impression that the internet is some sort of co-ordinating body. It is not so. In reality, the Internet does not exist as such.

The fact which you must know is that a computer which is connected to other computers in order to form the Internet has a unique name or address. This address is known as Domain Name System (**DNS**). More about it later on.

Now, you should be asking yourself :

. How are the interconnections and communication links between a myriad of computers all over the world organised/managed?

The voluntary agreements between the owners of a myriad of computers all over the world concerning the technical aspects such as the Internet Protocols and addressing methods (see glossary) have led to certain rules which are observed by the owners of networks. There a number of organisations such as:

- **The Internet Society**

- **Internet Engineering Task Force**

- **The Internet Assigned Number Authority**

who are able to communicate among themselves in the interest of devising voluntary acceptable rules concerning technical aspects. There are no international political pressures on the Internet, though in any individual country across the world, there may be some local legal restrictions concerning the storage, retrieval, manipulation and transfer of information in all forms on the Internet.

. Internet Service Providers (ISP)

Since the Internet has been proved to influence greatly all kinds of users, the Internet Service Providers (ISP) have their own rules concerning such important aspects as indecent advertising, sending unsolicited e-mail, obscene sex material, pornography and children, and hackers gaining unauthorised access to other users' information. Therefore, it is important for you when looking for an Internet service provider to ensure that your data held by the organisation in various files such as e-mail will be secured, free from computer virus, protected from unauthorised users, and the service on the whole is friendly and reliable.

In the United Kingdom, most ISPs are registered with the Nominet UK. There is also an association of ISPs known as ISPA. Thus, they are familiar with the technical and contractual details of the registration of domain names. In some other countries, there are similar organisations to whom ISPs are associated for the recognition of their status and the standard of services provided. You may prefer to do business with a member of ISPA, because it is their trade organisation.

. <u>Which Internet service provider should you choose?</u>

The Internet service providers have their computers interconnected to make up the Internet. This is the easiest way to visualise the Internet as it is there for you to use it. The Internet Service Providers link their computers via a high-speed link. Possibly, you have already seen advertisements of two big ISPs namely AOL and CompuServe. In fact, both companies have been amalgamated to become even bigger. It is in the press that they intend to keep operating their own line of services. World wide domination in this field! <u>You have to open an account with a service provider for dial-up access to the Net.</u>

These two large service providers also provide **on-line information** services, such as electronic conferencing system, electronic mail, and databases on hundreds of topics. In the broad sense, on-line system means the ability of a computer system to work interactively with its users. This way, the computer responds to each instruction given by the user, and prompts the user for information when necessary. In these days, on-line systems are common as most computers have some sort of databases.

Different users have different considerations for choosing a service provider. A private user, say a student, will prefer a service provider whose service charges are minimal or almost free, as he/she may not care too much about such aspects as continuity, and can always change the service provider. On the other hand, a business has to give serious consideration to such important aspects as listed:

- initial cost   - monthly cost   - reliability of data held
- accessibility - both linking its own computer to the ISP's computer and making use of the Net without any delays
- security of data held on ISP's computer system
- timely, efficient, reliable and user-friendly, technical support
- the ability of ISP to understand the changing needs of a business, and how to meet them without any fuss

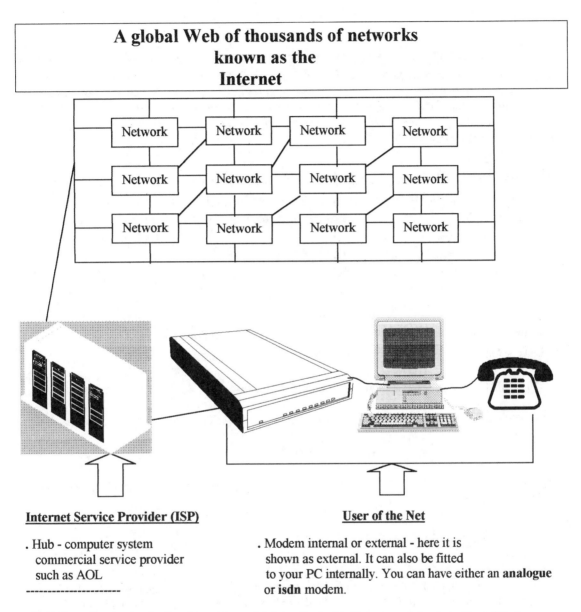

**A global Web of thousands of networks
known as the
Internet**

Internet Service Provider (ISP)   **User of the Net**

. Hub - computer system   . Modem internal or external - here it is
  commercial service provider   shown as external. It can also be fitted
  such as AOL   to your PC internally. You can have either an **analogue**
  -----------------------   or **isdn** modem.

. Telephone line is attached to the modem which is attached to the computer externally or fitted
  internally. For an **Isdn** modem, in the UK, BT can install for you either home highway or business
  highway for faster speed, if you can afford the extra costs of installing and running it. Your phone
  bill will be higher, if you use the home or business highway. First carry out cost and benefit analysis!

Diagram 2

. **ISDN** access link - your business may find it necessary to install for the sake of faster speed of data transmission an **I**ntegrated **S**ervices **D**igital **N**etwork (ISDN) link. It is a high-speed or highway telephone network that provides a faster communication link to the Internet. It may even prove cheaper than the ordinary telephone line, as you pay for it when you use it. If you are in the UK, try to get the latest information and offers available to BT customers for installing and using either home highway or business highway lines to be on the Net.

. **Domain Name** for your business. It is the name by which an individual or an organisation is known on the Internet. For instance: **sales@adrlondon.ltd.uk** is the e-mail address of the publishers of this book. In any e-mail address, the domain name comes after the symbol @. Thus

sales@<u>adrlondon.ltd.uk</u>

⇑

Domain name

This domain name ends with **.uk**. It indicates that it is a UK based e-mail address. The other three endings or formats of domain names for the UK are: **.co.uk**   **.org.uk**   **.plc.uk**

It is likely that you have seen a domain name ending with **.com**

This ending or format of domain name is widely used in the USA. The other international formats are:

.net   **.org**

The UK-based company or individual can have any of the international formats. There are no international barriers to stop you doing so.

Registering a domain name

You can register your domain name with a service provider, but It will cost you something (see below). You may find that your service provider includes the registering cost in their quoted price. It is in your own interest to talk to a number of service providers to find the right service at the right price for your requirements.

If your business is a corporate business, such as PLC or Limited, its name is already protected due to its incorporation as a public or private limited company. I have been advised by the Minister for Small Businesses and E-Commerce," Domain names in "**.uk**" are managed by Nominet UK, a not-for-profit organisation based in Oxford." You can contact **Nominet** directly at:

Nominet UK, Sanford Gate, Sandy Lane West, Oxford OX4 5LB

Telephone: 01865 33 22 11   Fax: 01865 33 22 99

e-mail: nominet@nominet.org.uk   website: http://www.nominet.org.uk

I have been further informed by the same minister," Nominet is not a Government body, and is not regulated by the Government, although we have a close informal relationship with them. Other domain names are managed by bodies in the appropriate country." You can find a list of these, together with links, at:

http://www.norid.no/domreg.html

In fact, you can directly register your Domain Name with the Nominet UK. The direct registration fee is £80 plus VAT. Transactions are taken either by telephone, fax or e-mail and will be processed within three working days, after which time the Domain Name will become registered for a period of two years. The registration fee covers the registration of a Domain Name for two years after which a renewal fee is levied. Nominet UK does not provide any legal, technical or other support.

You can also register your Domain Name in the **.uk** through an ISP firm. If you do so, you are asking them to act as your agent for your application to Nominet UK. If you do so, you will be entering into a binding contract at the same time. Contract 1 is between yourself and Nominet UK, and contract 2 is between yourself and your ISP as your agent. Nominet UK is not a party to the second contract. Thus, you must understand your rights and obligations, concerning your present and future business dealings with your agency(ISP firm). For instance, you may wish to change to a new ISP and take your Domain Name with you without paying any additional charges to your present ISP(agency). It is better to have your agreement in writing.

• Why should you rush now to register it?

You might have read in the national quality press that the longer you leave it to register your Domain Name the more difficult it will become. You may be disappointed to discover that the name of your choice has been registered by another person or business. In fact, people have set themselves up as businesses selling registered domain names in the same way as you can buy a limited company off the shelf. Many ISPs sell can sell you just a Domain Name.

• Is it possible to transfer your current Domain Name to another service provider?

Most service providers will be willing to accept your current Domain Name when you agree to do business with them. As stated above, you must make sure that you can transfer the Domain Name elsewhere without a charge.

• What is a Web site?

It is an interactive document. It is an electronic version of a document or photo, illustration or any other thing you can think of. For instance, a leaflet on this book can be a web site used for selling this book. If it is a web site, then it is in the electronic format, and on-line, where prospective customers can see it. In fact, on-line, the leaflet is just like a shop, where a customer can place an order, by filling in the order form. The order form is a part of this leaflet. You can find all kinds of information on the web. For example, you can make an airline booking from London to Moscow. In fact, it is highly likely that you will find some good bargains to travel across the world. There are very many web sites for you to visit.

One of the differences between web pages and traditional types of publishing is that web sites can contain hyperlinks(links for simplicity). A link is un underlined word or phrase, or an image. When you click it with a mouse it opens the required page. In fact, this required page can be anywhere on the Web. A great advantage of the web site is that it usually has forms for visitors to fill in. For instance, you can place an order for the purchase of C++ simplified by filling in the order form when you visit ADR web site. Many large organisations have built their web sites with a search facility in order to assist the visitor to find the required information.

• <u>How many E-mail addresses should you have?</u>

- It depends on your personal or business needs. For instance, a small
  business may require three e-mail addresses, say one for orders, enquiries and accounts. For example:

order@adllondon.ltd.uk	for sales orders
infor @adrlondon.ltd.uk	for information service
account@adrlondon.ltd.uk	for accounts

• <u>'adds-on' facility</u>

Your business may require some off-the shelf service, such as a payment system for transactions on Web for which you require a software package and your service provider should support it. Some companies provide transaction processing across the Internet. Such companies offer their services under the popular banner of secure payment system that operates over the Internet. If you install one, such a payment system can be integrated into your new or established site, but you will need the help of such a service provider for integrating it without any serious technical and payment problems. You have to discuss this payment system with your bankers as well.

If visitors to your web site have to fill in some forms, then you have to make sure that your ISP can provide you a free CGI script and E-mail replies in English without any codification. Often such services are known as public domain, free of charge and can include other facilities such as logging visitors to your site, and a guest book.   It is worth talking to a number of service providers in order to compare and contrast their range of services against your set criteria. It may be that by gathering sufficient information your requirements change and lead to a better plan for deciding with which Internet service provider to do business.

• How much one can expect per year for hiring web site hosting facilities?

Different companies offer different facilities. You have to get web site hosting packages from a number of Internet and Web service providers. For instance, one company offer 30 MB web space, multiple E-mail forwarding, web forwarding and registration of domain name for one year contract for £364.

Another company for the same service ask for £195. A third ISP's package for 100 MB space, regis-tering Domain Name, web forwarding, multiple E-mail forwarding for one year is offered for £99 per annum. So, charges vary greatly.

• Does it mean that the quality of service differs according to charges?

 You need to establish this before you enter into a binding contract with your ISP.

. The Web

At the beginning, I stated,

>   "the Web is the most exciting and popular part of the Internet."

Now, is the right place and time to expand this idea. By now you know that when someone says the Internet, it implies interconnected computers across the world. Of course, these interconnected comput-ers store masses of information. The Web is a method of accessing this stored information by anyone anywhere in the world by means of a computer system. The computer system can be a PC, which is equipped with some relevant software, a modem and a telephone line. Of course, the PC user has to have an account with the Internet service provider.

The Web has made it possible to ensure that the information stored on the Internet can be accessed by anyone. In general, the Web's appeal is that most people find it easy to make use of it. On the other hand, other parts of the Internet are not so easy to use, and require some technical skills and experience.

. How is the Information stored on computers around the Internet?

  - The information is stored in the **form of pages or documents** on computers. These pages may contain text, illustrations, photographs, animation, video, and sound clips. They are posted (stored) on the Web. No one can change their contents, except the publisher of these documents.

. Each document has **special codes.** The codes are written in HTML , which is an acronym for **Hypertext Markup Language**. The purpose of the HTML codes is two-fold as shown below:

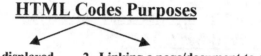

HTML Codes Purposes

1. How a document is to be displayed   **2. Linking a page/document to other documents**

. How can one view a Web page?

Two different types of software are needed at two different places to view a Web page on the Internet.

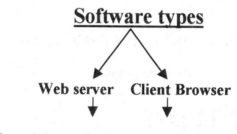

Software types

Web server   Client Browser

Software being used by the
computer holding the
Web page

Software being used by the computer
which is used to access the Web page
and some other pages which may be linked to it

. Web Server

Nothing is possible on the Internet without the web server. Thus, in order to access a vast amount of information world wide, you have to install a browser software on your computer. A **server** is a computer which serves other computers on the Internet. It can only do so through the web **server software**. The computer, on which a particular web page is located, is the server. See again diagram 1.

It is worth mentioning that in the context of the Internet and the Web, you may hear that there are many commercial Web Server service providers to allow you to use the Internet. It simply means the Internet service provider **(ISP)**. **Why?**

It is due to the fact that these service providers have their computers interconnected, and hold Web pages. These interconnected computers communicate with each other on the Internet. They serve each other on the Internet. A server runs most of the time, except when it requires servicing. A server communicates on the internet with the client program, which you know by now is called the **browser**. Sometimes, it is also called a **graphical Web browser**, because it operates by means of a mouse input device. The mouse moves a pointer to a required icon, menu or some graphics. Modern computers are graphical based, as you can use the mouse, have colours, pictures, sounds and a graphical display. For older computers, you can have a text-based browser. This book is concerned with modern computers. Thus, the graphical browser is simply called browser. **Is there a list of members of the Nominet?**

Members of the Nominet UKare ISP companies. A member list, 98 pages, is available on Nominet web site. The list is in random order and is re-ordered periodically.

. <u>What exactly does a browser do?</u>

For the user, the browser performs two specific **major** tasks. These are as follows:

- to decode the HTML code in the Web page; and

- to display the decoded page (document) for you to make use of it.

Once, the document has been decoded and the decoded page is currently displayed on the user's computer screen, then the browser interacts with the user, and **performs further tasks** described below:

- The user clicks the **hyperlink** , which is in the web page.

. <u>What is this hyperlink?</u>

Its purpose is to enable the user to link the current document to another required document on the Web or on the local system. It responds directly to the user's interest. The user clicks it with a mouse to go to another page. The link to a page anywhere on the Web requires the full URL for the page. The link to another page on the same system requires a path to the file in which the page is stored. The hyperlinks are shown in colours. Sometimes, due to background colours, a hyperlink may not be visible, but you can make hyperlinks stand out. Hyperlinks have different colours to represent their current state. For instance, a visited link is usually in purple. If your window has a purple background, it will not be visible. Without hyperlinks in documents, there will not be any connections to pages on the Web. The text you get when the link is made is called hypertext. Hyperlinks and hypertext are at the heart of HTML and make it so important to learn for developing your web site.

. <u>How does it happen?</u>

In response to the user's click, the **browser** communicates via the **HTTP (Hyper Text Transfer Protocol) network protocol** with the Web server, where the required document is stored. The required document can be anywhere on the Web. The link may take you to a page which is published by another publisher and kept on another computer on the Internet anywhere in the world. **Why?**

This is because a publisher of a document is not restricted to creating links only to his/her document. The hyperlink is like a jump to another related page of information. The browser requests for the specified document to be called up.

. How does the Web server respond?

In response to the browser's request for the specified document, the Web server via the HTTP protocol presents the required document to the browser.

. What happens next?

The browser now is able to interpret or decode the document, and presents it to the user in the required format. Now, the user is able to read the document. If the user wants to link this document to other pages, he can do so by clicking the hyperlink accordingly. The process can be repeated as long as the user is searching for the required information or service.

. Is it possible to trace all links which the user has tried ?

The hyperlinks can be traced back to the beginning of the hyperlinking process by the user. The browser keeps a record of all links the user made as he/she visited some documents.

. What is the advantage of keeping a record of hyperlinks by the browser?

This backtracking record can enable the user to know how he/she has been able to link to some documents in order to find the required information or service. It may be that the user has to visit a large number of pages kept on different servers in different countries. The user can return to a page several stages further back, if he/she wants.

. Which browser should you install on your computer?

There are a number of browser software packages on the market. You can obtain a browser software free of charge with some computer magazines, as **Freeware software**. If you do not pay for a piece of software, it is termed as freeware. When it costs you a nominal charge, it is called **shareware software**. The most commonly used browsers are Microsoft Internet Explorer and Netscape Communicator (originally known as Netscape's Navigator) from Netscape Communications Corporation. These two browsers dominate the market. There are many other browsers which are freeware or shareware. This book is not about browsers. It is highly likely that your Internet Service Provider (ISP) will supply you with one browser as part of the service (ask for it). For instance, on my computer, there is Microsoft Internet Explorer supplied by AOL. I also have Internet Explorer 4 as part of Microsoft Windows 98. Recently, I have acquired the latest version on Internet Explorer 5. If you have Windows 95 or Windows 98, you already have on your computer Microsoft Internet Explorer. For whatever personal reasons, you may be enthusiastic about browsers. In a super bookstore, you can find a number of books on browsers, especially on Microsoft Internet Explorer 4 and 5.

. <u>Microsoft Internet Explorer 4 and 5 versions</u>

If you do not have it, you can download it free at:

http://www.microsoft.com/ie

Anyway, it comes with Windows 98. This browser is the single interface to both the Internet and local windows system. In fact, your Windows 98 also includes a personal web Server. This is an excellentidea, as you can use it in order to test your Web pages on your own system. Once you have finalised your Web page, you can then put it on the World Wide Web for the world to see it. Windows 98 also includes Microsoft FrontPage Express and Web Publishing Wizard. You will learn more about them later on. If you have Windows 95, I recommend you to upgrade your Windows, as you can have all these tools for your working with the Internet. It is worth it.

You can also download from Microsoft Web site version 5. It is still comparatively new, but will soon become popular.

. <u>Netscape Communicator</u>

It runs on UNIX, Macs and PCs. It is a commercial Web browser. You can obtain an evaluation copy on Web at:

http://home.netscape.com

If you are installing it for your personal use, in that case, it is free for you. It is also free for educational institutions, but commercial organisations should pay for it, after the trial period of 30 days.

. <u>Are there any problems due to different browsers used by different users?</u>

It is true to say that most browsers are similar in their operations and easy to use. They all make use of

HTML and HTTP protocol. However, it must be noted that there are some differences in their designs and working, which may hinder your working with the Web. Some important differences are outlined below:

• Different extensions to HTML standard 4

The developers of Netscape, which is one of two the most commonly used browsers, discovered that HTML is not sufficient for formatting instructions, and thus extended the language by including their own **extensions**. This simply means Netscape displays documents in its own way. Since, there is a great rivalry between Netscape and Microsoft organisations, the developers at Microsoft have also added their own HTML extensions. So, the Internet Explorer displays documents differently.

The HTML is supposed to be a standard language. It has grown to the **current HTML 4. 0** standard, and both organisations have endorsed this standard, yet one can expect further extensions to HTML by these competitors for winning customers world wide. I believe one is right in thinking that soon one of these giants will introduce something new to their browser. To be almost certain, the other organisation in a matter of a few weeks will introduce their own new features. The race for winning customers all over the world will continue. The problem is that these different extensions to HTML can only be interpreted by the same browser.

• Old and new versions of browsers

The older versions of browsers tend to support the earlier levels (standards) of HTML. Thus, you will find out that all HTML 4.0 standard commands are not accepted by older versions of browsers. The whole idea of the Web page is that others can view it on their systems. If they cannot do so, then it defeats your objectives.

• How can a browser communicate with the Web server?

Web browsers communicate over the network with **Web Servers** by means of the:

Hyper Text Transfer Protocol which is widely known as **http**. It is also known as:

- **T**ransmission **C**ontrol **P**rotocol – **TCP** and

- **I**nternet **P**rotocol – **IP**

The network (Internet) protocol is a set of agreed symbols and rules that allow communication between computers in the network.

. Are there other protocols used on the Internet?

Yes, there are many other protocols used on the Internet. These protocols have their own rules and symbols. Three examples of such a protocol are **Gopher, FTP and WAIS.** These protocols have their own specific purposes. On the other hand, the **http protocol** incorporates numerous network protocols, and thus it is the **multipurpose** protocol. The Web browsers speak the **http** protocol. The **http protocol** enables the user by means of the browser to access all kinds of services on the Internet.

. What is the purpose of the URL?

URL is the acronym for Uniform Resources Locators. Its purpose is to take you to a particular required document on the Net. It creates a link. It is simply the full address of a page or document you are interested in on WWW. For instance:

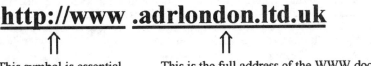

http://www .adrlondon.ltd.uk

This symbol is essential   This is the full address of the WWW document required
in this format

This particular URL will locate the page/document on the company called A.D.R.(London) Ltd., which is registered in the UK. In fact, URL is the key to finding and opening a page on WWW.

It is possible to install more than one browser on your machine. We can only hope that soon all browsers support the standard HTML without adding to it their own extensions. That has to be seen yet!

.Browsing

In order to locate and retrieve information on the Web, you have to **dip** into that area of the **WWW** that interests you on the Internet. This **dip** which is in fact a searching method is called **browsing**. It is also known as **surfing.**

. Search systems

A search system/engine is another piece of software with which you will work. It can help you to access the required information by any of the three search methods namely: search by category, search by subject and search within the Web page. There are many free search engines on the Internet. Some of the popular search engines are: Yahoo!, Lycos, HotBot, SearchUK, AltaVista. Yahoo! is the most popular search engine. Search engines, mailing lists and newsgroups are major categories in this area.

Yahoo's home page screen capture

Diagram 3

.Meta search engines

These search engines perform a search by means of more than one search engine simultaneously. Having found the required information, they collate it and then present it to you. They are much more powerful search engines. You can get more information about them from the world famous ISP Yahoo! Try now the following full URL:

www.yahoo.com/computers_and_internet/internet/world_wide_web/searching_the_web/all_in_one-search_pages

.Mailing lists

They are useful for exchanging E-mail with people who share your interest. Once you have subscribed to one or more mailing lists, you will start getting regular information and news on a regular basis via

E-mail. Mailing lists are, in fact, on almost any subject you are interested in. List members are fairly polite. If you do not wish to be flooded with E-mail messages, first subscribe to just one list. One of the most popular databases for obtaining mailing lists is **Liszt** on the Internet. It is itself a list of mailing lists at:

http:// www.liszt.com

There are about 100,000 mailing lists to choose from. The other popular source of obtaining mailing lists is the **List-Link database**. They can register you for free 15-day trial for mailing lists and their other sources of information. Find out more about them and their lists and other sources at:

http://www.list-link.com

Once you become a member of one of the selected mailing lists, you will receive a welcome message via E-mail. It will advise you how to cancel your subscription. Usually, a mailing list is free. If they ask you to pay, just search for another list. It is highly likely that you will find a free mailing list. A mailing list can be good to your business for marketing and eventually selling your products on-line. So, subscribe to at least one mailing list to assess your chances of doing business on the Net.

. <u>Newsgroups</u>

Another name for newsgroups is Usenet. Newsgroup has nothing to do with news in the real sense of the word. Newsgroups cover a vast subjects. You can always find many groups with your particular interest. Not all groups are serious enough. Some range of groups are professional to get answers to your questions. The first step is to find out those groups that are likely to be interested in your products or services which you wish to market. In the form of frequently asked questions **(FAQs)**, it is worth trying to introduce your business.

You may be reading this book for your personal web site development. In that case, you still have to search for those newsgroups which are free from information of dubious legality. Watch it carefully!

At the time of entering into a binding a contract with an ISP, find out if they have their news server for your use as part of your contract. Both MS Internet Explorer and Netscape Communicator can read news. For a good quality news reading, you may consider obtaining one, possibly from the Internet.

Chapter 2

Foundation of Web page design

The purpose of this chapter is to enable you to acquire the basic knowledge and skills of us-ing HTML in order to create your first, simple Web page. You will also learn how to use some of the essential tools which are part and parcel of your Windows 98 software.

. What is HTML?

HTML is an abbreviation for **Hyper**text Mark-up Language, which is used for presenting documents within the Web pages. It is not considered as a programming language, but **markup-language**. You can create and edit HTML documents by using any editing tools. You can use Microsoft Word for this purpose. Whenever, you access a **Web** document, follow the hyperlinks by using your mouse pointer, see animated images on your screen, and so on, all these things are created by using the HTML language. The HTML enables you

- to create pre-formatted text.

- to format documents - you can choose numerous typeface styles.

- to create hyperlinks – the hyperlinks allow you to point to such things as multimedia files, other Web documents.

- to create tables, lists, frames....

- to create graphical images and link these to other documents – you can link these to other documents all over the internet.

- interactive tasks – a user can perform various tasks. For example, form completion.

- other features – such as downloading and running of Web pages on your system.

The HTML language has its own set of symbols and rules that are part of http. The current version or standard is 4. Like any other subject area in the IT field, it is also being developed. This book uses the current version 4.

• <u>Creating your first HTML document</u>

The HTML documents contain plain text, **ASCII code.** ACSII or Ascii is an acronym for American Standard Code for Information Interchange. It has been widely used since it was introduced in 1963. It has 128 different character values in the range 0-127. These documents use special **markup codes**, which are embedded in the text. I have used Windows 98 WordPad (tool) for my HTML documents. If I wanted to use, say Microsoft Word for producing the HTML document, I could have done so. Thus, you can use whatever word processing tool is available on your computer. If you allow yourself, sufficient time, you can learn the basic skills of HTML as you prepare a few documents.

• <u>How can you distinguish the HTML document</u> <u>from any other plain document?</u>

The HTML document has HTML **tags**. HTML tags are markup codes, which are typed into the document. These markup codes are surrounded by special markers, which are the **angle brackets**, < and >. The following tags must be included in all HTML documents:

• <u>The <HTML > tag</u>

Your document must begin with the **declaration or opening** tag < HTML>, and it should end with the **closing** tag </ HTML>. It should be noted that the closing tag has a forward slash within the < >. If you omit it you may get an error message, providing you are using any of the HTML specialised editors (see below).

• <u>The <HEAD></u> and <u><Body> tags</u>

An HTML document must have a **head** and **body**. These divisions of the document enable the browsers to interpret the document correctly. What is included in the **head** of the HTML document?

It includes nothing more than some general information concerning the document. It looks like the following example:

```
<HEAD>
learning to use  HTML tags
</HEAD>
```

Example of <Body> tag

```
<BODY>
This is my first HTML document towards the design of my own Web site
</ BODY>
```

The **body** of the HTML document can have the bulk of the information that makes up your Web page. It looks as shown above.

. The <TITLE > tag

It is written within the <HEAD> section of an HTML document. Each document that is displayed by the Web browser should have its title shown in the top border of the browser window. Like other tags, it has an opening tag and a closing tag, as demonstrated by the following examples:

Example of <TITLE> tag

```
<TITLE>
My first Attempt
</ TITLE>
```

To summarise, each of these tags is in a pair: **<HTML> and </HTML>**. The HTML markup codes are **not case-sensitive**. A case-sensitive standard or language distinguishes between upper and lower case letters. I have used uppercase; but you can use lowercase, if you wish. In this book, I have also used in the same HTML document both upper and lower cases. Also, some people write HTML tags on the same line with other tags, such as **<html><head>**. I have not done so, because in my opinion it makes editing the document difficult. Now, is the right time to put theory into practice by preparing a workable HTML page.

. Running your first HTML document

So far, I have described the essential requirements for the simplest application in order to introduce HTML. We shall use this knowledge for the design of your first Web page. I have saved all my examples for this book in a folder called **Examples**. You should also save your examples in a particular folder for your own ease.

. Creating and saving the Web page (.html)

Once the Web page has been created, it has to be saved as a file. The file name ends with the html file extension. Thus, the file will be saved as:-

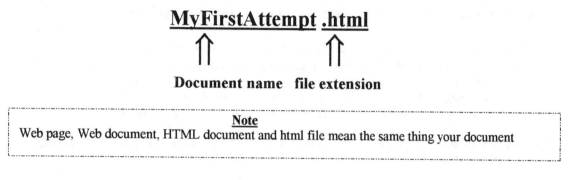

MyFirstAttempt .html

Document name   file extension

Note
Web page, Web document, HTML document and html file mean the same thing your document

---

. How do we create an HTML document?

You can use any **editor** in order to create an HTML document. Yes, there are also numerous specialised editors for this purpose. Some specialised editors can be obtained almost free. These editors can:

- enable you to create an HTML document

- check spellings of HTML words (keywords) automatically

- speed up the process of document creation

- provide you with some additional features such as templates , or codes. Codes you you can insert in your document by using function keys or pull down menus, and thus no keying manually.

- let you see what you create on the screen, providing it is a full blown editor. Such an editor formats a document as you create, and lets you see it on the screen, almost as it will appear in a Web browser

. Do you really need such a specialised HTML editor?

The frank answer is **no** for the following reasons:-

- restrains learning HTML - due to graphical design tools controlling code creation

- out of date soon, which means you must buy another one or up-date it

- may not be able to support all HTML tags, despite great promises

- may be too complex for your needs, and thus unwise investment in costly product

- HTML document can be created successfully by means of any standard text editor such
  as **NotedPad**, **WordPad**, **Word**, and similar plain text editors. These text editors can
  easily facilitate the learning of HTML in a short space of time and at the same time
  save your money. It is advisable to start learning with a simple text editor which is
  already available on your own PC - free of charge. Be wise with your resources!

My computer is running Windows 98. For creating my html document or Web page , I have decided to
make use of **WordPad** for this book for the following reasons:-

- it can handle several documents at the same time;

- it lists several files under File pull-down menu that have been used before, and any of them can be
  re-opened again to work with it; and

- besides the plain text, it can handle Microsoft Word formats text.

. <u>How do I start it?</u>

First open WordPad as shown below.

Click start $\rightarrow$ **select Programs** $\rightarrow$ **select Accessories** $\rightarrow$ **click WordPad**
as shown in diagram 1. This action will open WordPad. This is shown in diagram 2.

The **WordPad** has been opened as shown in diagram 2. Just observe the top left hand corner. At present, it reads Document – WordPad. The word **Document** will be replaced by the name of your html
file, once it has been keyed in and saved.

- Having opened the WordPad, just key in your document. You can also use another text editor
  available on your computer for creating and storing your source file. I have used WordPad, simply
  because I prefer it for the reasons given above.

. <u>Example 1</u>

In order to make good start, just enter the following simple html code in the WordPad shown in diagram 2. This code will create your simple Web page/document with the following **text:**

This is my first attempt towards the design of my own Web site.

WordPad selected

Diagram 1

. **The title of your Web page is :** My First Attempt

The html code created for this example is shown in diagram 3. It is simple but complete for the simplest Web page.

<u>**WordPad is now ready to be used**</u>

This will be replaced by the name of a saved html file

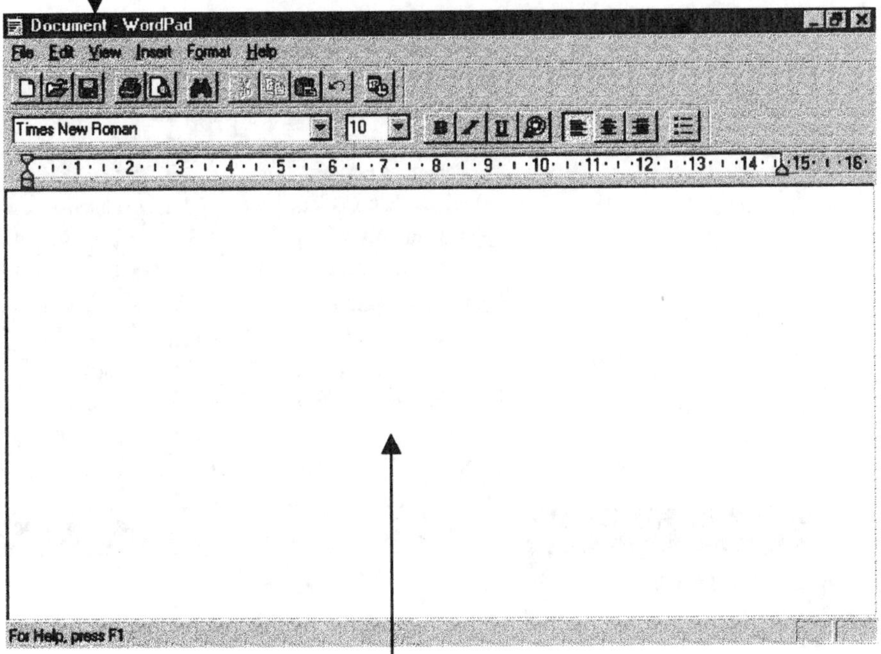

<u>**Ready for entering HTML code**</u>

<u>**Diagram 2**</u>

• <u>Explanation</u>

- In diagram 3, the HTML code starts with an **<HTML> tag**. It declares that it is HTML document.

- **<HEAD>** tag - it has no other information about the document, except to include the title tag.

- **<TITLE>** tag - it is followed by the title of your document. The title is followed by the closing tag **</TITLE>**.

- **</HEAD>** tag - There is no other information to go into the **head section** of this HTML document, and thus the next line contains nothing except the closing tag for this section.

- **<BODY>** tag - it begins the body section.

- There is only one line of text in this <body> section of this document.

- **</BODY>** is used to close this section. It is then followed by the HTML closing tag: **</HTML>**.

For this example, you do not need to code anything else. Indeed, it is a complete executable file which can be viewed with an Internet browser or any other browser. Before you can view it, you must first save it as demonstrated below.

WordPad displays HTML code for MYFirstAttempt document

```
MyFirstAttempt - WordPad
File  Edit  View  Insert  Format  Help

Times New Roman          ▼  11  ▼  B / U

<html>
<head>
<Title>My First Attempt</title>
</head>
<body>
    This is my first attempt towards the design of my own Web site.
</body>
</html>|
```

Diagram 3

Saving the coded html file

Having entered the html code in WordPad, the next step is to save it under an appropriate file name.

. **How?**

- I saved it under **MyFistAttempt . html** by taking the following actions:-

- click **File** on WordPad window $\longrightarrow$ select and **Save as** menu to open it as shown in diagram 4

- having opened the save as menu, select the folder in which you wish to keep your html files. My folder is called **Examples** as shown in diagram 4.

- select type as **Text Document**. This is essential as it will allow you to save your file in plain ASCII code

- in the box facing **file name**, enter your file name

- finally, click the save button in order to complete the save procedure. See diagram 4 for illustration.

Save as menu shown with the required selections and entries

My folder for storing my work for this book

Save in:	Examples
BoxedTable.hjtml	FontsCentered	SecondAppletjava
Calculations. java	FontsCentred	
Cities	FurtherJava,html	
ClipShape	MyOval.hml	
FirstApplet1.hmtl	MyRectangle	
FirstApplet1java	SecondApplet.javaa	

File name: MyFirstAttemot.html   Save

Save as type: Text Document   Cancel

This format creates   The html file to be saved by clicking   Save
Plain ASCII file

Diagram 4

.<u>Previewing your html document</u>

You can preview your html document by means of a Web browser. On my PC, I have installed AOL Version 5.0 Internet software. It includes Microsoft Internet Explorer Version 5. I use it to view document on the Internet. I can also use the same Internet Explorer provided by AOL to view documents on my screen, prior to public viewing on the Web site. In order to view your html file in the Web browser, the following steps are required:

- open the Internet Explorer (I have opened AOL software containing Internet Explorer).

- pull down the **File menu**

- select **Open** your folder in which you are storing your html files. In my case, it is **Examples**.

- locate the file required. In my case, it is **MyFirstAttempt.html**.

- select the required file.

The diagram 5 shows the file **MyFirstAttempt** ready to be viewed locally (off line)

- In order to display this file on your screen, click **Open**.

- Diagram 5 illustrates all the actions mentioned above in order to load the required html file for displaying it in the Web browser off line.

- Diagram 6 shows the html document. This document contains only one line of text.

This diagram shows exactly what your html file in diagram 3 contains, except the html mark up tags. The title, " My First Attempt" is displayed in the title bar of the browser. The file name together with full path is listed in the address box. The content of this document is just one line of text.

.<u>A notice</u>

I have described how to use the WordPad as my text editor for the purpose of creating and saving my HTML documents in Text format in my folder called Examples.

It does not mean that this is the only method of starting the WordPad. It may be that your WordPad is installed in a different way. However, you still have to use this or any other text editor.

Loading MyFirstAttempt as highlighted in the window

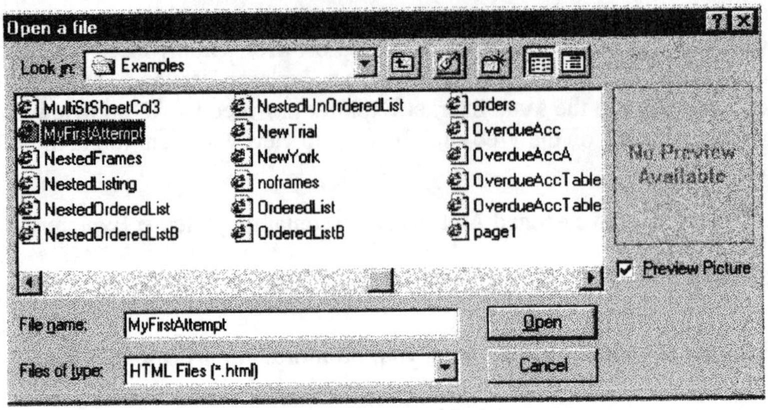

Open a file

Look in: Examples

MultiStSheetCol3	NestedUnOrderedList	orders
MyFirstAttempt	NewTrial	OverdueAcc
NestedFrames	NewYork	OverdueAccA
NestedListing	noframes	OverdueAccTable
NestedOrderedList	OrderedList	OverdueAccTable
NestedOrderedListB	OrderedListB	page1

No Preview Available

☑ Preview Picture

File name: MyFirstAttempt   Open

Files of type: HTML Files (*.html)   Cancel

Diagram 5

My First Attempt previewed in IE (Internet Explorer)

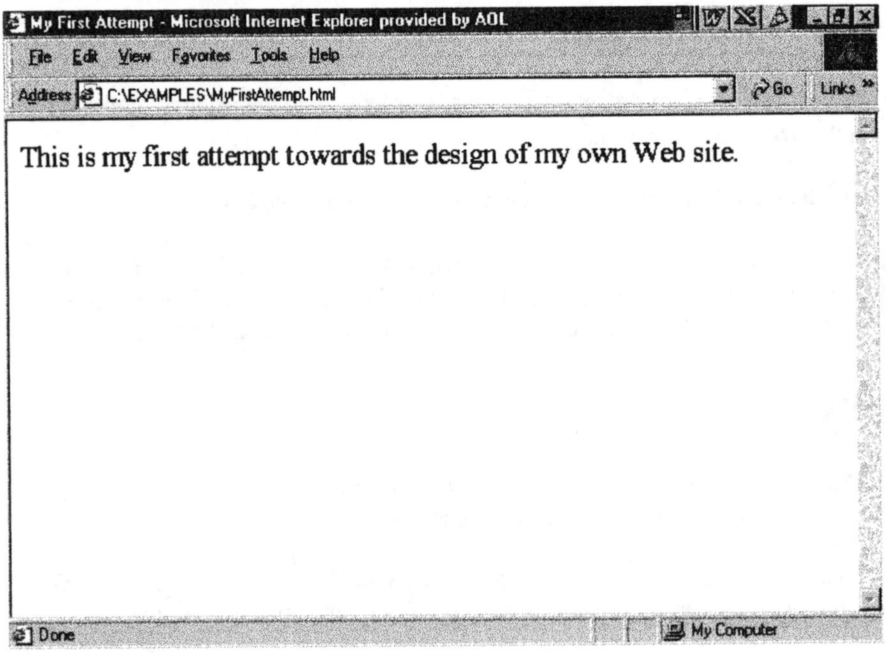

My First Attempt - Microsoft Internet Explorer provided by AOL

File Edit View Favorites Tools Help

Address C:\EXAMPLES\MyFirstAttempt.html   Go   Links

This is my first attempt towards the design of my own Web site.

Done   My Computer

Diagram 6

Chapter 3

Shaping your Web page

This chapter lays the foundation of understanding and using HTML basic styles and style sheets. It demonstrates the application of essential techniques for creating headings, paragraphs, line breaks, text alignment and character formatting with different text formatting tags. You should be able to apply these tools when developing your Web site.

I begin by raising the following four basic questions:

- **What do we mean by styles?**
- **What are HTML style sheets?**
- **Why do we use style sheets in a Web page?**
- **Are there any common problems in using style sheets?**

The idea of style is borrowed from the publishing world. Most likely you already know that a newspaper editor or the proprietor enforces a set of rules to be observed by all those who are involved with the writing, editing and printing of a newspaper in the organisation. These rules concern style of design, print, spelling, punctuation, hyphenation, and so on. For instance, spellings of places are always spelled in the same way in a particular publication. Similarly, a publisher, say of A.D.R. Student Simplified Series, has a set of rules for this series. For example, among other things, each chapter must have some practical examples in order to exemplify the idea introduced. These rules of styles are aimed at controlling the standards laid down by a particular organisation. Of course, these styles may be similar in many publishing organisations.

The HTML document design is also for a kind of publication for whatever purpose it may be designed. The individual writer or the organisation who generates such documents also has the desire to monitor the format of the HTML page in order to maintain a laid down standard. For the Web page designers, the HTML 4 has some rules or style sheets concerning many of its elements. By applying HTML style sheets one can exercise control over most features of an HTML document. For instance, by applying style sheets, among many other features, you can easily perform the following basic tasks:

- **format text** - it simply means defining the structure of text to be written in a Web page. It includes such things as font size, font types (boldface, italics, big…), headings, line breaks, underline text, margin settings. Thus, for instance, you can set spacing between letters words and lines.

- **specify colour** - selecting background colours, presenting text in different colours. For instance, you can set background for each paragraph in a document.

- **define text position** - positioning text in the document in the desired place.

Thus, with style sheets one can control the appearance of the text, specify the element's position on the document and the layout of a web page. Yes indeed, style sheets are easy to use, and can be applied in all kinds of HTML documents. You can define a style sheet; you can change your style sheet as well. The change in a style sheet can affect all pages in a document.

. <u>Differences in implementing style sheets</u>

However, there is one drawback, which is due to the fact that not all browsers have implemented the same set of style sheets. The reason for this difficulty is due to the fact that there are a number of different style sheets developed by different companies. Each set of style sheets has its own methods, and extends the current version of the HTML in its own way. The commonly known set of style sheets is known as Cascading Style Sheets **(CSS)** Version 1. It has been recommended by the World Wide Web Consortium **(W3C)**, but has not been either fully or correctly implemented by browser manufacturers. To make life more difficult, CSS2 in being developed, whilst CSS1 is not yet fully supported. Here, the idea is to extend the existing CSS1 features for improved overall document control.

Microsoft Internet Explorer version 3.01 partially supported CSS1, its version 4.0 supports more CSS sheets than version 3.01 has. The version 5.0 has not yet fully implemented CSS. The other well-known browser, namely Netscape has not yet fully implemented CSS as well. Even so, you can still use some features without unduly worrying that your browser may fail to work.

It is widely known that so far, most browsers' manufacturers support a few features of style sheets. Also, you should note that most older browsers do not support style sheets. I hope that by the time you read this book, more browsers will have implemented some more style sheets, which are really helpful to Web page designers for the overall control of Web pages. Style Sheets are implemented in the following chapters. Now, it is time to illustrate some of HTML 4.0 features by means of solved examples.

. <u>Creating headlines</u>

The tag which is used for making a headline is called the headline tag (also heading tag). For ease of learning, I classify headline tags in table 1. Each level has its own opening and closing pair of tags. According to convention these tags are written in upper case letters although sometimes, I have written these in both upper and lower case letters, and the code operated successfully. Browser software does not see the visual layout of the text as human eyes can see it. It is for this reason that you have to use these headline tags to tell the browser how headlines should appear in your document. As shown in Table 1 above, heading tags must be followed by their closing tags.

Headline Tags

Level	Tag	Size	Use
1	<H1> or < h1> </h> or </h1>	largest headline	often in use for top level heading
2	< H2> or < h2> </h2> or <h2>	large headline	often in use for secondary level heading
3	< H3> or < h3> </h3> or <h3>	small headline	often in use for third level heading
4	<H4> or < h4> <h4> or <h4>	smaller headline	seldom in use due to size too small
5	< H5> or < h5> < /H5> or <h5>	smallest headline	seldom in use due to very small size
6	<H6> or <h6> </h6> or </h6>	tiniest headline	seldom in use due to tiniest size

Table 1

. Example 1

This example demonstrates how to create headlines of different sizes in your document by implementing all six **headline tags.**

. Explanation

The HTML code shown in diagram 1 below is designed to create six different headlines. When you study this code carefully in order to key it in your own PC to practise you will see that the structure of this code is based upon the essential techniques introduced in Chapter 1. I will analyse each line of this code now:-

- The code starts with the **opening** HTML tag **<html>**. This is to open or declare the document.

- It is followed by the **head** tag. A Web page must have a head. It is needed as it enables the browser to correctly interpret the document. Within the head section, the **title** tag **<Title>** is enclosed. The title tag is immediately followed by the title given to this document. It is **Largest to smallest headlines**.

- At the end of the text for this title, there is a closing title tag **</Title>**.

- The next requirement is to declare the **body** of a Web page. This is done by the tag **<body>**. In the last chapter, it is stated that the body contains much of the information that forms your Web page. In this example, the body contains all six heading tags: For instance:

```
<h1>
    h1 or H1 displays the largest size headline. This is level 1.
</h1>
```

This will be the first line of information in this Web page called **Largest to smallest headlines**. Once again, notice that the text for this heading is enclosed within the opening and closing tags of level 1 heading tag. Now, examine the rest of this code to discover that the pattern is repeated for each type of heading.

- The body of HTML code has to be closed. This is achieved by **< /body>** as shown in this diagram. It is also required to place **</html>,** the closing HTML tag, at the end of the whole HTML code. This is to remind you that **<html> and </html>** are used in a document as a pair.

. Previewing document: headlinSizes.html

The code shown in diagram 1 was saved as headlinSize.html file. I have viewed it successfully by means of the Internet Explorer. Of course, this can also be viewed on-line as a part of a Web page.

The document is shown in diagram 2. It can be seen that an HTML code is excluded from this display. It shows only the required information in the desired format.

The HTML code for example 1

```
<html>
<head>
<Title>Largest to smallest headlines</Title>
</head>
<body>
<H1> h1 or H1 displays the largest size headline. This is level 1. </H1>
<h2> h2 or H2 displays a larger size headline. This is level 2. </h2>
<H3> h3 or H3 displays a large size headline. This is level 3. </H3>
</h4> h4 or H4 displays a small size headline. This is level 4. </H4>
<H5> h5 or H5 displays a smaller size headline. This is level 5. </H5>
 <h6> h6 or H6 displays smallest size headline. This is level 6. </h6>
</body>
</html>
```

Diagram 1

You can see that each heading is on a separate line.

. What is the reason for this occurrence?

It is because of the fact that a headline creates **an automatic line break**. There are some other ways of creating line breaks which you will learn soon.

You might have already noticed that headline text created by heading tags <3> to <<6> is smaller than regular text size. For this reason, their use is rather limited.

. Example 2

This example further illustrates the use of headline tags. The idea is to show you the practical use of these tags by giving a simple example. It creates only two lines of text:

Address for reply:-

Daniel Lancaster @ home.com

The HTML code is shown in diagram 3 below. It was previewed successfully as shown in diagram 4 on the next page. It is strongly recommended that you key in HTML codes presented in this book in order to learn by doing. This way, you will develop your practical skills and gain self-confidence in your own learning.

See example 8 for using address tag <ADDRESS> ....</ADDRESS> for writing author's address and may be the date of the last update, usually shown at the bottom home page.

In diagram 2, you can see that the headline of Level 6 is too small.

Largest to smallest headlines Previewed in IE

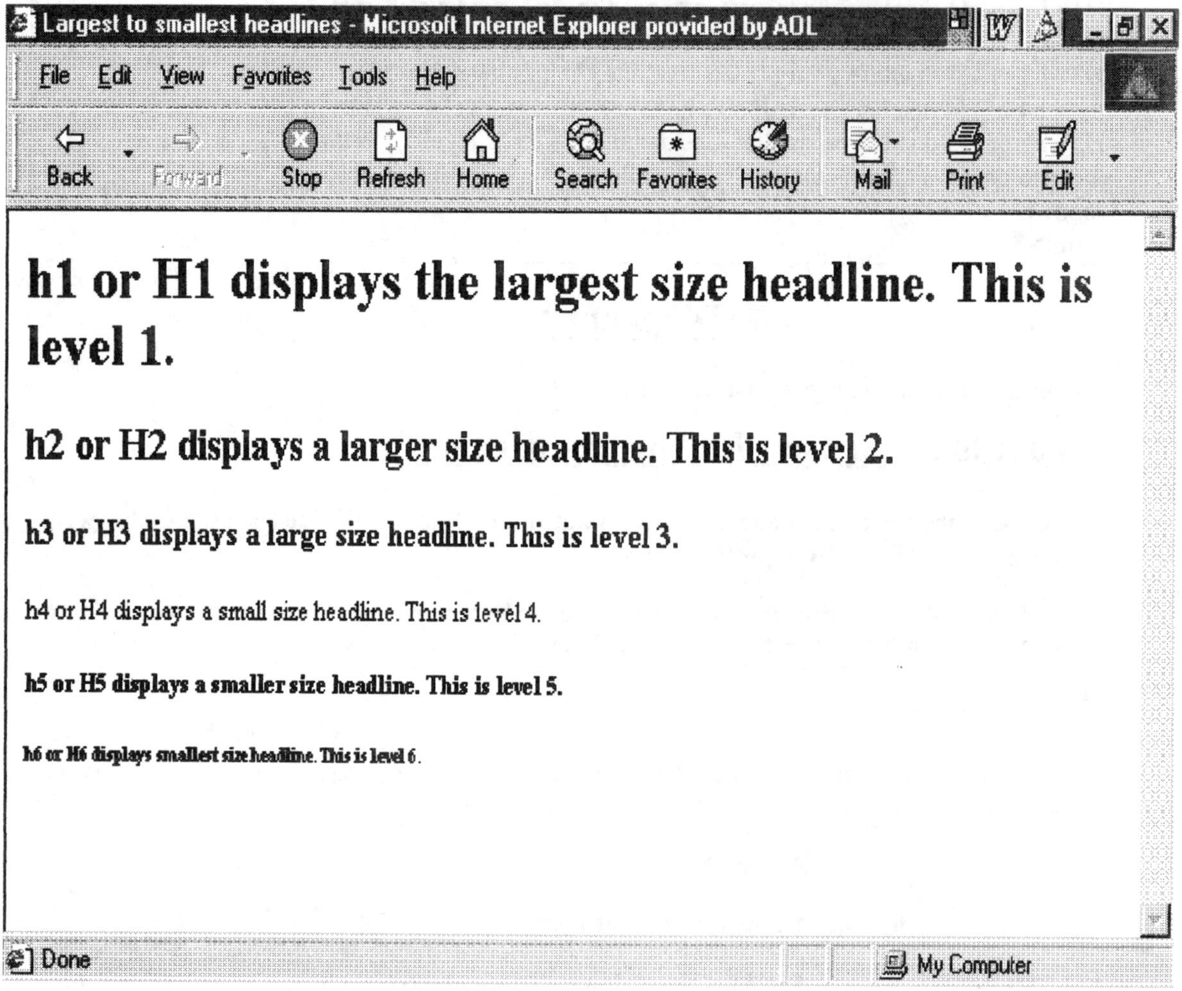

h1 or H1 displays the largest size headline. This is level 1.

h2 or H2 displays a larger size headline. This is level 2.

h3 or H3 displays a large size headline. This is level 3.

h4 or H4 displays a small size headline. This is level 4.

h5 or H5 displays a smaller size headline. This is level 5.

h6 or H6 displays smallest size headline. This is level 6.

Diagram 2

HTML code for example 2

```
<html>
<head>
<title> Another example of using heading tags</title>
</head>
<body>
<h1>
          Address for reply:-
</h1>
<h2>
          Daniel Lancaster @home.com
</h2>
</body>
</html>
```

Diagram 3

. Paragraph Formatting

Here, the idea is to learn how to organise text into paragraphs so that your text can be shown correctly in the desired format by different browsers on a variety of computers with varying graphics capabilities. You know well that not all browsers and computers are universally of the same type, and thus do not always render documents as you wish. It is, therefore, necessary to mark paragraphs.

. How do we achieve this aim ?

You can place a **paragraph tag** <p> at the beginning of each paragraph. This tag also has its closing tag </p>.

. Is it necessary to place a paragraph closing tag at the end of each paragraph?

The quick answer is **no**. You will soon learn why its use at the end of each paragraph is not always required. Firstly, study example 3 on the next page which implements paragraph tags. This example also includes the use of other tags which you have learnt so far.

Another example of using heading tags previewed in IE

Diagram 4

. Example 3

This example illustrates the rule of making paragraphs with the aid of paragraph tags **<p></p>**. The HTML code shown in diagram 5 is aimed at making the following paragraphs for a web page called paragraph formatting.

The Human Brain
The human brain is as big as a coconut, the shape of a walnut. It has two hemispheres, which are covered in a thin skin of deeply wrinkled grey tissue called the cerebral cortex.

Each infold on this surface is known as sulcus, and each bulge is known as gyrus. The surface landscape of each individual's brain is slightly different, but the main wrinkles - like nose - mouth grooves and crow's feet on an ageing face - are common to all and are used as landmarks.
For further Information: TheBrainSurgeon @home.com

. Explanation

The diagram 5 contains HTML code for this example. This code is similar to the code you have already seen in our previous examples, but its structure deserves the following explanation.

- **<h2>The Human Brain** - this line of text does not end with the closing tag of heading level 2 - **</h2>**. The reason for its exclusion is that a new paragraph starts with the paragraph tag **<p>** on a new line.

- **<h2>** starts a new line. For this reason, it is unnecessary to place **</h1>** in this and similar situations.

- The paragraph "the human......cortex." Does not end with the closing paragraph **tag </p>**.

. Why is this so?

Because at the beginning of the next paragraph is the paragraph opening tag <p>. In such circumstances, there is no need to place both the opening and closing paragraph tags one after the other.

- It is worth noticing that the next paragraph, "Each....landmarks." ends with **</p> tag**. The reason for placing this tag here is that I want to separate this paragraph with the next one line paragraph.

- The html code for this example was tested locally by means of the Internet Explorer **(IE)**. It was tested successfully as is evident from diagram 6.

. Lines Break
 ...</BR>

So far, you have learnt how to separate paragraphs or single lines from each other by means of:

- closing headline tags   - closing paragraph tag   and

- placing any of the opening headline tags at the start of a paragraph or a line

These techniques create a blank line or white space between two lines or paragraphs, which may not be desirable. You can achieve a line break without any blank line, by using line break tag <BR> or <br>. In addition to line break tags, you can also use other tags to achieve the same effects. Be patient, as you will meet this topic again.

. Is there a pair of tags for underlining a text? Yes.

It is implemented in example 4. You can use <U>...</U> tags to underline your text enclosed within these tags. This will save you from drawing a line manually.

HTML code for example 3

```
<html>
<head>
<title> Paragraph formatting </title>
</head>
<body>
<h2>
    The Human Brain
<p> <h3>
The human brain is as big as a coconut, the shape of a walnut. It has two hemispheres, which
are covered in a thin skin of deeply wrinkled grey tissue called the cerebral cortex.
<p> Each infold on this surface is known as sulcus, and each bulge is known as gyrus. The
surface landscape of each individual's brain is slightly different, but the main wrinkles - like
nose - mouth grooves and crow's feet on an ageing face - are common to all and are used as
landmarks.</p>
For further Information: TheBrainSurgeon @home.com
</h3>
</body>
</html>
```

Diagram 5

.Example 4

Why am I learning HTML markup language?
The idea is to develop my own web site. My new knowledge and skills will enable me to control costs
of developing, running and up-dating it. Furthermore, I like new challenges. Learning is good for your
brain. It keeps your brain active and alive. The Web site developers are rather expensive. Some insist
on a long time contract. Why should you buy something which you can make yourself cheaper and
better? Think!!!

You are asked to re-organise the text shown below in the shaded area in order to present it with the
following requirements:

- use level 2 heading tag to create an underlined heading with the first sentence in this text. This
  heading must end with a line break, so that it is separated from the text that follows it.

- apply level 3 heading tag to start a block of text with the words "The idea ", and continue keying in text until you reach "challenges." This block of text should end with a line break. Start a new line with "Learning", and continue until "alive."

- start a new paragraph "The web.....better?", end it with a line break and finally key in "Think!!!".

This example is discussed below the diagram 6.

Paragraph formatting previewed in IE

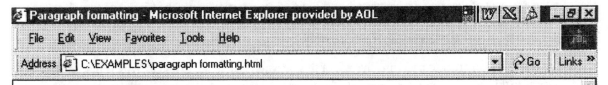

Paragraph formatting - Microsoft Internet Explorer provided by AOL

File Edit View Favorites Tools Help

Address C:\EXAMPLES\paragraph formatting.html   Go   Links »

The Human Brain

The human brain is as big as a coconut, the shape of a walnut. It has two hemispheres, which are covered in a thin skin of deeply wrinkled grey tissue called the cerebral cortex.

Each infold on this surface is known as sulcus, and each bulge is known as gyrus.The surface landscape of each individual's brain is slightly different, but the main wrinkles - like nose - mouth grooves and crow's feet on an ageing face - are common to all and are used as landmarks.

For further Information: TheBrainSurgeon @home.com

Done   My Computer

Diagram 6

. <u>Explanation</u>

- The HTML code for this document is given in diagram 7. The structure of this HTML file follows the same pattern, which you have already seen in previous examples. However, tags that are introduced in this code need to be discussed in order to understand the reason (s) for using them as such in specific places.

- **Why am I learning HTML markup language?
**

  In this segment of the code, I have placed, at the end of the question mark, the break line **tag
**. Why? It was essential here. Otherwise, the line drawn would have appeared next to the question mark,instead of underlying the text of this question.

- The line drawn in order to underline the text of this question has **no** tag to end it. Why is that so? he answer to this question becomes apparent, if you just read the next line, which is **<h3>**. Whenever, any of the headline tags starts a paragraph or a line, it automatically creates line break.

- There is no need to place </h2> before <h3>. Why? The closing tag </h2> is unnecessary here, as the line drawn to underline the question is separated from the next paragraph by <h3>.

- Will it be all right, if I place </h2> prior to <h3>? If you do so, your code will work fine. Anyway, if your file is much bigger than this document, you will be wasting a lot of time in entering it. It does demonstrate that in such cases closing tags are not always necessary. <u>If you prefer to use closing tags at all times, you can do so.</u>

- Consider this section of HTML code **<p>The web…..better?
, and discover why I used <BR> here instead of <p> (or <P>). In this particular case, the implementation of <BR> is correct as I wanted to join the next line containing "Think!!!" to this paragraph. Once again, using </p> tag would have created an empty line or white space between the last line of this paragraph and the line containing **Think!!! This was not required.

These examples have illustrated not only the use of tags introduced so far, but also the reasons for using them, and when appropriate avoiding their use.

. <u>Character Formatting</u>

The HTML can let you control the appearance of your text by means of different typefaces. The application of some of these tags is illustrated below. Some writers label them as phrasal elements. They also come in pairs. Some typeface tags are listed in Table 2.

HTML code for example 4

```
<html>
<head>
<title> Using Line breaks </title>
</head>
<body>
<h2>
      Why am I learning HTML markup language?<BR>

      _____

<h3>
   The idea is to develop my own  web site. My new knowledge and
   skills will enable me to control costs of developing, running and
   up-dating it. Furthermore, I like new challenges.<br>
   Learning is good for your brain. It keeps your brain active and alive.
<p>
   The web site developers are rather expensive. Some insist on a
   long time contract. Why should you buy something which you can
   make yourself  cheaper and better?<BR>
   Think!!!
</body>
</html>
```

Diagram 7

.Example 5

This tag renders text in boldface.
This is Italic type
This style is called bold or emphasis. It puts strong emphasis on a regular text.
See Page 35. This is an example of citation or reference. It is shown in italic font.
This is another tag which you can use for italic typeface.
This tag is good for underlying any text. Thus, it has underlined even these two sentences. It was re-
quired by me.

The prime aim of this example is to demonstrate how to use different typefaces. The above text has to be rendered in different typefaces which are also written in the shaded area. Use different type faces which are listed in table 2 in order to convert this text into the HTML markup code for testing it locally in the Internet Explorer (IE). **(Due to limited space here, example 5 continued below the diagram 8).**

Using Line breaks previewed in IE

```
Using Line breaks - Microsoft Internet Explorer provided by AOL        □ ☑ ☒ △ _ ☐ ☒
 File   Edit   View   Favorites   Tools   Help
 Address  C:\EXAMPLES\UsingLineBreaks.html                    ▼  ↗ Go   Links »
```

Why am I learning HTML markup language?

─────────────────────────────────────

**The idea is to develop my own web site. My new knowledge and skills will
enable me to control costs of developing, running and up-dating it.
Furthermore, I like new challenges.**
Learning is good for your brain. It keeps your brain active and alive.

**The web site developers are rather expensive. Some insist on a long time
contract. Why should you buy something which you can make yourself
cheaper and better?**
Think!!!

```
 Done                                              My Computer
```

Diagram 8

. Explanation - example 5

The idea is to display the text shown above in the shaded block as six different paragraphs (only the
last paragraph has more than one line). Each paragraph must have different character/text format. These
should be written by using the following tags in pairs respectively.

\<B\>, \<EM\>, \<CITE\>, \<STRONG\>, \<I\> and \<U\>

- By now, you should find HTML code for this requirement shown in diagram 9 above self-explanatory. In order to make six paragraphs, it was essential to apply <P> and </P> in places shown in diagram 9.

- The preview of this document locally is shown in diagram 10. It meets all requirements.

- The HTML code in diagram 9 has closing tags for all six typeface tags. It is interesting to know the answer to the following question:

- ## What would have happened if closing tags were omitted?

In this case, the text in your first paragraph (just one line here) would have displayed in the required character format, and all other text would have appeared in italic form. Thus, it is important to use closing tags in such circumstances.

This example also further exemplifies the application of some other HTML tags already introduced. This will enable you to evaluate your own knowledge gained so far, and improve your practical HTML skills; providing you run this code like other previous codes on your own PC system. The HTML code is shown in diagrams 9 and 9A.

Once again, I keyed tags in both upper and lower case letters (see below). The browser has correctly interpreted my HTML document. If you prefer using upper or lower case letters only, you can do so by all means.

HTML Code for example 5

```
<html>
<head>
<title> character formatting </title>
</head>
<body>
<B>
        This tag renders text in boldface.
</B>
<EM>
        <P> This is italic type </P>
</EM>
<strong>
```

Diagram 9

HTML Code for example 5 (cont.)

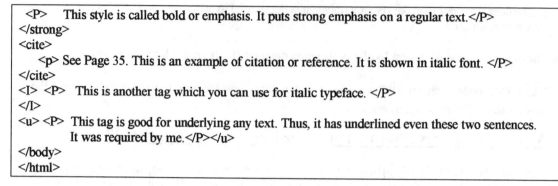

```
<P>     This style is called bold or emphasis. It puts strong emphasis on a regular text.</P>
</strong>
<cite>
    <p> See Page 35. This is an example of citation or reference. It is shown in italic font. </P>
</cite>
<I> <P>   This is another tag which you can use for italic typeface. </P>
</I>
<u> <P>  This tag is good for underlying any text. Thus, it has underlined even these two sentences.
        It was required by me.</P></u>
</body>
</html>
```

Diagram 9A

Character formatting previewed in IE

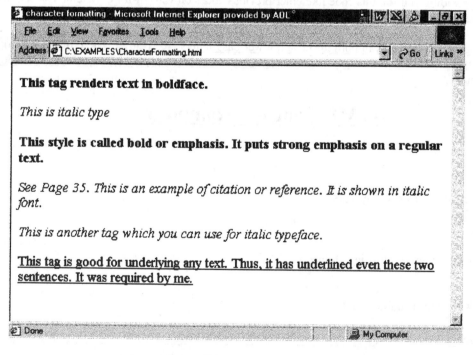

Diagram 10

. <u>Practical Hints</u>

Without the dedicated HTML editor, you can only find out HTML errors when you are trying to preview your document locally (in IE or any other browser). It is therefore advisable to look for mistakes in your HTML code. For instance, if you key <CIT> for some text to appear in this format. It will not render as such, because the browser will not recognise it as <CITE>. However, it is not too difficult to spot such mistakes. The good thing is that you can use both upper and lower case letters for tags. This has already been proven through the worked examples discussed so far.

<u>Some Typeface Tags -Text formatting tags</u>

Opening Tag	Closing Tag	Purpose
<B>	</B>	to render **bold** text
<CITE>	</CITE>	to mark text for a reference or citation purpose usually rendered in *an italic font*
<CODE>	</CODE>	to indicate HTML or Program code. The text is rendered in a fixed width font
<EM>	</EM>	to render characters in *italics* with regular emphasis
<I>	</I>	to render text in italic
<STRONG>	</STRONG>	to format characters in **boldface.** Strong emphasis
<U>	</U>	to underline text

<u>Table 2</u>

. <u>Example 6</u>

This example is designed to demonstrate the application of some text formatting tags simultaneously in the same paragraph in order to highlight a word or a phrase. The text used for this example is shown in the shaded area on the next page.

Memory

Memory is many different things:

It is the picture that comes into your mind when you think of your school days; the feeling of unease associated with a place where something frightening once happened to you; and the knowledge you hold that London Bridge is over the River Thames in London, England.

In order to understand memory you have to look at individual cells because that is where memories are made.

The above text should be displayed with the following enhancement:

- heading - "Memory" to be written in **boldface** and <u>underlined</u>.

- paragraph - "Memory…. England." should be shown as citation, with London Bridge highlighted in **boldface**.

- paragraph - "In…made." Should be written in regular emphasis italics, but individual cells should be highlighted by using **boldface**.

- paragraph - "There…. subject." It should be in italic style, with the exception of caught, which must be in boldface and <u>underlined.</u>

. <u>Explanation</u>

The HTML code for this example is in diagram 11, whose structure is worth discussing now.

To change the appearance of a word or a phrase or the whole sentence in a paragraph means stopping the flow and appearance of the text up to the point from where the alteration to the paragraph is to be made. For this reason, in paragraph "Memory… England", the closing tag **</cite>** is inserted to cease the flow of this text at word **that**. But, **London Bridge** is enclosed within **<B> and </B>** so that it can be written in boldface font.

The flow of this paragraph must continue in the same font with which it is started. Thus, **<cite>** is written next to **</B>**.

The same method of altering the appearance of text as required is applied for the next two paragraphs. Now, you should examine and key in the HTML code shown in diagram 11 in your PC system to see how its mechanism works. You should note the order of placing tags in their correct places in this code.

This document was previewed successfully. You can see the outcome in diagram 12.

HTML code for example 6

```
<html>
<head>
<title> Different typefaces </title>
</head>
<body>
<B><u
                    Memory
</u></B.>
<cite><p>
Memory is many different things:

It is the picture that comes into your mind when you think of your school days; the feeling of
unease associated with a place where something frightening once happened to you; and the
knowledge you hold that</cite><B> London Bridge </B><cite>
is over the River Thames in London, England. </p></cite>
<EM> <P>
      In order to understand memory you have to look at </EM><B> individual
      cells</B>,
<EM>
      because that is where memories are made.
</EM>
<I> <P>
      There are two types of attention: the automatic engagement of the senses that occurs
      when your eye is </I> <B><u> caught </B></u>

<I> by a flash of movement; and the deliberate turning of the mind to a subject.</I></P>
</body>
</html>
```

Diagram 11

. Are there some more text formatting tags?

Yes, there some more tags. You have seen here some of these tags in action. But, the other tags are also implemented in the same way. For the sake of simplicity, text formatting tags can be classified as shown below:

Different typefaces previewed in IE

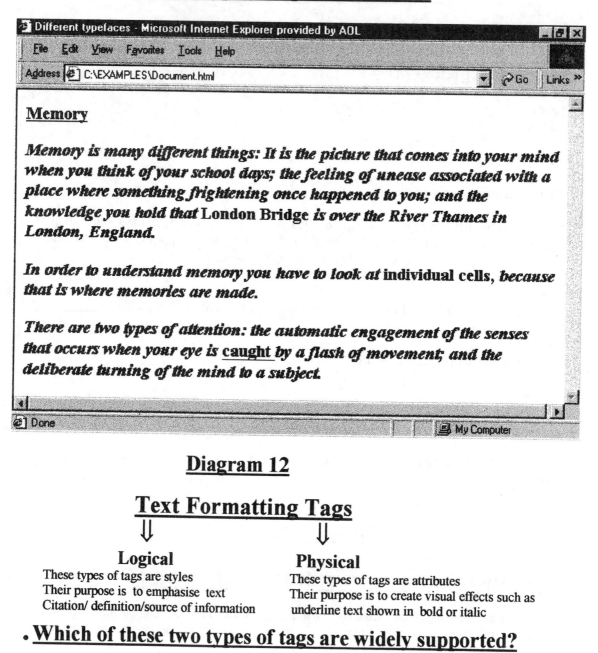

Diagram 12

Text Formatting Tags

⇓   ⇓

Logical   **Physical**

These types of tags are styles   These types of tags are attributes
Their purpose is to emphasise text   Their purpose is to create visual effects such as
Citation/ definition/source of information   underline text shown in bold or italic

. <u>**Which of these two types of tags are widely supported?**</u>

Logical tags (style sheets) are not as widely supported as physical tags. It may be that by the time you read this book the use of style sheets is already more popular than at the time of writing this book. Anyway, you have already seen both logical and physical tags working together in a document. You will meet these and other tags again.

. Text Alignment

Automatically text is aligned to the left ends of lines. In other words, the text begins to the left of your screen. In HTML, you can create left, right, centre and justified alignment positions by means of the alignment option. But, the current version of HTML4.0 adopts style sheets by deprecating the align option. Even so, you can still use it. In fact, it is still advisable to apply the alignment option, as not all browsers have correctly and fully implemented CSS, as we have already discussed this matter above. This option is safer, as it works on both new and old browsers.

Text Alignment

Option	Meaning	Format of use
right alignment	aligns text to the right of the page	`<P ALIGN ="RIGHT">text...</P>`
center alignment	aligns text in the centre of the page	`<CENTER> text...</CETER>`
left alignment	aligns text to the left of the page	`<P ALIGN = "LEFT"> text... </P>`

Table 3

There are other aspects of alignment such as creating tables, and images. These are discussed later on at the appropriate time and place in this book. Now, examine the following examples for their application.

. Example 7

The text shown below in the shaded area has to be re-presented in order to meet the following requirements:

- "Plug-ins" must be an underlined heading in the centre of the Web page. It should be larger than the rest of the text.

- start a new paragraph "The most... images successfully." It should be left justified (alignment), and display in italics.

- display in the centre of your screen/page text "There are many.....are free." This should be displayed as a citation/quotation in boldface.

- the remaining text " One can...system." Should be displayed as right justified in regular typeface.

- run this code HTML code in order to preview it in IE or any other browser on your system.

Plug-in
The most popular browsers can handle text found on a Web site. They can also handle some kind of images. You can also copy from the Internet such things as sound clips, but your browser may not be able to do much with them. Anyway, there is no shortage of programs called plug-ins, which work with browsers. A plug-in can enable the browser to handle things such as graphics and images successfully. There are many plug-ins software on the market. Many of them are free. One can copy a free plug-in to one's own computer from the Internet. Again, there is one big issue, which is to do with **proprietary** - a Plug-in program may work with only a particular software or hardware, and thus may not meet your requirements. On the other hand, many dozens of plug-ins are available to choose one program which can work with your PC system.

HTML code for example 7

```
<html>
<head>
<title> Text Alignment Example</title>
</head>
<body>
<center>
<h2>
<u>
        Plug-ins</u>
</h2>
</Center>
<I> <P>
```

Diagram 13

HTML code for example 7 (cont. from diagram 13)

The most popular browsers can handle text found on a Web site. They can also handle some
kind of images. You can also copy from the Internet such things as sound clips, but your
browser may not be able to do much with them. Anyway, there is no shortage of programs
called plug-ins, which work with browsers. A plug-in can enable the browser to handle things
such as graphics and images successfully.
</P>
</I>

<B>
<cite>
        There are many plug-ins software on the market. Many of them are free.
</cite>
</B>

<P align = "right">
    One can copy a free plug-in to one's own computer from the Internet.
    Again, there is one big issue, which is to do with **proprietary** - a Plug-in
    program may work with only a particular software or hardware,
    and thus may not meet your requirements. On the other hand, many dozens of plug-ins
    are available to choose one program which can work with your PC system.
</P>
</body>
</html>

Diagram 13A

. Explanation

The required HTML code for example 7 is shown in diagrams 13 and 13A. It was saved, and then
tested by means of the Internet Explorer. It was previewed successfully, and it is shown in diagram 14.
The structure of this code is pretty much the same as you have already met. However, you must study it
carefully in order to learn how I have coded each requirement. In diagram 14, the first paragraph is left
justified (left alignment). There was no need to code it as

<P align = "left"> text </P>

. <u>Why?</u>

There is no need to use the left alignment attribute, because left alignment is automatic. If you wish you can use it, you can do so.

. <u>Can you implement full justification in HTML?</u>

Yes, you can make use of **<P align = "justify"> text </P>**.

It will align the text to both sides (left and right) of the document. In practice, its use is not common on the Web. The reason is that in most browsers the spacing between letters is imprecise, and that the text fully justified does not look good. You can experiment with it to see how it looks in browser.

. <u>What are attributes?</u>

The simplest meaning of attribute is an additional information that can be attached to a tag. It is used to modify the tag. For instance:

< P align = "value" > text </P>

In this example, value represents an attribute, which can be left, right, centre, or justify. You will meet this topic again.

. <u><ADDRESS>......</ADDRESS></u>

The purpose of this tag is simply to allow the author to provide his/her address for contact with any other detail , such as the date when the page updated the last time. It is your decision what and how much information you wish to write here. It renders text in *italic font*, as demonstrated by example 8 below.

. <u><BIG> ...</BIG></u>   displays character 2 points bigger than normal size.

. <u><SMALL> ...</SMALL></u> It generates text just the opposite of the BIG, that is 2 points smaller than the normal text.

These two text appearance font or typeface styles are also very useful. Their use is shown in example 8.

Text Alignment Example previewed in IE

```
Text Alignment Example - Microsoft Internet Explorer provided by AOL        W X A _ 8 X
 File   Edit   View   Favorites   Tools   Help
 Address  C:\EXAMPLES\Plugins.html                              ▼  Go   Links »
```

Plug-ins

The most popular browsers can handle text found on a Web site. They can also handle some kind of images. You can also copy from the Internet such things as sound clips, but your browser may not be able to do much with them. Anyway, there is no shortage of programs called plug-ins, which work with browsers. A plug-in can enable the browser to handle things such as graphics and images successfully.

There are many plug-ins software on the market. Many of them are free.

One can copy a free plug-in to one's own computer from the Internet. Again, there is one big issue, which is to do with proprietary - a Plug-in program may work with only a particular software or hardware, and thus may not meet your requirements. On the other hand, many dozens of plug-ins are available to choose one program which can work with your PC system.

```
 Done                                                          My Computer
```

Diagram 14

. Example 8

Thinking
Millions of us die early each year from clogged arteries and other complications of obesity. Our drive to pleasure is killing us. Children respond appropriately to facial expressions almost from the time they are born, but they get progressively better at it as they get older. Most of us are surprisingly poor at detecting dishonesty from facial expression. PeoplePsy @ Psycho.com Last update: 30.03.2000

Use the text shown above in the shaded box and perform the following tasks:

- **underline** "Thinking" - make it a headline of **level 2 size** for placing it in the centre of the page.

- the paragraph "Millions...killing us."- whole text should be displayed in **BIG** and **BOLD** styles, with the exception of "obesity" , which must be written in *italic style and underlined.*

- the paragraph "Children … expression." - it must be displayed in **small font style**, with the exception of "dishonesty", which must be made bold and underlined.

- PeoplePsy @ Psycho.com Last update: 30.03.2000 should appear as a separate paragraph in the form of **author's address** and when the page was last updated.

HTML code for example 8

```
<html>
<head>
<title> Address & update Infor </title>
</head>
<body>
<center>
<h2>
<u>
       Thinking</u></h2> </Center>

<P> <BIG><B>Millions of us die early each year from clogged arteries and
          other complications of<I><U> obesity.</U></I> Our drive to pleasure is killing
          us.</BIG></B></P>
<P><Small>

Children respond appropriately to facial expressions almost from the time they are born,
but they get progressively better at it as they get older. Most of us are surprisingly poor at
detecting<B><u> dishonesty</B></u> from facial expression.</small></P>
<Address>
          PeoplePsy @ Psycho.com<BR>
          Last update: 30.03.2000</Address>
</body>
</html>
```

Diagram 15

Address & update previewed in IE

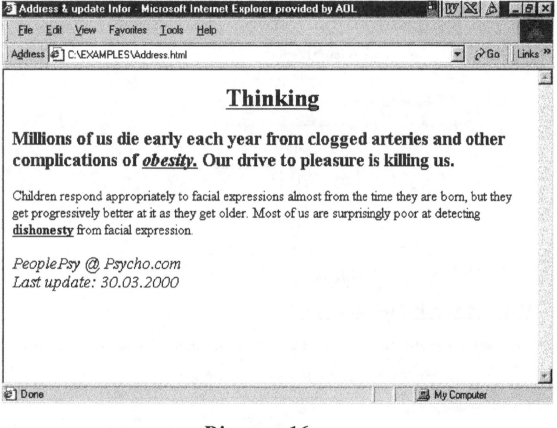

Diagram 16

. Explanation

The HTML code for these tasks is given in diagram 15. Once again, the structure of this HTML file is similar to the previous codes, but it also demonstrate how to implement some more features of HTML 4.0 together with some other features you have already seen.

BIG, **SMALL** and **ADDRESS** tags can also be written in lower case letters. When your address consists of several lines, in that case, you must end each line with **
** tags. You should now experiment with this code to extend your experience and skills. It was tested and previewed in IE successfully, as shown in diagram 16 below.

. Font sizes

You can use the <FONT.....></FONT> tag to change the size of the font. The Table 4 lists font sizes. You can write font sizes in lower case letters as well. SIZE = *n*, where *n* ranges between 1 - 7.

Font Sizes

Font Range	Size in point
1	8
2	10
3	**12** default size
4	14
5	18
6	24
7	36

Table 4

. How can you declare font sizes?

- There are two ways of declaring font sizes. One way is to use font range between 1 - 7. For instance:

< FONT SIZE = 4 > It is in fact point 14 </FONT>

- The other method is to apply:

<BASEFONT SIZE = > <BASEFONT> - the default font size(3), and then declare the required font size as **SIZE = +/n** , where lies in the range -4 to +4. For instance: <FONT SIZE = - 1>

This is not a good way of setting the font size </FONT> This method is least recommended for changing font size. **Why?** The Font size tag should be avoided for changing font sizes, as it can cause unpredictable problems. For instance, browsers for languages other than English do not use English fonts, and changing this way can create problems.

Furthermore, it may be that for your work the precise size of fonts is an important factor, and thus changing the font size by this method may prove least satisfactory for you requirement. It is a good idea to use style sheet. By the time you read this book, style sheets will be possibly widely implemented.

HTML code for example 9

```
<html>
<head>
<title> Font Sizes</title>
</head>
<body>
<P><Font size = 7>
                Guaranteed Security </font></P>
<P><B><font size =  5> There are now a growing number of transaction processing compa-
nies across the Internet.</font></B> </P>
<p><font size = 4>You must get in touch with several such companies, and some of their cli-
ents to assess their services and guaranteed security for all money transactions . </font></P>
<P> <B><I> <font size =6> End of warning!!!</font></I></B></P>
</body></html>
```

Diagram 17

. Example 9

The code shown in diagram 17 is designed to demonstrate the application of **font size tags** in a document. It also gives you another chance to see how some other tags, once again, are implemented in order to generate the required document.

Guaranteed Security
There are now a growing number of transaction processing companies across the Internet.
You must get in touch with several such companies, and some of their clients to assess their services and guaranteed security for all money transactions .
End of warning!!!

. Explanation

The above text has to be coded in HTML in order to display it in the same form, but by using different fonts for each paragraph. These requirements are:

- "Guaranteed Security" - in font size 7.

- "There ....Internet." - change font to size 5.

- "You …transactions." - change again to font size 4.

- ""End of warning!!!" - change to font size 6.

Now, you should carefully study the code in diagram 17 to see how the above requirements are coded. The HTML file was successfully previewed in IE as shown below in diagram 18.

Font Sizes previewed in IE

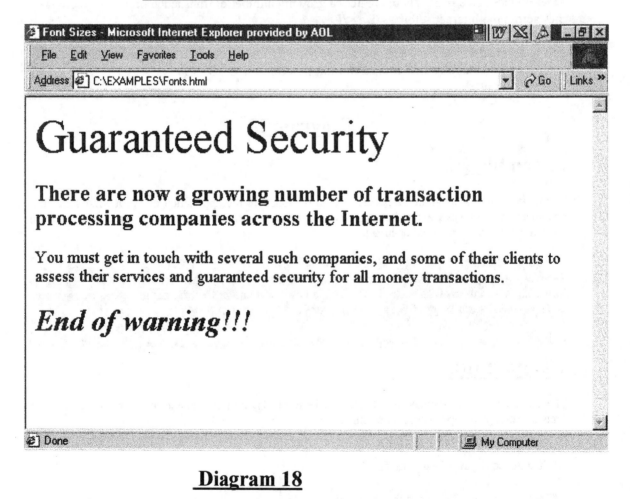

Diagram 18

You will meet fonts again with style sheets application soon. Be patient! Now, learn how to create **lists.**

Chapter 4

Including lists in your Web Page

This chapter should enable you to learn how to design lists with a view to including them in your Web documents.

. Creating Lists

You have already seen how to create and shape text in a variety of ways. Often text is also in the form of a list. In HTML, you can create three types of list:

. Ordered List   . Unordered List   and   . Glossary List

These are defined in Table 1.

. What is TYPE option?

The TYPE is an attribute. This attribute is implemented with **ordered** and **unordered** lists. It can be written in both upper and lower case letters. For instance in the following case:

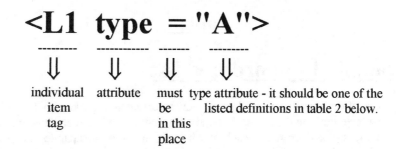

$$<L1 \quad type \quad = \quad "A">$$

individual	attribute	must	type attribute - it should be one of the
item		be	listed definitions in table 2 below.
tag		in this	
		place	

This will generate a list starting with the capital letter **A**. The type attribute should be put in action with any of the definitions shown in table 2; when creating an ordered list.

<u>List Types</u>

Ordered	Unordered	Glossary
• forming a sequence of either numbers or alphabetical letters	• it is also called bulleted list	• its purpose is to allow you to give a brief description of each list item
• both upper and lower case letters are allowed	• bullets may be CIRCLE, SQUARE and DISC	
• a number as a starting point can with using be given	• It is created with <UL> tag - unordered tag <UL>....</UL>	• It is created by using the following tags:
		<DL>...</DL> for creating the list itself.
• It is created with **<OL>** - ordered tag and with <L1> for individual items within the list **<OL ...</OL>** and **<L1>...</L1>**	• **<L1>** for individual items **<L1>...</L1>** within the list <UL>....</UL> and < L1>...</L1>	• **<DT>...</DT>** pair is for defining each list item
		<DD> ...</DD> pair is for defining data for each list item
• TYPE option is allowed	• TYPE option is permitted	
• use upper or lower case letters	• use upper or lower case letters	

<u>Table 1</u>

• <u>Example 1 - unordered list</u>

The purpose of this example is to illustrate how to create an unordered bulleted list in such a way that for the first three items in the list, each item begins with a circle bullet. This group of items is separated by the next group of three items, each of which is, again, on a separate line, and each begins with a square bullet. Each group of three elements should have its own underlined headline, created with level 2 a pair of headline tags. <u>Please go on to next page, below Table 2</u>

Type attribute definitions

Type	Definition
A	creates upper case letters
a	generates lower case letters
I	for big Roman numbers
i	for small Roman numbers
1(number one)	it is for default - no need to set it with attribute

Table 2

. Explanation

The code for example 1 is shown in diagram 1. Although the prime objective of this example is to enable you to learn how to create an unordered list, you still have to apply your knowledge gained so far in order to design the structure and flow of the required code. In fact, the code which is new begins with the following segment of the code shown in diagram 1.

- **<UL type ="circle">** . Here, circle is a bullet which displays a hallow circle, before each list item appears. This declares that the list is "unordered ", and each line starts with a bullet of hallow circle type. Indeed, in this case, **"UL"** is essential tag to signal the beginning of the unordered list.

- Having set the basic requirement for both type of listing and the bullet type, the next thing is to code the actual list items. This is achieved as: **<LI> Chris Butler </LI>**

. What can happen if the tag contains an error?

Here, you should really use list items tags <LI>...</LI> as a pair, and this pair should be written without any kind of error. If you do not observe this rule, the bullet will be displayed without any list item against it. This is undesirable. For instance, if you write list item closing tag as **<LI**, the bullet will appear with out any list item. One can easily type 1(one) for I (letter I), which will not generate the required information. Try yourself, and see what you get.

- The closing unordered list tag **</UL>** should be placed at the end of each group of list items. Now, you should practise with this code. This code was tested with the aid of IE, and its preview is shown in diagram 2 above.

HTML code for example 1

```
<html>
<head>
<title> Unordered List</Title>
</head>
<body>
<center>
 <h2> <u>
            An example of unordered list</u></center>

<u> Using circle as bullet</u></h2>
                    <UL type ="circle">
                            <LI> Chris Butler</LI>
                            <LI> Susan Johnson</LI>
                            <LI>  James Taylor</LI>
                </UL>

<h2><u>  Using square as bullet</u></h2>
                    <UL Type =" SQUARE">
                            <LI> London </LI>
                            <LI> Birmingham</LI>
                            <LI> Manchester </LI></UL>
</body>
</html>
```

Diagram 1

. Example 2 - ordered list

The aim of this example is to demonstrate how to create an ordered list. It has two sub lists. Each sub list is separated from the other, and has its own underlined heading created with level 2 heading tags. The first sub list is **lettered list,** which is created with letters, starting at **A**. It has only three list elements. The second sub list is a **numbered** list, starting at number **7**. It has four list elements, which should be displayed in Arabic numbers (7,8,9,10). Please go on to next page, below Diagram 2.

Unordered List previewed in IE

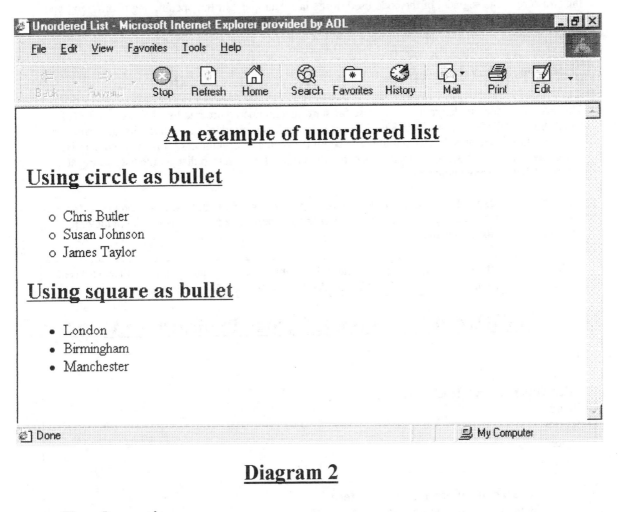

Diagram 2

. Explanation

The HTML code for this example is in diagrams 3 & 3A. Of course, you have seen similar code before, but the important point is to detect in what ways it is different from the last code in diagram 3. Apart from headlines, the following are core differences.

. <OL type ="A">   **.....................(a)**

this segment of the code is for declaring that it is an ordered list of lettered order. It creates a list, using capital **A**, as its initial letter for the lettered sequential series of items in a list. Its structure looks like the structure of the segment of the code used in the last example, but the opening tag is different, and that the attribute value within " " is not any of the bullet types, but one of the definitions shown in table 2. This is why it is different and performs a different task.

• **<OL Type "1" START =" 7">**   .... **(b)**

This part of the code in diagram 3 is the base for starting a numbered ordered list. The word **START** is an attribute in HTML. The attribute START is used when it is desired to commence a list at a particular number. Thus, it declares the initial number to begin the sequence of numbers for an ordered list. Here, "I"(number one) is necessary in order to meet the requirement, which is to display the list starting at number 7, but as Arabic numbers.

The code for this example was tested in IE. The preview is shown in diagram 4. It was previewed successfully, Now, it is your turn to key in this code in order to see its mechanism works for achieving the objectives set for this example 2.

A Practical Note - the number **1** is the default for Arabic numbers. Thus, you do not have to use it in (b) above. You can declare as: **<OL TYPE START =" 7">.** It will work alright.

HTML code for example 2 (cont. in diagram 3A)

```
<html>
<head>
<title> Ordered List</Title>
</head>
<body>
<center>
 <h2>
<u>
          An example of ordered list </center>
          Using upper case letters starting at A</h2></u>
<OL type ="A">
              <LI> London is a capital city in Europe.</LI>
              <LI> Birmingham is situated in the middle of England.</LI>
               <LI> Berlin is also a capital city in Europe . </LI></OL>
```

Diagram 3

Diagram 3A: HTML code for example 2 (cont. from diagram 3)

```
<h2><u>Using small Roman Numerals starting at 7</u></h2>
<OL Type "I" START =" 7">
                    <LI> USA </LI>
                    <LI> Russia</LI>
                    <LI> United Kingdom</LI>
                    <LI> France</L></OL></body></html>
```

Preview of Ordered List in IE

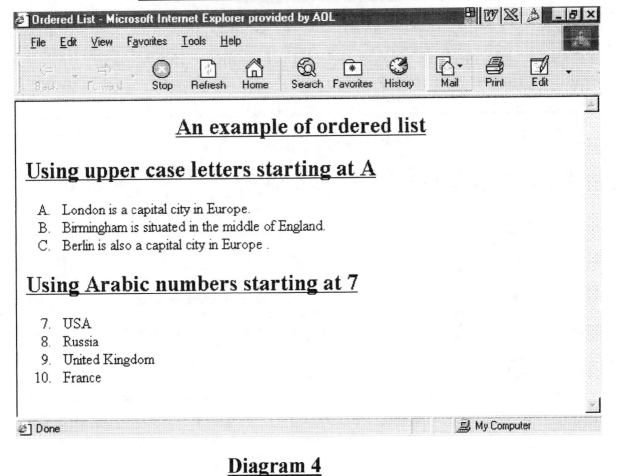

Diagram 4

. Nested Lists

What is a nested list? It is a list within a list. A nested list can prove invaluable in presenting complex relationships of components in a complex system. It can help to analyse a complex task into its components. Each component can be further analysed into its sub-components, and each sub component of a sub-component can be analysed until the desired level of analysis has been reached. You can apply ordered or unordered lists techniques in order to create a nested list, which can show all such relationships. You can also combine both ordered and unordered list features to create a nested list.

. How do you create a nested list?

Examples 3,4 and 5 are designed to demonstrate how this is achieved.

An example of nested ordered list together with some explanatory notes shown in reversed(white) background

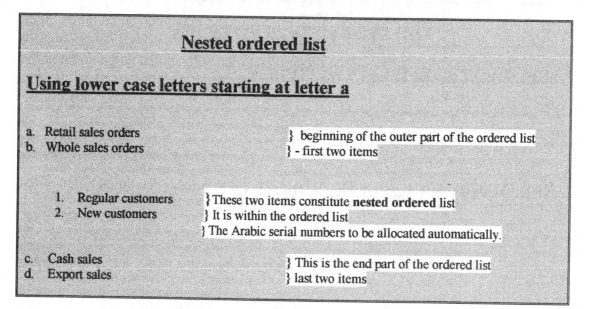

Nested ordered list

Using lower case letters starting at letter a

a. Retail sales orders   } beginning of the outer part of the ordered list
b. Whole sales orders   } - first two items

    1. Regular customers   } These two items constitute **nested ordered** list
    2. New customers   } It is within the ordered list
                            } The Arabic serial numbers to be allocated automatically.

c. Cash sales   } This is the end part of the ordered list
d. Export sales   } last two items

This clearly illustrates the principle of creating a nested list. The inner part can have a number of levels, depending on the complexity involved. Perhaps, you have already guessed that the inner part will become outer part, if you have another level of nesting within this ordered list, and so on. BY applying this principle one can create complex nested lists.

. Example 3

The purpose of this example is to create an HTML document in order to generate a nested ordered list by using the data and format of the above example. The required format should not include explanatory notes, but it must include both headings and paragraphs. This document should be tested in the Internet Explorer to preview it locally.

. Explanation

The code for this example is listed in diagrams 5 & 5A. This code does not introduce any new HTML features, except a method for creating a nested ordered list. Thus, your acquired knowledge and skills of applying HTML should enable you to follow the code with relative ease. You should particularly examine how a list within a list is coded.

There are two lists in this code, but only one pair of opening and closing tags for the ordered list. **Why?** The answer can be deducted from the list shown above in the shaded area. You can see that in the shaded area there are four list items in the outer list, but from only one list item namely **whole sales** further two list items namely, **Regular customers** and **New customers** are derived. Thus, there is only one level of break down to create just one inner list form one list item only.

For this reason alone, here, you have only one</OL> closing tag, which is at the end of the outer list. This marks the end of the ordered list.

- In diagram 5, on two occasions, you can see paragraph markers <P> and </P>. The idea is to form two paragraphs in the body of the list in order to match the format shown in the shaded area.

- The preview is shown in diagram 6. It matches the required format.

HTML code for example 3 (cont. in diagram 5A)

```
<html>
<head>
<title> Nested ordered List </Title>
</head>
<body>
<center>
 <h2> <u>
Nested ordered  list</u></h2></center>
```

Diagram 5

HTML code for example 3 (cont. from diagram 5)

```
<h3>
<u>
      Using lower case letters starting at letter a </h3></u>
<OL type ="a">
                <LI> Retail sales orders</LI>
                <LI> Whole sales orders</LI>
<p></P>
<OL>

                <LI> Regular customers</LI>
                <LI> New customers</LI></OL>
<P></P>

                   <LI> Cash sales</LI>
                   <LI> Export sales</LI>
</OL>
</body>
</html>
```

Diagram 5 A

- **How do we get nested list numbered 1-2 when the ordered list began with "a" a lower case letter?**

In HTML, the default is the Arabic number system. Since the ordered list itself began with **"a"** in lower case, the system created the inner list/nested list by using default Arabic numbers. On the other hand, if you begin the list as **numbered ordered** list, the system will generate both the whole list and the inner/nested list with the Arabic numbers. **Why?**

Because the Arabic notation is in its default mode. Thus, it does not change default unless you change it through the code.

• **Unorderd nested list**

By now, you are familiar with nested list development method. In order to generate an unordered nested list, you still have to create the outer list, and within which you must generate the inner list. The example 4 discussed below diagram 6 illustrates the technique involved in creating such a list.

Nested ordered list document previewed in IE

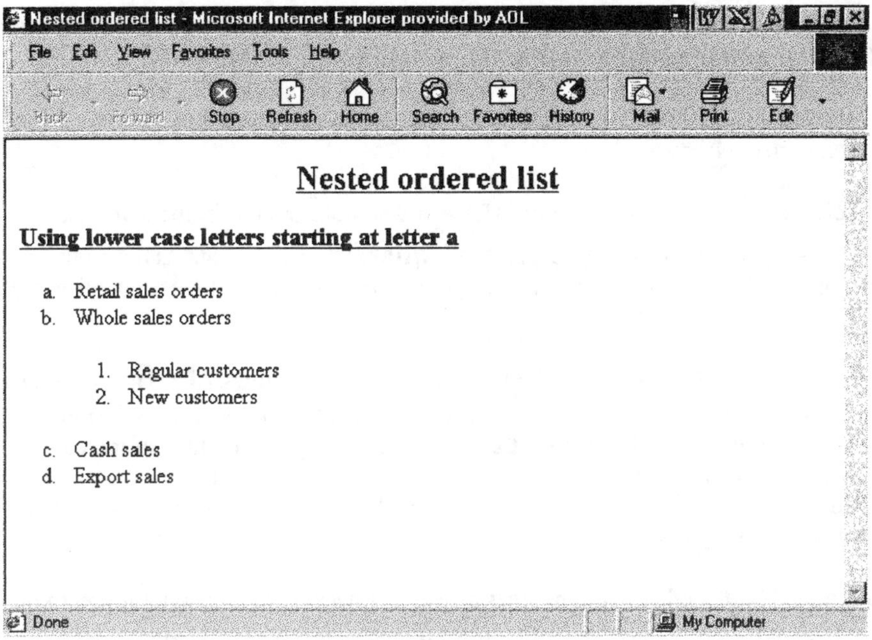

Diagram 6

. Example 4

This example illustrates how to create a nested unordered list as shown below. In this example, a square is used as a bullet. Note that filled circles will appear in the preview as hallow circles.

Nested unordered list

Computer programming
- Java Simplified
- C++ Simplified

Computer hardware
- Printers
- Hard Disks
- Display Units

Computer manufacturers
- Internet working
- Web Sites for business

Internet for home users

. Explanation

The flow of the code in diagram 7 is very similar to the code in the last example, but the following discussion should assist you to understand how to generate nested lists within the unordered list:

- This example has three bulleted inner lists , and thus it requires careful placing of relevant markup tags in their correct places.

- The opening and closing tags for the outer list are <UL> and </UL>. Of course, the outer list begins with <UL>. Its starting point is : **<UL type ="square**">, which contains the required attribute: **square** for the bullet. This way, the outer list is initiated first, as all three nested lists are accommodated within it.

- The first item in the outer list is coded as: **<LI> Computer programming</LI>**. This list item has its own sub-list. This sub-list consists of two items, which are Java Simplified and C++ Simplified. In fact, this sub-list is the first inner list. It is for this reason that it begins with the unordered opening tag <UL>, and contains both list items. Each list item is enclosed within <LI>…</LI> tags. In order to indicate the end of the inner list, it is essential to place the closing tag </ UL> at the end of this and other inner lists.

- This process is repeated for the other two inner lists as well. However, you must not forget to place the closing tag </UL> at the end of each inner list (warning repeated!),otherwise you will not achieve the required output. For instance, if you do not place the closing tag </UL> at the end of the last inner list, you will get the last item, which is **Internet for home users**, of the outer list displayed as the last item of the last inner list. This is wrong, as it is not required in this format. The preview of this document is shown in diagram 8, which meets all requirements.

If you are not sure about the meaning of "bulleted list", you should read list types in table 1.

. Mixed nested lists - example 5

By now, you have some experience of creating ordered, unordered and nested lists. You have also seen that nested lists can be created by starting another list, which can be either ordered or unordered. Indeed, you can also create mixed nested lists, by using both ordered and unordered list tags. The example 5 is designed to demonstrate the technique of creating a mixed nested list for the following data.

    1. Computer programming

        . C++ Simplified
        . Visual C++ 6
        . Java Simplified

2. Computer hardware

. Electrical components
. Electronic components
. Disk drives
. Mechanical parts-box/cabinet

The prime objective of this example is to create nested mixed ordered and unordered list, which will reproduce the above data in a list called **Mixed nested ordered & unordered list**. It is discussed below diagram 8.

HTML code for example 4

```
<h3>
<u>  Using a square as a bullet </u></h3>
<UL type ="square">

<LI>  Computer programming </LI>
              <UL>
                        <LI> Java Simplified</LI>
                        <LI> C++ Simplified</LI> </UL>
<P></P>
<LI>  Computer hardware</LI>
              <UL>
                         <LI> Printers</LI>
                        <LI> Hard Disks</LI>
                        <LI> Display Units</LI> </UL>
<P></P>
<LI>   Computer manufacturers </LI>

              <UL >
                        <LI> Internet working</LI>
                        <LI> Web Sites for business</LI> </UL>
<P></P>

<LI> Internet for home users</LI>
</UL>
</body>
</html>
```

Diagram 7

Nested unordered list previewed in IE

```
Nested unordered list - Microsoft Internet Explorer provided by AOL

 File   Edit   View   Favorites   Tools   Help

  Back    Forward    Stop   Refresh   Home    Search  Favorites  History    Mail    Print    Edit
```

Nested unordered list

Using a square as a bullet

- Computer programming
  - o Java Simplified
  - o C++ Simplified

- Computer hardware
  - o Printers
  - o Hard Disks
  - o Display Units

- Computer manufacturers
  - o Internet working
  - o Web Sites for business

- Internet for home users

```
Done                                                          My Computer
```

Diagram 8

This preview shows each item in the list started with a square bullet. This has happened so, because of this segment of the code: **<UL type ="square">**. On the other hand, each list item in all three nested lists automatically began with a hallow circle. Note that filled circles have appeared in this preview as hallow circles.

. Explanation - example 5

The code for creating a mixed nested ordered and unordered list is shown in diagram 10. The code is self-explanatory. You have already seen the implementation of all these markup tags several times.

Anyway, the special feature of this code starts at the ordered list opening tag **<OL>**. This tag signals the beginning of the ordered list, which is created as the outer list. Thus, the mixed nested list started with the ordered type list. Within this outer list, the unordered nested lists are created. You should carefully note how each unordered list is enclosed within <UL>...</UL> in order to have two sub lists/inner lists within the outer ordered list.

The document was previewed successfully in the IE. The preview is shown in diagram 9A. You can see two inner lists are displayed within the outer list. It demonstrates that the whole list is created within <OL>... </OL> tags.

When mixing tags, you must take extra care, especially, when line break and headline tags are involved. **Why?**

These tags can result in unexpected problems.

. Is it always necessary to implement closing tags?

Sometimes, you do not need a closing tag of any kind. For instance, there is no need to place</UL> or </OL> before </BODY> tag. On the other hand, if you do not place, say </UL> tag, at the end of the following code segment in diagram 10, you will not get data displayed in the required format.

```
<UL>
    <LI> C++ Simplified</LI>
    <LI> Visual C++ 6</LI>
    <LI> Java Simplified </LI>
```

The result will be different than expected, and it will appear as shown below in diagram 9.

Certainly, this is not the required format of the mixed ordered & unordered list. The required format is shown in diagram 9A, with which you can compare the above preview. This preview was obtained without </UL>.

The required list should have an outer ordered list, containing two unordered or bulleted list. This is shown in the preview in diagram 9A.

Thus, it is better to use closing tags in such circumstances instead of relying upon exceptions to rules. Furthermore, if you use tags in pairs (opening and closing tags), you will find it easy to check the accuracy of your HTML code.

. Can a list contain multiple lines of text for a list item or items?

Yes indeed, you can have more than one line of text for any item or all items in your list.

Diagram 9: The top illustration is not the required format as explained above.

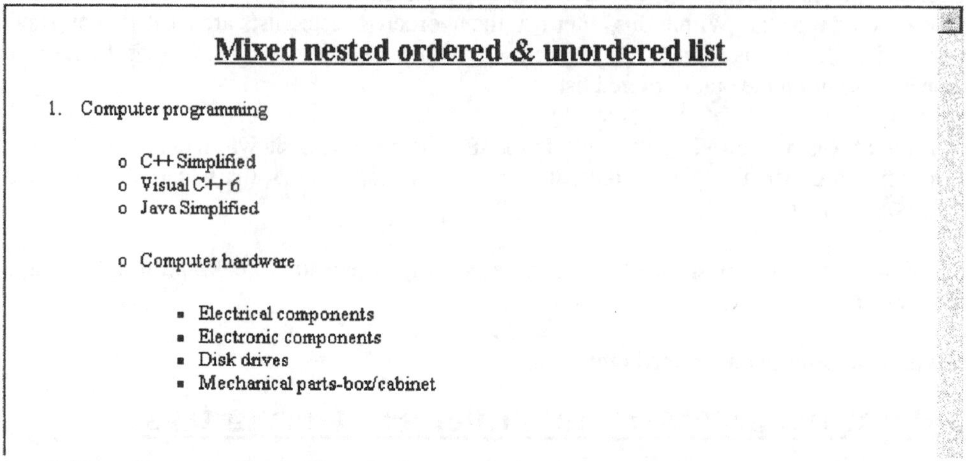

<u>**Mixed nested ordered & unordered list**</u>

1. Computer programming

   o C++ Simplified
   o Visual C++ 6
   o Java Simplified

   o Computer hardware

      ▪ Electrical components
      ▪ Electronic components
      ▪ Disk drives
      ▪ Mechanical parts-box/cabinet

Mixed nested ordered & unordered list previewed in IE

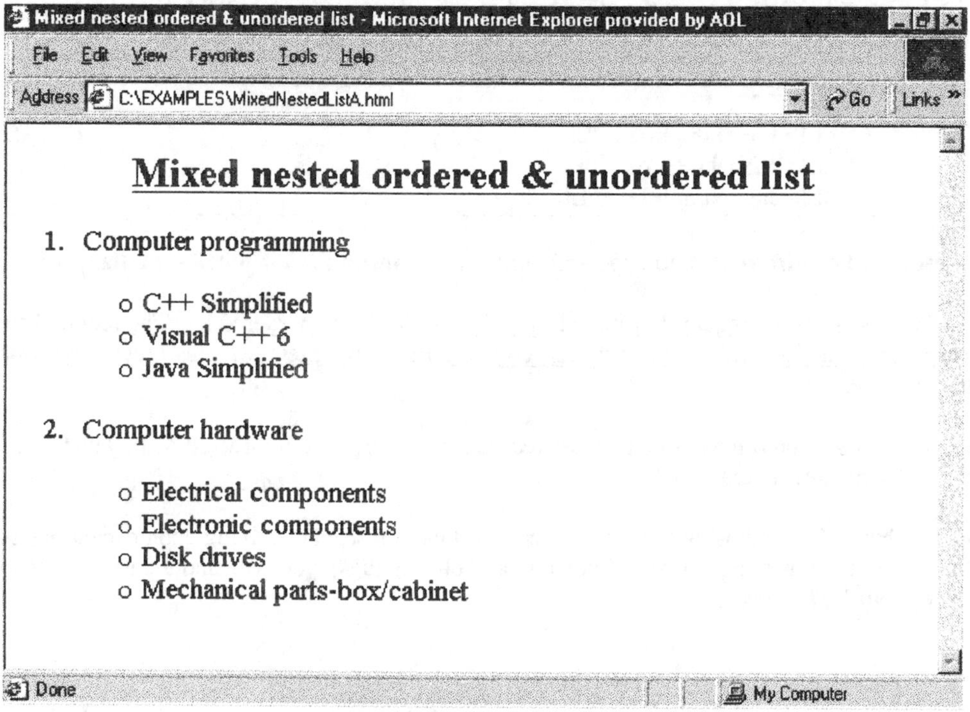

Mixed nested ordered & unordered list - Microsoft Internet Explorer provided by AOL

File   Edit   View   Favorites   Tools   Help

Address C:\EXAMPLES\MixedNestedListA.html   Go   Links »

Mixed nested ordered & unordered list

1. Computer programming

   o C++ Simplified
   o Visual C++ 6
   o Java Simplified

2. Computer hardware

   o Electrical components
   o Electronic components
   o Disk drives
   o Mechanical parts-box/cabinet

Done   My Computer

Diagram 9A

HTML code for example 5

```
<html>
<head>
<title> Mixed nested ordered & unordered list</Title>
</head>
<body>
<center>
 <h2><u>Mixed nested ordered & unordered  list</u></h2></center>
<OL>
     <LI>  Computer programming</LI>
     </UL>
<P></P>
       <UL>
              <LI> C++ Simplified</LI>
              <LI> Visual C++ 6</LI>
              <LI> Java Simplified </LI>
</UL>
<p></P><LI> Computer hardware</LI>
<P></P>
       <UL>
              <LI> Electrical components</LI>
              <LI> Electronic components</LI>
               <LI> Disk drives</LI>
                <LI> Mechanical parts-box/cabinet</LI>
         </UL>
</OL>
</body>
</html>
```

Diagram 10

. Glossary list

A glossary is another kind of list. It is very useful for creating lists which have some references or de-scriptive phrases to be followed by related definitions or values or data. It can be used with other features of HTML for a variety of types lists. For instance, on the next page, in the shaded area, there is an example of its use. I have reversed parts of this shaded area, so that you can see the explanation easily.

. <u>Example 6</u>

The code in diagrams 11 & 11A is designed to generate the information in its present format shown in the shaded area below. This code excludes everything which is shown in reversed background.

<u>An example of glossary with an explanatory note shown in reversed background</u>

<u>An example of glossary list</u>

A Program   first descriptive phrase/description/ just a phrase

It is a set of instructions that tells a computer what to do.   value/definition of the 1ˢᵗ descriptive phrase

A computer   second descriptive phrase

It is a machine that obeys instructions given by a program.   value of the second descriptive phrase

PCs   third descriptive phrase

The most common computers are a variety of PCs.   value/definition of the 3ʳᵈ descriptive phrase

Cost   fourth descriptive phrase

You can buy a PC for just £500.   value/definition of the 4ᵗʰ descriptive phrase

Note: Value or definition or defining data all these mean the same.

.<u>Explanation</u>

The structure of the code in diagrams 11 and 11A is similar to the codes you have met in this chapter. Therefore, it is expected that you can grasp easily how this coding began in order to create the required list in its present format . As far as the actual glossary list is concerned, you need to use some new markup tags which you have not yet used in any of the previous HTML documents, but these are shown in table 1. However, it is important to state as follows.

- To start the glossary list, you must place **<DL>** tag at the beginning of the segment of the code, which is the first descriptive phrase in the list. In this example, it comes before coding: **A Program,** which is the first descriptive phrase. It is coded by using a pair of tags for defining each list item. The following is the segment of the code for it:

<DT> A Program</DT>

- Having started the glossary list, the next step is to code any definitions or values or defining data that follow the descriptive phrase. To do so, for each list item, you must implement a pair of tags <DD> and </DD>, which define data/value/definition for each list item. For the first descriptive phrase, it is coded as shown below:

<DD> It is a set of instructions that tells a computer what to do.</DD>

This first descriptive phrase has only one definition/value/defining data, and thus the next step is to code the next descriptive phrase and its defining data.

- This above process is also applicable to other list items and their defining data.

- At the end of the last defining data, you must place the glossary closing tag **</DL>**.

Once again, it is suggested that you key in the code shown in diagram 11 to learn by practising. The preview of this document is shown in diagram 12. Now, compare it with the required glossary list in its required format shown in the shaded area on the last page.

HTML code for example 6 (cont. in diagram 11A)

```
 <html>
<head>
<title> Glossary list</Title>
</head>
<body>
<center>
 <h2> <u>
       An example of glossary list </u></h2></center>
<DL>

      <DT> <u> A Program</u></DT>
      <DD> It is a set of instructions that tells a computer what to do.</DD>
```

Diagram 11

HTML code for example 6 (cont. from diagram 11)

```
<p></P>
        <DT><u>  A computer</u></DT>
         <DD> It is a machine that obeys instructions given by a program.</DD>
<p></P>
        <DT><u>PCs</u> </DT>
        <DD> The most common computers are a variety of PCs.</DD>
<P></P>
        <DT><u> Cost</u></DT>
        <DD> You can buy a PC for just £500.</DD> </DL>
</body></html>
```

Diagram 11A

Glossary list previewed in IE

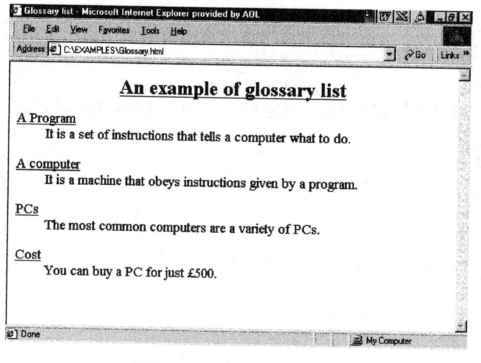

Diagram 12

Chapter 5

Colours & style sheets - 1

The aim of this chapter is to enable you to understand text and background colours, create text and background in different colours and to use HTML single style sheet rules for setting up text and background colours. The reader should be able to decide for oneself to use whether a simple colour scheme or whether to set up mixed colours for the Web page.

. Setting Colours

You have possibly seen some Web pages, and noticed how colourful these pages were. You can create attractive Web pages by applying different colours and their combinations to both the text itself and the background. The 16 standard (or simple) colours, to choose from for your Web page, are shown in table 3. The style sheets can be used to set both text and background colours. By applying hexadecimal values, in theory you can specify colours from a palette of 24 million colours. **What?** Not for me thank you! In fact, it is highly likely that your system is capable of no more than 256-colour default display. It is a wide range of colours. Wide enough for most needs!

. How is the combined colour generated?

The colour display unit of your computer system has a great number of pixels. A pixel is a single tiny dot on a display unit (screen). All screen images are made up of a collection of pixels. These pixels are so tiny and so close to each other that a human eye cannot distinguish one from the other. Each pixel is capable of either **off (dark)** or **on (illuminated in colour if it is a colour screen)**.

. The RGB colour model

The RGB colour model defines colour in terms of **red**, **green** and **blue** components. Thus, the primary colours or lights are red, green and blue. These colours can be combined in order to generate a combined colour. When RGB components are mixed in <u>equal amount of light intensity they produce white</u>. When RGB components are combined in other proportions they generate a mixed colour representing the proportional amount of intensity of light of RGB components. This is how you can create virtually countless mixed colours.

In order to represent the intensity of red, green and blue lights/colours in the mixed colour, the mixed colour is specified by a number or value. This number itself consists of three different sets of numbers, each representing the intensity of red, green and blue in the mixed colour. The system used to describe this mixed colour is called **hexadecimal** (base 16). The hexadecimal numbering system is commonly used in the computing field. The reason for preferring this numbering system is that it can represent any number between 0 - 255 with just two hex digits in accordance with the hexadecimal system. For instance:

- **000000** - it represents **black colour** as it has no RGB components. Just no colour

- **FF0000** - it means **red colour** as it has 100% red light, and the other two are not present

- **FFFFFF** - this represents **white colour** - no other colours in it

Table 1 contains the hexadecimal equivalent of 16 standard colours. The hexadecimal numbers are known as hexadecimal the **triplets** or hexadecimal pairs or **hex pairs**. In passing, there is no harm in mentioning that the base 16 is easier to use in the computing field than base 10. For example, it is easier to convert a hex number into binary and vice versa. You should know by now that binary numbers are the backbone of computer systems. In table 1, you can see that hex pairs begin with the symbol # in order to distinguish them from other numbering systems. Sometimes, hex pairs are within the " ", but without quotes numbers are also permissible.

Standard HTML Colours

Colour Name	Hex Pair Triplet	Colour Name	Hex Pair Triplet
Black	#000000	Gray	#808080
White	#FFFFFF	Lime	#00FF00
Red	#FF0000	Olive	#808000
Green	#008000	Yellow	#FFFF00
Blue	#0000FF	Maroon	#800000
Navy	#000080	Purple	#800080
Silver	#C0C0C0	Fuchsia	#FF00FF
Teal	#008080	Aqua	#00FFFF

Table 1

These are standard Windows colours. You can use names for displays on a 16-colour monitor. For complex colour schemes, you have to apply the hex pair values. The biggest drawback is that different manufacturers have different standards. For instance, Netscape has countless colours. Scores of browsers do not even have the same colour names. However, there is one important aspect which must not be overlooked which is the fact that the most manufacturers base their colour systems on 256 different colours. These are almost the same throughout the industry. Thus, it is a good idea to design Web pages using these colours.

• Is it a good idea to use simple colours to improve the visual attraction of your Web page?

In my opinion, yes, it is. The reason for this suggested simplicity is that there are many different browsers and often several different versions of the same browser in use across the Internet. You may have the latest version of a particular browser running on your computer system, and thus your Web page on your system appears brilliant. On the other hand, the same document, on someone else's system with a rather older version of the same browser or a different browser, may look dull, or may not even display clearly the image(s) in your document.

Another important reason for using simple colours instead of applying a complex colouring scheme and complex graphics is that the whole idea for, say a commercial Web page, is to interest a visitor in your products, so that a sale can take place. If your Web page uses extravagant brilliant colours to the extent that the attraction lies primarily in presentation rather than for what the document is designed for, then it will defeat the prime objective of doing business on the Net.

Therefore, your design of Web page must get your message across on the Net. It is, therefore, recommended to design your Web page simply with a standard colour scheme. This way, it is most likely that your colourful visual presentation will be rendered across the Internet in the same way and as you want. Remember, the whole idea is to communicate with viewers, with the main aim to do business with them. You should always bear in mind that you are investing both time and money in your Web page design for your business, and thus its complex colourful visual presentation must not hinder your principal goal.

• How do you set text and background colours?

You have learnt the use of < **BODY**> **tag** as a markup for the beginning and ending of the body section of the HTML document. The body tag plays more than one role. It can also be used for setting colour attributes. There are five colour attributes which are implemented with the **<body>** tag. These are listed in table 2.

• What are link, vlink and alink in colour terminlology?

- A link or LINK - it refers to an ordinary link on a page.

- a vlink or VLINK - it is a link that has been followed.

- alink or ALINK - it refers to a current link which is in the process of connecting.

Usually on the white background:

. LINK is set to **blue**   . VLINK is set to **purple**   . ALINK is set to **red**

<BODY> tag colour attributes

Colour Attribute		Function
BGCOLOR 0r bgcolor	=	Sets the background colour for the whole page
TEXT or text	=	Sets the normal text colour
LINK or link *	=	Sets the colour of the link not yet visited
VLINK or vlink *	=	Sets the colour of the visited link
ALINK or alink *	=	Sets the colour of the current or active link

The following examples will enable you to see how these features work in practice.

. <u>Example 1</u>

This simple example is designed to show you how to construct an HTML file for generating text in colour on a colourful background, and display the underlined text in the centre. It generates the following message:

The white text is displayed on blue background

. <u>Explanation</u>

The code is listed in diagram 1. The body tag contains the required colours for both the text and the background. You should carefully note the construction of the following segment of the code. If you make a mistake such as omit " " you will not get the required result. Without the browser editor, you must check your document for such errors. There is no comma or any other symbol between these two attributes within the < >. The same rule applies, if you have more than two colour attributes with their values enclosed with the < >.

<body bgcolor = "0000FF"   Text = "FFFFFF">

↓   ↓

hex value for blue colour   hex value for white colour

HTML code for example 1

```
<html>
<head>
<title> Applying colours </title>
</head>
<body bgcolor ="0000FF"   Text= "FFFFFF">
<center>
<u><h2> The white text is displayed on blue background</h2></u></center>
</body>
</html>
```

Diagram 1

Applying colours previewed in IE

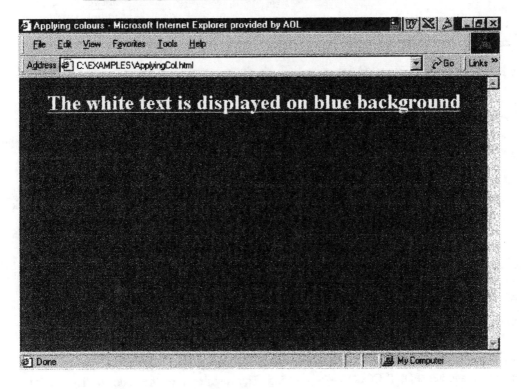

Diagram 2

- The closing body tag</body> is still used to mark the end of <body> tag.

The html document was previewed in IE as shown in diagram 2. Obviously, the blue colour is invisible as such, but most certainly, your colour display unit will illuminate it.

. Example 2

The purpose of this example is to show you how to use names of colours, <font >...</font> tags, and use different colours on the same page.

- **Teal background** - this message should be displayed on a teal background, using the fuchsia colour, underlined and in the centre of the page.

- **This is in font colour white.** - this sentence should be displayed in the centre of the page, on a teal background, but in white colour using the colour option within the <FONT> tags.

. Explanation

The HTML code for example 2 is given in diagram 2 below. The code requires the following discussion.

- The <BODY> tag - it sets both the background colour for the entire page, as well as the colour of **Teal background**. It demonstrates that you can declare colours by their standard names. There is no need to surround them with " " marks.

- **<FONT Color = >** - the colour option can be given within this tag. It is useful tag when you have to display one or more aspects of a Web page in different font colours, and on the same back ground which applies to the whole page. The segment of the code:

   <Font color = white> This is in font colour white.</font>

- It is important to place the closing tag </font> at the end of the section, where a specific colour requirement ends.

. What will happen if you do not place the closing </font> tag?

The colour set for a particular section will continue to affect the remainder of the page until it is changed by another<FONT COLOR = - - - >tag. The remainder of the code in diagram 3 is self-explanatory. The code was previewed successfully. The preview in IE is shown in diagram 4.

HTML code for example 2

```
<html>
<head>
<title> Applying colours 2</title>
</head>
<body bgcolor = Teal text = Fuchsia >
<center>
<U>
<h1>
    Teal background</h1></u>

 <h2><Font color = white> This is in font colour white.</font></h2></center>
</body>
</html>
```

Diagram 3

. Style sheets

In chapter 3 styles and style sheets were outlined. Style sheets can enable you to control the appearance of Web pages. By means of style sheets, you can format your text, font sizes and types, spacing between lines, word and letters, control margin, background colours, and so on. In fact, style sheets can be applied to all aspects of HTML 4.0. The most popular style sheet language is

Cascading Style Sheet (CSS) version 1.

The reason for its popularity is that the leading browsers' manufacturers have implemented it. The Internet Explorer and Netscape Navigator have adopted it, but the manner of adoption differs, and thus both browsers interpret style sheets in their own way. One can only hope that by the time you read this book these differences are minimum. The older browsers under version 4 cannot handle style sheets at all. It means that older browsers and those do not support CSS will set aside your style sheet markup code. Now, it is the right time and place in this book to learn how to apply style sheets in your HTML document.

. How can you use style sheets to set text
and background colours in a Web page? *Now read on after diagram 4*

Applying colours 2 previewed in IE

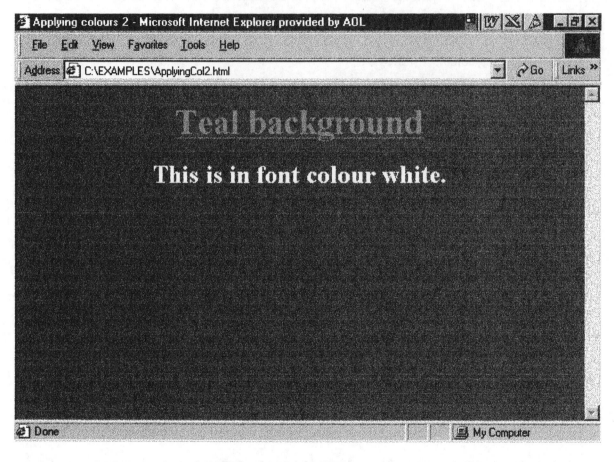

Diagram 4

.Setting up text and background colours

Firstly, it is of paramount importance to understand the **general syntax rule** for applying style sheets. The general syntax rule consists of two parts. These parts are:

. **selector** - it sets the scope of the style. For instance, **H2** can be used as a selector, whose scope is to create a headline of level 2. Thus, the selector is the name of the tag.

. **declaration** - it is within the **curly braces {...}**, which consists of some HTML features concerning the required typographic style. For instance, **{ font-size: 14; font-style:Bold}**

In fact, the purpose of the declaration is to set the typographical effect of the selector. For example:

H3 { font-size:20; font-style:*italic*}

This HTML code will result in setting the headline in level 3 **(scope)**, but in font size 20 using *italic* style typeface **(typographical effect)**.

The general format of the syntax used for setting a style sheet is given below. The declaration has its own two components, which are also illustrated below.

selector {declaration }

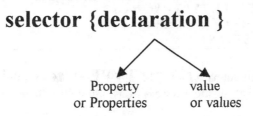

Property   value
or Properties   or values

It is important to note that the declaration is **not** within the angle brackets. **You have been warned!**

In the following HTML code, you can identify each component in the syntax of style sheet rule:

H2{ font-size : 14 ; font-style : Bold}

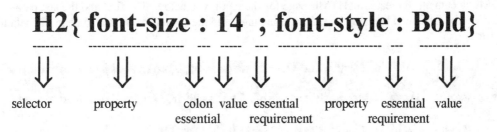

selector   property   colon value essential   property   essential value
                          essential   requirement   requirement

- The property can be single properties or more than one property

- The semicolon is used to separate pairs of property and value from the other property and its value

- Property and value are used as a pair

- Within the pair is a colon to separate its elements

. <u>How can you place style sheet definition in your Web page?</u>

The style definition or style information or style blocks all these phrases means the same that is style sheets feature for using these in the Web page. There are three modes of including style sheet definition into a Web page. Here, first, the embedded style sheet is implemented, because it is the most reliable mode of controlling many aspects of HTML documents.

. <u>Embedded Style Sheet</u>

The embedded pair of tags is <STYLE>....</STYLE>. It is inserted in the **Head** part of the Web page. Within it, the style sheet definition is placed. It forms a block of style sheet information/definition. This information affects the style preferences in the **whole HTML** document. Its simplest form is as shown on the next page.

```
<STYLE TYPE = "text/css ">
    selector {declaration}
    </STYLE>
```

Often, you need to expand this simplest form. The **TYPE ="text/css"** - it is an essential attribute. It is required to specify that you are using **css** (Cascading Style Sheets language).

. <u>Example 3</u>

This example is designed to demonstrate the effects of inserting embedded style sheet information into the HTML document. It creates an HTML page for the text given below. The first and the last paragraphs are to be formatted by using level 3 headline tags, and the second paragraph to be in the default text format.

This is an example of embedded style sheet. This paragraph is displayed in level 3 headline, using font size 14, in italic style. [embedded style sheet rule]
This is outside the scope of embedded style sheet rule. This is why it is rendered in default font size and style.
This is another headline in accordance with the embedded style sheet rule.

. <u>Explanation</u>

The HTML code for this example is listed in diagram 5.The segment of the code shown below indicates the place where the style sheet information is placed in the **HEAD** section of the HTML document.

```
<head>
    <STYLE TYPE="text/css">
    H3{font-size:14pt;font-style:Italic} </style></head>
```

Here, you can see how the selector and declaration have been implemented.

. The preview of this Web page is given in diagram 6. You can see that the embedded style sheet affects only those style preferences in the whole document which are formatted by using level 3 headlines across the document. It does not affect all style preferences in the entire document. This is evident in paragraph 2 in which the text is rendered in the default format.

HTML code for example 3

```
<html>
<head>
<title> Style sheet</title>
<STYLE  TYPE="text/css">
                            H3{font-size:14pt;font-style:Italic}
</style>
</head>
<body>

 <h3>
 This is an example of embedded style sheet. This  paragraph is displayed in level 3 headline,
using font size 14, in italic style. [embedded style sheet rule]</h3>
<P>
        This is outside the scope of embedded style sheet rule. This is why it is  rendered in
default font size and style.</P>

<p></P> <P></P>

<h3>
        This is another headline in accordance with the embedded style sheet rule. </h3>
</body>
</html>
```

Diagram 5

. Example 4

The prime objective of this example is to demonstrate that you can expand style sheet information to more than one **general syntax** rule in the same document.

See explanation and code below diagram 6.

Style Sheet previewed in IE

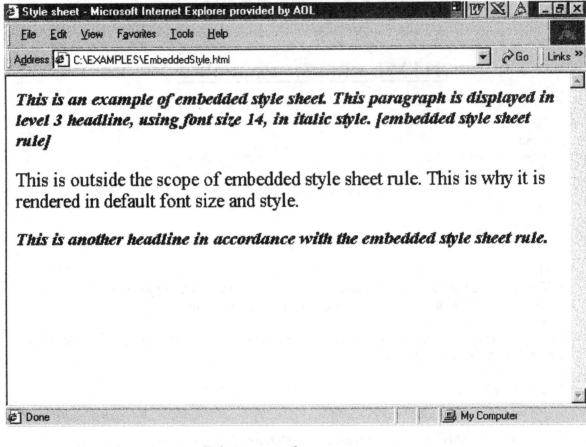

Diagram 6

. Explanation

The code shown in diagram 7 is designed for this purpose. It illustrates that in the same document two different selectors and declarations can be implemented successfully in order to control the appearance of the Web page. The embedded style sheet information is entered in the code by the following segment of the code.

In accordance with it, wherever in the same document any of these selectors are met, the text is formatted and displayed as per each declaration respectively.

```
<STYLE  TYPE="text/css">
H3{font-size:20pt;font-style:ITALIC}
H2{font-size:16pt;font-style:STRONG}<style>
```

• The document is called Style sheet 2. You can see its preview in diagram 8.

HTML code for example 4

```
<html>
<head>
<title> Style sheet 2</title>
<STYLE  TYPE="text/css">
H3{font-size:20pt;font-style:ITALIC}
H2{font-size:16pt;font-style:STRONG}
</style></head>
<body>
<h3>  This is level 3 headline.</h3>
<P></P>
<h2><U> This is level 2 headline.</h2></U>
<P></P>
<h3>Another level 3 headline - Style sheet in operation.</h3>
<h2><U> Another level 2 headline. Style sheet works fine.</U></h2>
</body>
</html>
```

Diagram 7

• Practical Hints

• By now, you must know that a style sheet information has the following three elements namely, selector, property and value.

• Property + value = declaration. This declaration makes up the style.

• The element called selector tells the browser about declaration, and in turn the browser works out the style coded in the declaration.

Style Sheet 2 previewed in IE

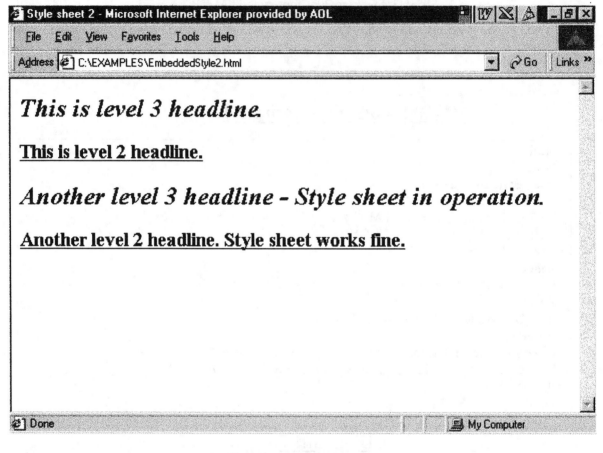

Diagram 8

. Applying style sheets to set text & background colours

You can implement style sheet rules to set text colours, background colours, images, selected parts of the page, paragraphs, and the entire page. The **general syntax rule** for applying style to set text and background colours is pretty much the same, but extended to include more relevant information. The following is the general syntax format for the single style sheet rule to be inserted into the HTML document in order to **change text colours:**

```
<HEAD>
        <STYLE TYPE="text/css">
        BODY { color: value}</STYLE>
</HEAD>
```

- The following is the general syntax format for the single style sheet rule to be inserted into the HTML document in order to **change background colours:**

```
<HEAD>
        <STYLE TYPE="text/css">
        BODY { color: value; background-color:value}
</STYLE>
</HEAD>
```

You may be wondering why the keyword BODY is used in these cases instead of selector. The answer is that a selector is a name of a tag. Here, the BODY is a tag. You have already met <BODY> tag.

By value, it implies any of the 16 standard HTML colours. You can also use colour values in the range 0 to 255. In addition, if you wish, you can also implement RGB triplets as values. So, the choice is yours. You are already familiar with these colour terms.

. **Example 5**

The aim of this example is demonstrate how to display in the Web page the following message. The message should be written in white colour, and displayed on a green background in the format shown below.

It is displayed on green background, but this writing is in white colour.

The HTML code for this example is given in diagram 9 below.

. **Explanation**

The code for this example is shown in diagram 9. The following segment of this code sets the style, background and text colours.

```
<style type="text/css">
body {color: white; background:green}
```

- In CSS application, you cannot use **BGCOLOR** for background. You must code either of the two following ways:

Background-color: name the colour of your choice　Or

　　　　background: name the colour of your choice

- There is no need to say :　　**Font color = white** as in diagram 3.

In CSS application:　　**Color = white**　is sufficient as shown in diagram 9.

- In CSS application:　you can use lower or upper case letters.　The document Applying different colours was previewed in IE successfully, This is in diagram 10.

HTML code

```
<html>
<head>
<title> Applying different colours</title>
<style type="text/css">
body {color: white; background:green}
</style>
</head>
<body>
<h1> It is displayed on green background, but this writing is in white colour.</h1>
</body>
</html>
```

Diagram 9

.Multiple style sheets

The last two example have provided a guideline for setting up the single style rule. By applying CSS, you can also set up multiple style sheet rules/ definitions in your HTML document.

Applying different colours previewed in IE

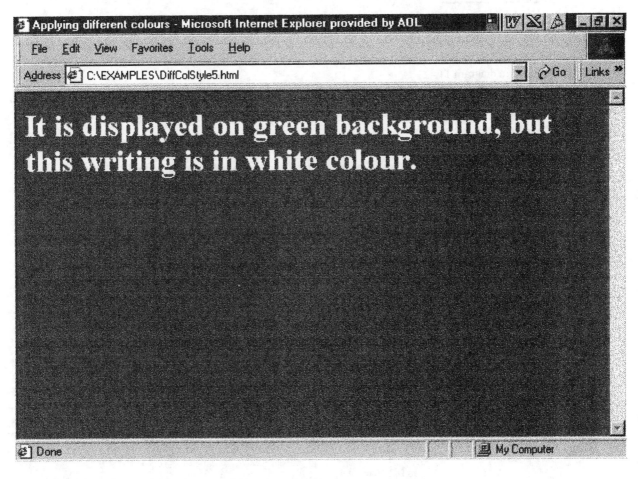

Diagram 10

. Example 6

This example is designed to demonstrate the technique of inserting several style sheet rules in a HTML document in order to generate on a colour background several text in different styles and colours. In this example, three different style sheet rules are applied to three different headlines, which are displayed on a single colourful background, but each line has its own style and colour.

. Explanation

The HTML code for this example is in diagram 11 & 11A. The code is written in such a way that you have more practice of writing HTML documents, and that you can apply your skills of HTML acquired so far. The new feature introduced by this document is highlighted in diagram 11. See the shaded area in diagram 11.

- As you have no doubt gathered, it is embedded style sheet using multiple style sheet information.

Why?

Because the declaration of style sheet rules is in the head section of the document. In addition, in accordance with the style sheet rules, when the relevant headline meets, the rule is implemented.

- It is suggested that when you practise with this document, you should amend this code by including three different tiny paragraphs at different places in the document, using these three headline tags respectively. You will then learn that these rules apply in accordance with the definition of the embedded style sheet rule.

- It was previewed in the Internet Explorer successfully as shown in diagram 12.

HTML code for example 6 (cont. in diagram 11A)

```
<html>
<head>
<title> Multiple styles sheet - colours</title>

<style type="text/css">
body{background: yellow}
                    H1{color: red}
                    h2{color: blue}
                    h3{color: gray}
</style>
</head>
<body>
<center>
<h1>
```

Diagram 11

HTML code for example 6 (cont. from diagram 11)

```
<u>
    Learn by doing!
</u></h1></center></BR>
<h2>
      Practise! Practise! Practise!
</BR></h2>
<center>
<h3>
    Skills are acquired by doing.
</h3></center></body></html>
```

Diagram 11 A

Multiple style sheet -colours previewed in IE

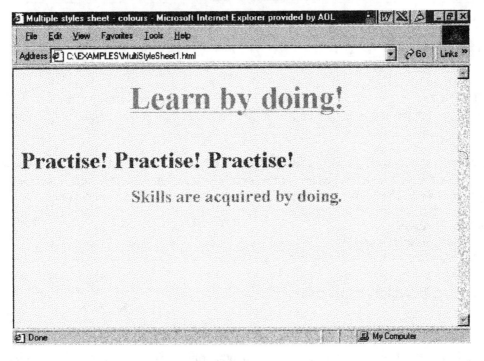

Diagram 12

. <u>Example 7</u>

The purpose of this example is to write the HTML code for the text given in the shaded area, and test it in the Internet Explorer, in order to preview it locally. You should use different colours for both top and bottom headings, and two paragraphs. The whole text should be displayed on a colour background using any colour other than the colours set for text for headings and the middle part of this whole text block.

J. H. BOSS Accountants

<u>30 minutes free advice.</u>
<u>We are here to help!</u>

Consultancy service - business and personal taxation, VAT returns, book-keeping service for small firms, financial advice and financial reports preparation.

<u>ESTABLISHED 1900</u>

. <u>Explanation</u>

- The HTML code for this task is shown in diagram 13, and the document was previewed in the IE successfully. The preview is in diagram 14. This is another example of an embedded style sheet.

- Although the structure of this HTML file is similar to the file you have seen in the previous case, this example further introduces the idea of implementing style sheet rules for setting font types and their sizes as well. The following segment of the code sets the style sheet multiple rules.

```
<style type="text/css">
body{color = fuchsia; background:yellow}
H2{color:blue}
h3{color:teal}
h4{font-size:22pt;font-style:italic;color:FF0000}
```

- Above, you can see **h4{font-size:22pt;font-style:italic;color:FF0000}**. In this rule, hexadecimal notation for the colour red is coded. In other rules, colours are named. It means that in the same document you can use both colour names and hexadecimal notations.

HTML code for example 7

```
<html>
<head>
<title> Multiple styles sheet - colours 2</title>

<style type="text/css">
body{color = fuchsia; background:yellow}
H2{color:blue}
h3{color:teal}
h4{font-size:22pt;font-style:italic;color:FF0000}
</style></head>

<body>
<center>
<h1><u>
                    J.H. BOSS Accountants
<h2>

            30 minutes free advice. <BR>
            We are here to help!
</center>
</h2>
</u>
</BR>

<h3>
            Consultancy service -
            business and personal taxation, VAT returns, book-keeping
            service for small firms, financial advice and financial reports
            preparation.

</h3>
<center><h4><u>
    ESTABLISHED 1900
</u></h4></center>
</body>
</html>
```

Diagram 13

You should run this code on your system so that you can analyse its structure, and advance your own skills of developing HTML documents for designing, and putting them on-line for public viewing.

Multiple styles sheet -colours 2 previewed in IE

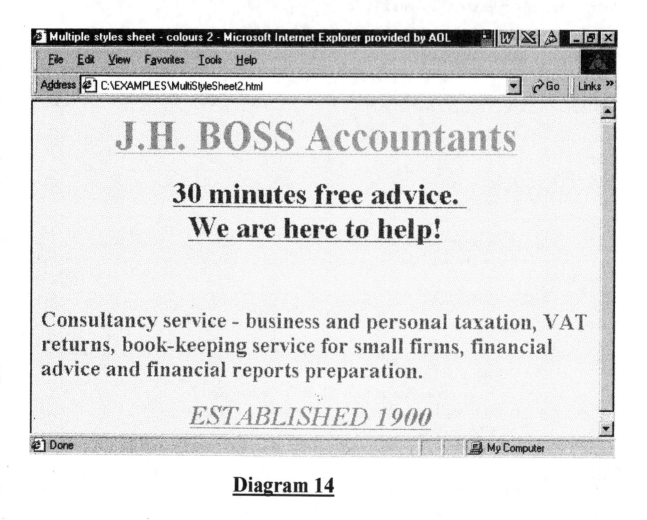

Diagram 14

.Contrasting headlines and backgrounds

By now you have worked with a number of embedded style sheets. They are fine for affecting HTML style preferences across the entire document. On the other hand, there are occasions when you want to design a document with contrasting headlines and background. In such cases:

in-line style sheet rules

are applied. By means of in-line style sheet rules, anywhere in the document, you can override an embedded style rule. **WHY?**

The reason is that an in-line style sheet rule affects only a selected section of the document. Examples 8 and 9 are aimed at demonstrating the use of in-line style sheet rules.

. **Example 8**

In order to demonstrate the application of in-line style sheet rules, this example creates five different headlines on five different colourful backgrounds. The following text in the same format, but with different font sizes and style is created, displayed, and viewed locally in the Internet Explorer.

Screen centre
font size 20 bold style in red on aqua background.

This paragraph starts at left margin.
Font size 18 italic white on navy background. Size

20 blue italic on red background.

Size 16 regular font navy on lime background.

Size 18 bold grey on yellow background.

. **Explanation**

The HTML document is in diagram 15 and its preview is shown in diagram 16. The general format for setting styles for font size, style and colour together with the background colour is as follows:

**< p style "color: color name/hex; font-size: value; font-style: value; background: name/hex">
followed by the text to be coded**

In this code, <P> tag is essential, as it is used here to define the required styles. In this HTML file, it has to be coded five times in order to create five different contrasting headlines and backgrounds. Each headline is just like a paragraph, and thus <P> tag moves the action to the next paragraph.

- In accordance with this general format, the following is the HTML code for the first paragraph:

<P style="color:red; font-size:20pt;font-style:bold;background:00FFFF" >
    **Screen centre
**
    font size 20 bold style in red on aqua background.

This process is repeated for the other four paragraphs by using their respective preferences.

- The rest of the document follows the same pattern. Certainly, once again, it enables you to practise your acquired knowledge and skills of developing HTML document.

- This HTML document was previewed in IE successfully. Try it yourself. Surely, you can appreciate that for seeing the effects of colours, you must key in this document, and preview it locally (IE).

- <u>Have you noticed the omission of the closing paragraph tag</></u>?

You do not need it, because each segment of the code setting styles for font size, styles, colour and background colour starts with a paragraph opening tag <P>. If you prefer to implement </P>, you can do so.

<u>HTML code for example 8 (cont. in diagram 15A)</u>

```
<html>
<head>
<title> in-line style sheet - colours</title>
</head>
<body>
<center>
<U>
<P style="color:red; font-size:20pt;font-style:bold;background:00FFFF" >
      Screen centre<BR>
      font size 20 bold style in red on aqua background.</U>
```

<u>Diagram 15</u>

HTML code for example 8 (cont. from diagram 15)

```
</center>
<p style="color:white; font-size:18pt; font-style:italic;background:000080">

    This paragraph starts at left margin.<BR>
    Font size 18 italic white on navy background.

<p style="color:blue; font-size:20pt; font-style:italic; background: red">

    Size 20 blue italic on red background.

<P STYLE="color:navy; Font-size:16pt; Font-style:regular; background: lime">
    Size 16 regular font navy on lime background.

<P style="color:gray;font-size:18pt; font-style:bold; background: yellow">
    Size 18 bold grey on yellow background.</P>
</body>
</html>
```

Diagram 15 A

. A word of warning!

When you key in this code, you must pay special attention to all symbols used in this code. Since the browser will not comment on any omission or incorrect use of any of these symbols, you can waste invaluable time searching for a minute error which occurred during the key in process. You may find that due to such an error, one of your headlines has not appeared as required. In this case, you look for an error in its <P....> tag.

. Font Properties - In this examples, some of font properties and values are implements.
For a list of these and other properties and values, see appendix.

For-size, and **font-style** are two examples of font properties. Similarly, **Italic**, and **bold** are two examples of font values.

. If there is no need to include in the paragraph < P---------- > font different properties and values, you can still write in-line code for a particular headline. For instance:

<P STYLE ="color: navy; background: lime"> This is in navy colour on lime background.

This amendment will generate a headline in navy colour on lime background, but using the same font property and value, which the default found is set. You can experiment with it, and see what you get.

In-line style sheet -colours previewed in IE

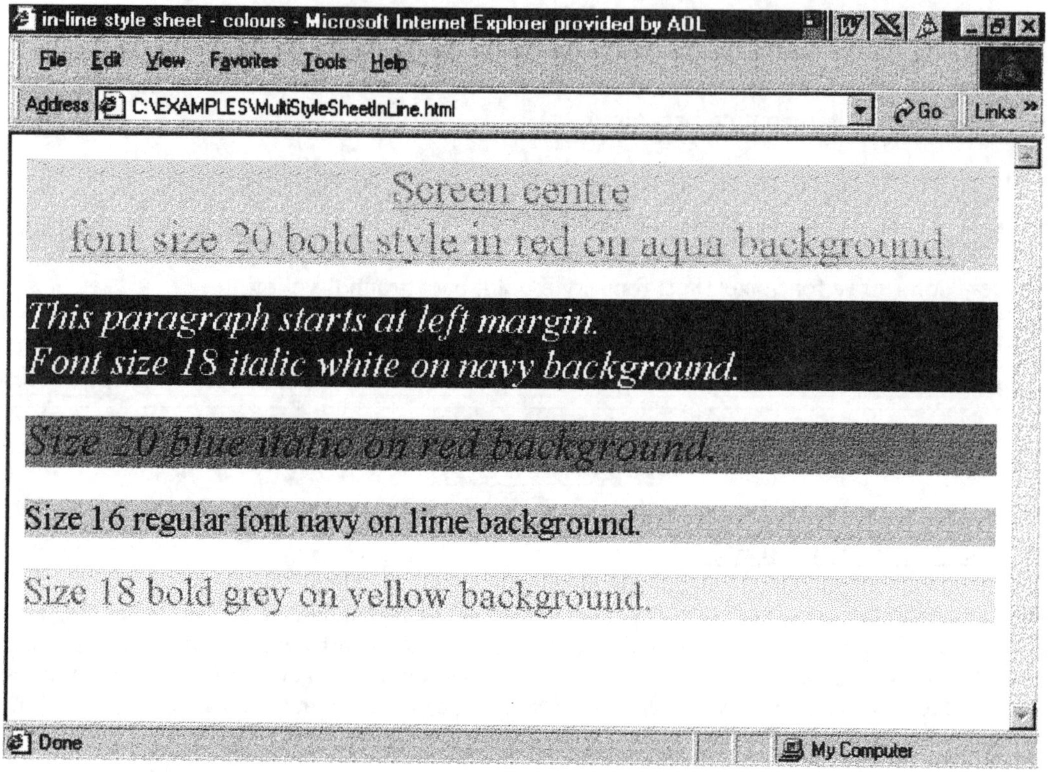

Diagram 16

.Example 9

To write an HTML document for converting the following book cover into a Web page. You should view it locally by means of the IE. The cover should be generated in the same format. You should apply standard colours scheme for both text and background (s). Style sheet rules, both embedded and in-line, must be implemented in the coding of this document.

. A Suggestion

The HTML document is shown in diagram 17. In your own interest, as self-evaluation of your learning and skills, you should develop your own HTML document, save it and then preview it in the Internet Explorer or any other browser on your machine.

I previewed it successfully. You can see my preview in diagram 18, only when you have previewed your own HTML document. Remember our motto. learn by doing!

This chapter has introduced the application of standard colours, and cascading style sheets (CSS). The style sheets have been used to apply colours in the HTML documents, font property and values. Style sheets can be applied to all features of HTML. 4.0. You will see their application again in this book.

There is another type of style sheet, which is known as **linked style sheet**. This can be applied to any group of documents. There is no space for further discussion in this chapter.

HTML document for example 9

```
<html>
<head>
<title> Learn to program in C++</Title>
<style type ="text/css">
body{background: white}
h2 {color:black}
h3{{color:red}
</style></head>
<body>
<center>
<h3><u>
     A.D.R. Student Simplified Text Series <BR>
</u></h3>
<h2>
       C++ <BR>
       Simplified<BR>
</h2></center>
<h3>
   * Text exemplified with code and solution<BR>
   * Learn fast through practical examples    <BR>
   * Gain confidence in your C++ programming skills <BR>
   * Explore Java and compare it with C++ <BR>
</h3>
<center>

 <P style ="color:white; font-size:14 pt;font-style: bold; background:blue" >

                    Second Edition 1998
                    ISBN 1901197 999
                    Best Buy £14.99
 </P>
 <h3>

                      For <BR>
              Students and Beginners<BR>
                      By<BR>
                  Adam Shaw<BR>
<u>            A.D.R.(London) Ltd
 </u> </h3></center>
</body>
</html>
```

Diagram 17

Learn to program in c++ previewed in IE

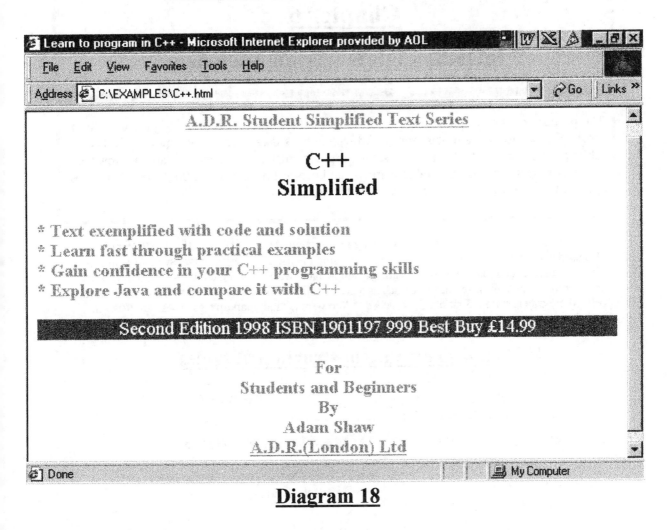

Diagram 18

Chapter 6

<u>Including tables in your Web page</u>

The purpose of this chapter is to enable you to acquire the basic knowledge and skills of creating information in a tabluar format, which contains data in rows and columns. In HTML tables are also used in Web pages for some purposes other than presenting data in a rows and columns format. For instance, table markup can be used for controlling the layout of images. You will learn elsewhere how to create such tables.

Tables are a means of organising, and presenting information. At the same time, in HTML, tables are also used extensively for page layout. Before discussing the use of tables for page layout, it is necessary to understand the mechanism of creating a simple table with rows and columns. A table with rows and columns is just like a spreadsheet, such as Microsoft Excel. A row and a column intersect to form a cell, where data is stored. First of all, you need to know some table markup tags. These are listed in table 1 together with their respective functions.

<u>HTML tags for the construction of tables</u>

Tag	Function
. <TABLE> ...<TABLE>	Mark the beginning and end of a table
. <TH> ...</TH>	For setting a heading of a table and marking the end of the heading
. <TR> ...</TR>	Use it for marking the beginning and end of a row
. <TD>...</TD>	For data entry from left to right and marking the end of data entry into cells. This way, columns are created

<u>Table 1</u>

Table formatting attributes

Attribute name	Tag	Meaning
. ALIGN	<TH ALIGN ="LEFT">	. It is used for controlling the position of the text in a cell.

	<TD ALIGN ="RIGHT">	. It can also let you align text by using it with any of the following:
		    . VALIGN - to control vertical alignment within a cell.
		
		    . CHAR - to control spacing around a particular character in a cell.

. WIDTH	< TABLE WIDTH ="70" "UNITS= RELATIVE">	. It is used for controlling the table width. It can take any of the attributes listed below, but with UNITS attributes :-
		    . Pixels - screen pixels
		    . Relatives - percentage of the page width (browser window>.

. COLSPAN	<TD COLSPAN =3>	. It is used to set the number of columns a cell spans. It merges columns. This example creates a column which is three columns wide.
. ROWSPAN	<TH ROWSPAN =2>	. It is used to set the number of rows a cell spans. It merges rows. This example creates a row which is two rows high.
. BORDER	<TABLE BORDER>	. It creates a box like table with a thick border.
. CAPTION	<CAPTION>	. It is used to set the title of a table. It is valid only when it is within a table tag <TABLE>.

Table 2

•Formatting tables and cells in tables

Any of the attributes listed in table 2 above can be placed in the <**TABLE....**> tag.

•What happens if the width is not specified?

The width attribute sets the width of the table in **pixels** or **percentage** of the page width, which is a percentage of the browser window (Relatives - see above). When the width is given the table is constructed automatically wide enough to hold its specified contents. If the table is a large table, and the width is not declared in that case, the table will be created to fit in the window of the browser.

•How are the contents of cells placed in the table?

In a table, by default, the content of a cell is aligned (placed) to the left, and vertically to the middle of each cell.. This can be altered for each cell by implementing the required option in < **TD** > in accordance with the following rules:

- • ALIGN tag - for setting the horizontal alignment; and

- • **VALIGN** tag - for setting the vertical alignment.

•Can you alter the background colour?

Yes, you can do so for each cell by using the <**BACKGROUND**> tag.

•Is it also possible to change the background colour of a cell?

You can change the colour of any cell of your choice in a table. This action may be necessary in order to highlight a particular cell. You can achieve this by using the tag - <BACKGROUND>.

•Can one set spacing between cells?

You can set spacing or distance between rows and columns by applying the following rules:

- • **CELLPADDING** - this will set the space between the cell contents and borders. The space or distance is measured is in pixels.

. **CELLSPACING** - this sets the space between cells. The distance is measured in pixels.

. <u>Are there HTML 4.0 tools for applying width and other table attributes to groups of columns?</u>

Here, the idea is to make a group of some columns by applying <COLGROUP....> tag. To this COLGROUP, you can then apply table attributes such as alignment.

These are some of the table attributes. In addition, some other attributes also apply to tables.

The following examples are designed to demonstrate the application of both tags and their attributes which are shown in table 2.

In addition to these tags, there are a number of attributes which are implemented when formatting tables. These attributes (options) can be used whenever there is a need to do so in <TABLE.......> tag. Some of these attributes together with their meanings are shown in table 2.

. <u>Example 1</u>

To write an HTML document for creating a skeleton of a table by using the following text. You must also save it and then preview it locally.

<u>**Monthly Account Statement**</u>

<u>Date</u>	<u>Invoice No.</u>	<u>Amount</u>	<u>Date</u>	<u>Payment Method</u>	<u>Amount Paid</u>

. <u>Explanation</u>

- The required HTML document is in diagrams 1& 1A. Since all headings have to start at the centre of the page/screen, <Center> opening tag is placed before the opening <Table> tag.

- The <Table> tag is then used in order to mark the beginning of the table.

- **<Caption><h1><u> Monthly Account Statement </U></h1>** is written outside the scope of any of the three core table markup tags. **Why?**

Simply because it does not form the body of the table structure. **<Caption...>** is one of the attributes listed in table 2. You can see that it does not end with its closing tag </Caption>.

•<u>What is the reason for its omission?</u>

There is an empty line between the table heading and the line containing names of columns. In order to achieve this white space. <p></P> tags are placed side by side in the correct place in this code. This rule has been already applied several times before in this book. The paragraph tag <P> starts a new paragraph and thus there is no need to put </Caption> tag to mark the end of this segment of the code. If you want to place it in the interest of some desired consistency of using markup tags in pairs, you can do so. This will not cause any harm and your code will perform its task.

- One of the core table tags <TR> is implemented to start the row for the setting of column names. Thus, it begins the row for writing the name of each column.

- Each name of a column is within <TH>...</TH>.

- At the end of the closing tag</TH> of the last column name, you must place </TR> to mark the end of the row.

•<u>Can you write table tags and attributes in lower case letters?</u>

Yes indeed, you can use either upper or lower case letters. Most likely, you know by now that I have used both cases in my HTML documents without any problem.

- The HTML document was saved as usual and previewed in IE. The preview is shown in diagram 2. This example has illustrated the use of three out of four core table markup tags. This example has shown you the technique of designing a skeleton of a table with rows and columns. This idea is taken further through the next example, which demonstrates how to construct an entire table with rows and columns of data.

<u>HTML code for example 1(cont. in diagram 1A)</u>

```
<html>
<head>
<title> Creating a table</title>
</head>
<body>
<center>
```

<u>Diagram 1</u>

HTML code for example 1(cont. from diagram 1)

```
<Table>
<Caption><h1><u> Monthly Account Statement</U></h1>
<P></P>
<TR>
<h2>
<TH ><u>
         Date </u><TH>
<TH><u>
         Invoice No.</u><TH>
<TH> <u>
         Amount </u><TH>
<TH><u>
         Date</u><TH>
<TH><u>
         Payment Method</u><TH>
<TH><u>
         Amount paid </u></TH></h2> </TR></Table></center>
</body></html>
```

Diagram 1A

. Example 2

In the skeleton table drawn in diagram 2, you should enter the following six rows of data in the same format. For the completion of this task, you must write a new HTML document, save it and finally preview it by means of any other browser, if you do not have IE. **The explanation for example 2 is given below diagram 2.**

Data for example 2

Date	Invoice No	Amount	Date	Payment Method	Amount Paid
15.03.00	C00123	£75.99	12.05.00	Bank Transfer	£75.99
08.03.00	C00205	£144.00	12.05.00	Cheque	£139.00
10.04.00	C11678	£234.75	12.05.00	Cheque	£1279.70
10.04.00	C11680	£120.66	12.05.00	Cash	£ 120.66
11.04.00	C11720	£467.00	12.05.00	Bank Transfer	£467.00
12.04.00	C12777	£985.11	12.05.00	Cheque	£985.11

HTML document called table previewed in IE

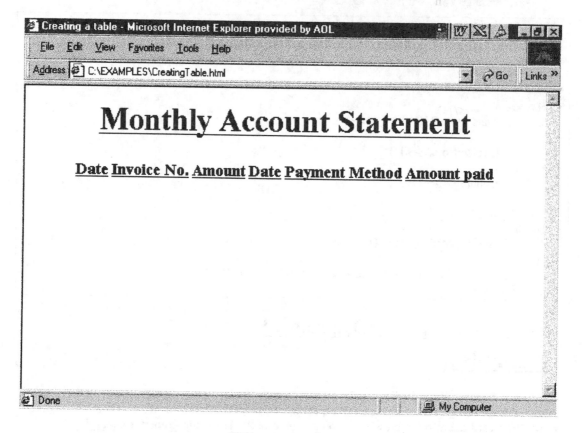

Diagram 2

. Explanation

As far as the setting of a table heading and names of each column are concerned, there are no new tags applied, other than those used in the previous example. The data items are entered by implementing the pair of the core table tag **<TD>...</DT>**.

- To enter data items for each row, you must first place <TR> tag at the beginning of each row. It signals the beginning of a row. It is followed by data entry tag<TD>, which is ten followed by the data itself. At the end of each data item, you must put the closing tag</TD>. The data entry is from left to right.

- Since there are six individual data items in each row (for six different columns), you must code each data item separately. The segment of the code required for creating first row is listed below:

```
<TR>
<TD>15.03.00</TD>
<TD>C00123</TD>
<TD>£75.99</TD>
<TD>12.05.00</TD>
<TD>Bank Transfer</TD>
<TD>£75.99</TD>
<TR>
```

You might have noticed that the above code does not end with </TR> closing tag. There is no need for it as the next row begins with <TR> opening tag for the next row, which automatically starts on the next line. If you finish your data entry for each row with </TR>, it will not do any harm.

- Since this example has six rows, you must repeat the above coding process for each row, but obviously, using the relevant data for each row.

- The full code is listed in diagrams 3, 3A & 3B. Its construction should be carefully studied, so that you can grasp its flow. The document was saved, and then previewed in IE successfully. Its preview is shown in diagram 4.

- Figures in diagram 4 are displayed in accordance with the default setting, which is starting from the left.

HTML code for example 2 (cont. in diagram 3A)

```
<html>
<head>
<title> A table with data </title>
</head>
<body>
<center>
<Table>
<Caption><h1><u> Monthly Account Statement</U></h1>
<P></P>
<TR>
```

Diagram 3

HTML code for example 2 (cont. from diagram 3)

```
<TH ><h3><u>  Date </TH><h3></u>
<TH><h3><u> Invoice No.</TH><h3></u>
<TH><h3> <u>Amount </TH> <h3></u>
<TH><h3> <u> Date</TH><h3> </u>
<TH><h3> <u>  Payment Method</TH><h3></u>
<TH><h3> <u> Amount paid </TH><h3> </U>
<TR>
<TD>15.03.00</TD>
<TD>C00123</TD>
<TD>£75.99</TD>
<TD>12.05.00</TD>
<TD>Bank Transfer</TD>
<TD>£75.99</TD>
<TR>
<TD>08.03.00</TD>
 <TD>C00205</TD>
<TD>£144.00</TD>
<TD>12.05.00</TD>
 <TD>Cheque</TD>
<TD>£139.00</TD>
<TR>
<TD>10.04.00</TD>
<TD>C11678</TD>
<TD>£234.75</TD>
<TD>12.05.00</TD>
<TD>Cheque</TD>
<TD>£1279.70</TD>
<TR>
<TD>10.04.00</TD>
<TD>C11680</TD>
<TD>£120.66</TD>
<TD>12.05.00</TD>
<TD>Cash</TD>
<TD>£120.66</TD>
<TR>
<TD>11.04.00</TD>
<TD>C11720</TD>
<TD>£467.00</TD>
<TD>12.05.00</TD>
```

Diagram 3A

HTML code for example 2 (cont. from diagram 3A)

```
<TD>Bank Transfer</TD>
<TD>£467.00</TD>
<TR>
<TD>12.04.00</TD>
<TD>C12777</TD>
<TD>£985.11</TD>
<TD>12.05.00</TD>
<TD>Cheque</TD>
<TD>£985.11</TD>
</Table></center></body></html>
```

Diagram 3B

A table with data previewed in IE

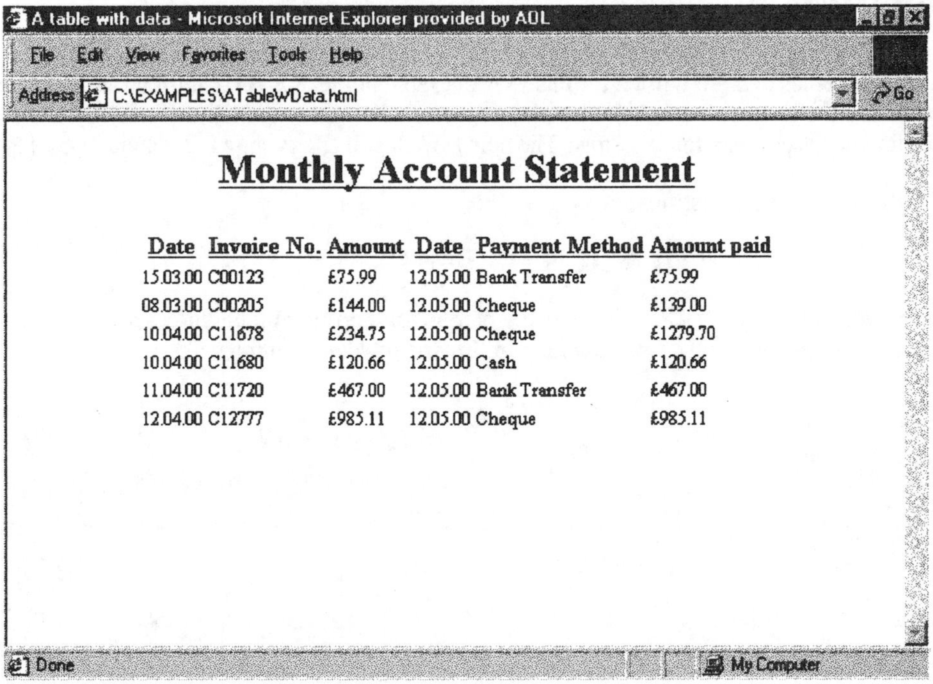

Monthly Account Statement

Date	Invoice No.	Amount	Date	Payment Method	Amount paid
15.03.00	C00123	£75.99	12.05.00	Bank Transfer	£75.99
08.03.00	C00205	£144.00	12.05.00	Cheque	£139.00
10.04.00	C11678	£234.75	12.05.00	Cheque	£1279.70
10.04.00	C11680	£120.66	12.05.00	Cash	£120.66
11.04.00	C11720	£467.00	12.05.00	Bank Transfer	£467.00
12.04.00	C12777	£985.11	12.05.00	Cheque	£985.11

Diagram 4

.Alignment of data in cells

.Is it possible to control data in cells by justification?

By implementing any of the table formatting attributes which are shown in table 2 you can control the text position in a cell. The example 3 is designed to demonstrate how you can achieve right justification in data cells.

.Example 3

This example is based on the data used in the last example. Here, the idea is to improve the appearance of data in cells, so that the contents of each cell are aligned to the right side of the column. In other words, to perform right justification.

. Explanation

The code in diagram 3 has to be re-written for this example, so that the **ALIGN** attribute, which enables you to control the justification in cells for placing data from right to the left can be written in the correct places for each set of data for each row. The new HTML full file is shown in diagrams 5 & 5A.

The general format for the right justification is

<TD ALIGN ="RIGHT">

but it should be within the pair <TR>...</TR>tags, which is for starting and ending of a row. The following segment of the code is for the first data item in the first row and column cell.

```
<TR>                          ⇒  to start a row
 <TD ALIGN="RIGHT">           ⇒  to set right justification
 15.03.00</TD>                ⇒  to insert the actual data value
...............
...............
</TR>                         ⇒  to mark the end of a row
```

This process is repeated for each data item. All rows are coded in the same way. Now, study the whole HTML document, save it on your own machine, and preview it. I previewed it successfully as shown in diagram 6.

HTML code for example 3 (cont. in diagram 5A)

```
<html>
<head>
<title> A table with alignment</title>
</head>
<body>
<center>
<Table>
<Caption><h1><u> Monthly Account Statement</U></h1>
<P></P>
<TR>
<TH ><h3><u>
          Date </TH><h3></u>
<TH><h3><u>
          Invoice No.</TH><h3></u>
<TH><h3> <u>
          Amount </TH> <h3></u>
<TH><h3> <u>
          Date</TH><h3> </u>
<TH><h3> <u>
          Payment Method</TH><h3></u>
<TH><h3> <u>
          Amount paid </TH><h3> </U>
<TR>
<TD ALIGN="RIGHT">15.03.00</TD>
<TD ALIGN ="RIGHT">C00123</TD>
<TD ALIGN="RIGHT">£75.99</TD>
<TD ALIGN="RIGHT">12.05.00</TD>
<TD ALIGN="RIGHT">Bank Transfer</TD>
<TD ALIGN="RIGHT">£75.99</TD>
<TR>
<TD Align="Right">08.03.00</TD>
 <TD Align ="Right">C00205</TD>
<TD Align ="Right">£144.00</TD>
<TD Align="Right">12.05.00</TD>
<TD Align ="Right">Cheque</TD>
<TD Align ="Right">£139.00</TD>
```

Diagram 5 A

HTML code for example 3 (cont. from diagram 5)

```
<TR>
<TD Align ="Right">10.04.00</TD>
<TD Align ="Right">C11678</TD>
<TD Align ="Right">£234.75</TD>
<TD Align ="Right">12.05.00</TD>
<TD Align="Right">Cheque</TD>
<TD Align="Right">£1279.70</TD>
<TR>
<TD Align="Right">10.04.00</TD>
<TD Align="Right">C11680</TD>
<TD Align ="Right">£120.66</TD>
<TD Align ="Right">12.05.00</TD>
<TD Align="Right">Cash</TD>
<TD Align="Right">£120.66</TD>
<TR>
<TD Align ="Right">11.04.00</TD>
<TD Align="Right">C11720</TD>
<TD Align="Right">£467.00</TD>
<TD Align="Right">12.05.00</TD>
<TD Align="Right"> Bank Transfer</TD>
<TD Align="Right">£467.00</TD>
<TR>
<TD Align="Right">12.04.00</TD>
<TD Align="Right">C12777</TD>
<TD Align="Right"> £985.11</TD>
<TD Align="Right"> 12.05.00</TD>
<TD Align="Right">Cheque</TD>
<TD Align="Right">£985.11</TD>
</Table></center></body></html>
```

Diagram 5 A

. Controlling columns and rows

You have seen a number of previews of tables generated in this chapter. You have most likely noticed that the columns are too close to each other. Now, is the right time and place in this chapter to intro-duce the application of table attributes namely, **COLPSAN and ROWSPAN**, These attributes have to be implemented within <TH...> and <TD.....> codes. These attributes can enable you to design complex tables with data spread in accordance with the width and height set as desired by you. The next ample illustrates the application of this attribute.

A table with alignment previewed in IE

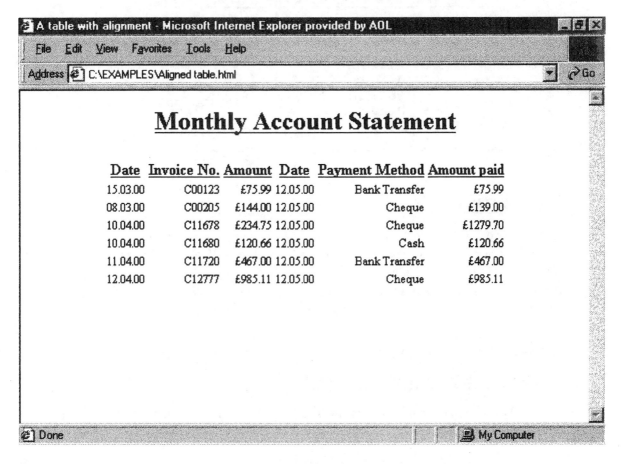

Diagram 6

. Example 4

The purpose of this example is to demonstrate the application of the attribute COLSPAN in the construction of a table. The data, which has to be coded for this table, is shown in the shaded area be-low. The whole table together with its title must be displayed in the centre of the screen. The width of each cell is four columns wide. In addition, the data in each cell is placed in the centre of a cell.

Data for example 4

Number of hours worked week ended 01.06.2000	
Day	**Hours**
Monday	23
Tuesday	15
Wednesday	20
Thursday	12
Friday	20

. **Explanation**

The structure of this HTML file is pretty much the same as HTML files for other examples in this chapter. Nevertheless, it introduces the use of an important attribute of table formatting, together with applying other HTML features learnt so far.

- It is required to centre the table in the middle of the screen. To meet this requirement, the <center> tag is placed as the first item in the <BODY> section of this document.

. <u>Is there a table formatting tag which can centre the entire table on the screen?</u>

Yes, you can declare centre justification using the **ALIGN** attribute in the <TABLE.....> tag. Its general format is given below:

<TABLE ALIGN ="CENTER">

- Column headings - the following segment of the code creates headings.

```
<TH COLSPAN=4><h2><u>Day </h2></u></TH>     ..........................⇒ creates column Day
<TH COLSPAN=4><h2><u> Hours</h2></u></TH>    ..........................⇒ creates column Hours
```

Here, it is important to specify both levels of headings (if you want other than default), and underlining (if you wish). Such requirements should be within the pair of tags **<TH.....> -----</TH>**, as shown above. If you try to place these requirements elsewhere in this document, these headings will not be underlined and placed in the centre. In fact, they will start at the left side of the screen (automatically left justification occurred). You can experiment to see what you get. Good luck!

- **The other two requirements are concerning:**

    - the width of each cell - you have to make each cell four columns wide, and

    - place the actual data item in the centre of each cell.

These two requirements for the first data item of the first row are coded as shown below:

<TD COLSPAN = 4 ALIGN = "center"> Monday</TD>
↑   ↑   ↑
essential   essential   " " essential

This code is repeated for the remaining data items which constitute this table, but by using relevant data value. The document was previewed successfully in the IE, as shown in diagram 8. Once again, it is strongly suggested that you run this code on your machine to analyse its mechanism, test it, and evaluate your own skills in creating HTML documents. The preview is shown in diagram 8.

. <u>Is it possible to draw a border around a table?</u>

You can draw a box like a border around a table. You will soon learn about how to draw a border.

<u>HTML code for example 4 (cont. in diagram 7 A)</u>

```
<html>
<head>
<title>Controlling rows and columns</title>
</head>
<body>
<center>
<u>
<h2>
```

<u>Diagram 7</u>

HTML code for example 4 (cont. from diagram 7)

```
        Number of hours worked week ended 01.06.2000 </u></h2>

<TABLE>
<TR>
<TH COLSPAN=4><h2><u>Day </h2></u></TH>
<TH COLSPAN=4><h2><u> Hours</h2></u></TH>
<TR>
<TD COLSPAN=4 ALIGN="center"> Monday</TD>
<TD COLSPAN=4 ALIGN="center">23</TD>
<TR>
<TD COLSPAN=4 ALIGN="center">Tuesday</TD>
<TD COLSPN =4 ALIGN="center" >15</TD>
<TR>
<TD COLSPAN=4 ALIGN="center">Wednesday </TD>
<TD C<Td COLSPAN=4 ALIGN="center">12</TD>
<TR>
<TD COLSPAN=4 ALIGN="center">Friday</TD>
<TD COLSPAN=4 ALIGN="center" >20</TD>
</center></Table>
</body>
</html>
```

Diagram 7 A

- The preview of "Controlling rows and columns" is in shown in diagram 8 on the next page.

Overdue Sales Accounts

Account No.	Overdue Amounts £s
1010	10000
1134	11500
1050	20000
3456	12500
5050	20040

Controlling rows and columns previewed in IE

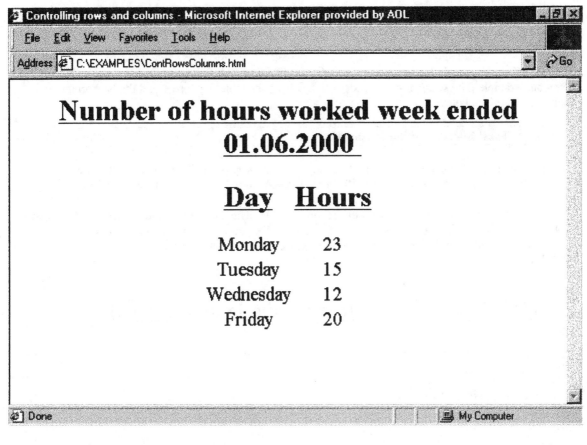

Diagram 8

. Boxed table

. Example 5

Example 5 is designed to create a boxed table which will contain the information shown in the shaded area, below diagram 7A, together with its heading. The other requirements are as follows:-

. To create each cell which is four columns wide.

- A figure in each cell should be right justified.
- The background colour of the table is yellow or any other colour of your choice.

.Explanation

The HTML markup code for example 5 is shown in diagrams 9 & 9A. It is similar to the code in the previous example. The segment of the code which sets up the table, its border and the background colour yellow is given below.

```
<Table Border  bgcolor =yellow>
```

It is important to note the structure of this segment of the markup code. The preview of the document called a boxed table is shown in diagram 10. Now, it is your turn to run it on your own system.

You have now learnt how to draw a border around a table. This is a very useful attribute, which can help you to design a table which looks like a box and enable you to present complex information in an easy to understand format. The border attribute is associated with other options namely FRAMES and RULES.

HTML code for example 5 (cont. in diagram 9A)

```
html>
<head>
<title>A boxed table</title>
</head>
<body>
<center>
<Table Border bgcolor =yellow>
<Caption><h2><u>Overdue Sales Accounts</h2></u><h3>
<TR>
<TH COLSPAN=4> Account No.</TH>
<TH COLSPAN=4>Overdue Amount £s</TH>
<TR>
<TD COLSPAN=4 ALIGN="center">1010</TD>
<TD COLSPN=4 ALIGN="center">10000</TD>
```

Diagram 9

HTML code for example 5 (cont. from diagram 9)

```
<TR>
<TD COLSPAN=4 ALIGN="center">1134</TD>
<TD COLSPN =4 ALIGN="center" >11500</TD>
<TR>
<TD COLSPAN=4 ALIGN="center">1055 </TD>
<TD COLSPAN =4 ALIGN="center">20000</TD>
<TR>
<TD COLSPAN=4 Align="center">3456 </TD>
<TD COLSPAN=4  align="center">12500</TD>
<TR>
<TD COLSPAN=4 align ="center">5050</TD>
<TD COLSPAN=4 ALIGN="CENTER" >20040</TD>
</h3></Center></Table> </body></html>
```

Diagram 9A

A boxed table previewed in IE

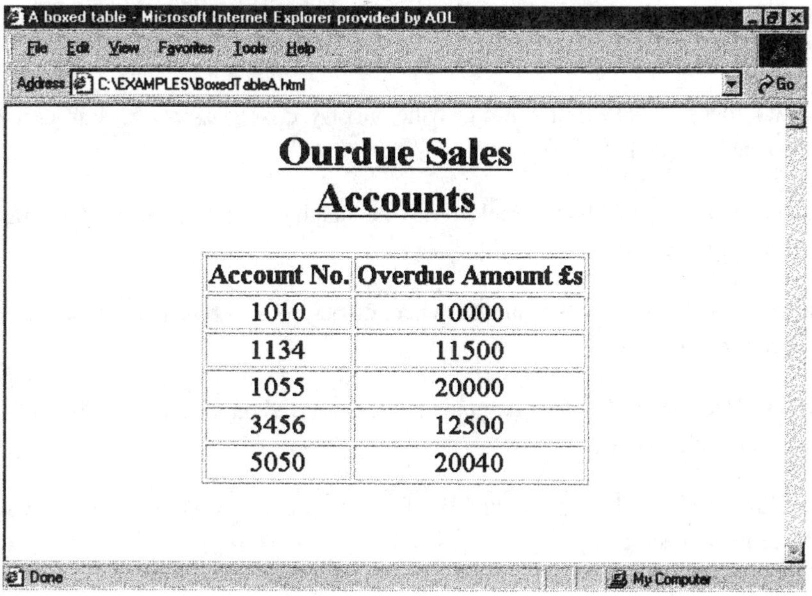

Ourdue Sales
Accounts

Account No.	Overdue Amount £s
1010	10000
1134	11500
1055	20000
3456	12500
5050	20040

Diagram 10

. <u>Example 6</u>

This example is designed to illustrate how to apply the **<BORDER....>** option together with some other options learnt so far. The aim of this practice is to perform the following tasks:

<u>Section A</u>

- Use the same information which is for creating the above boxed table.
- By applying some style sheets features of cascading style sheets, create the table title in black.
- Use level 2 heading tag with font size 18-point and in *italic* style for writing the title.
- The title should be underlined and displayed in the centre of the browser's window.
- Override the black colour option for the table, so that text in the table is displayed in the colour red.

<u>Section B</u>

- The table must have a border around it, and the table must be aligned in the centre of window.

- The heading of each column should be in the cell which is four columns wide, displayed on a white background, but must be aligned in the centre of each cell.

- The cells in the first row should be four columns wide, displayed on a maroon background, but must be aligned in the centre of each cell.

- The cells in the second row should be four columns wide, displayed on a green background, but must be aligned in the centre of each cell.

- The cells in the third row should be four columns wide, displayed on a blue background, but must be aligned in the centre of each cell.

- The cells in the fourth row should be four columns wide, displayed on a silver background, but must be aligned in the centre of each cell.

- The cells in the fifth row should be four columns wide, displayed on a yellow background, but must be aligned in the centre of each cell.

The above information is self-explanatory. By now, you should be able to write the required HTML document yourself , prior to examining it in diagram 11. The preview is given in diagram 12. Try it first yourself.

HTML code for example 6

```
<html>
<head>
<title>A colourful boxed table</title>
<Style type="text/css">
h2{color:000000; font-size:18pt;font-style:italic}
body{color:red}</style></head>
<body>
<center>
<u>
<h2>
                    Overdue Accounts</h2></u>
<Table Border align ="Center">
<TR >
<TH COLSPAN=4 BGColor ="White"> Account No.</TH>
<TH COLSPAN=4 BGColor="White">  Overdue Amount £s</TH>
<TR >
<TD COLSPAN=4 BGColor ="maroon" ALIGN="center">1010</TD>
<TD COLSPN=4 BGColor="maroon" ALIGN="center">10000</TD>
<TR>
<TD COLSPAN=4 BGColor="green" ALIGN="center"> 1134</TD>
<TD COLSPN =4 BGColor="green" ALIGN="center" >11500</TD>
<TR>
<TD COLSPAN=4 BGColor="blue" ALIGN="center">1055 </TD>
<TD COLSPAN =4 BGColor="blue"  ALIGN="center">20000</TD>
<TR>
<TD COLSPAN=4 BGColor="silver" Align="center">3456 </Td>
<Td COLSPAN=4  BGColor="silver" align="center">12500</TD>
<TR>
<TD COLSPAN=4 BGColor ="yellow" align ="center"> 5050</TD>
<TD COLSPAN=4 BGColor="yellow" ALIGN="CENTER" >20040</TD></Center>
</Table>
</body>
</html>
```

Diagram 11

A colourful boxed table previewed in IE

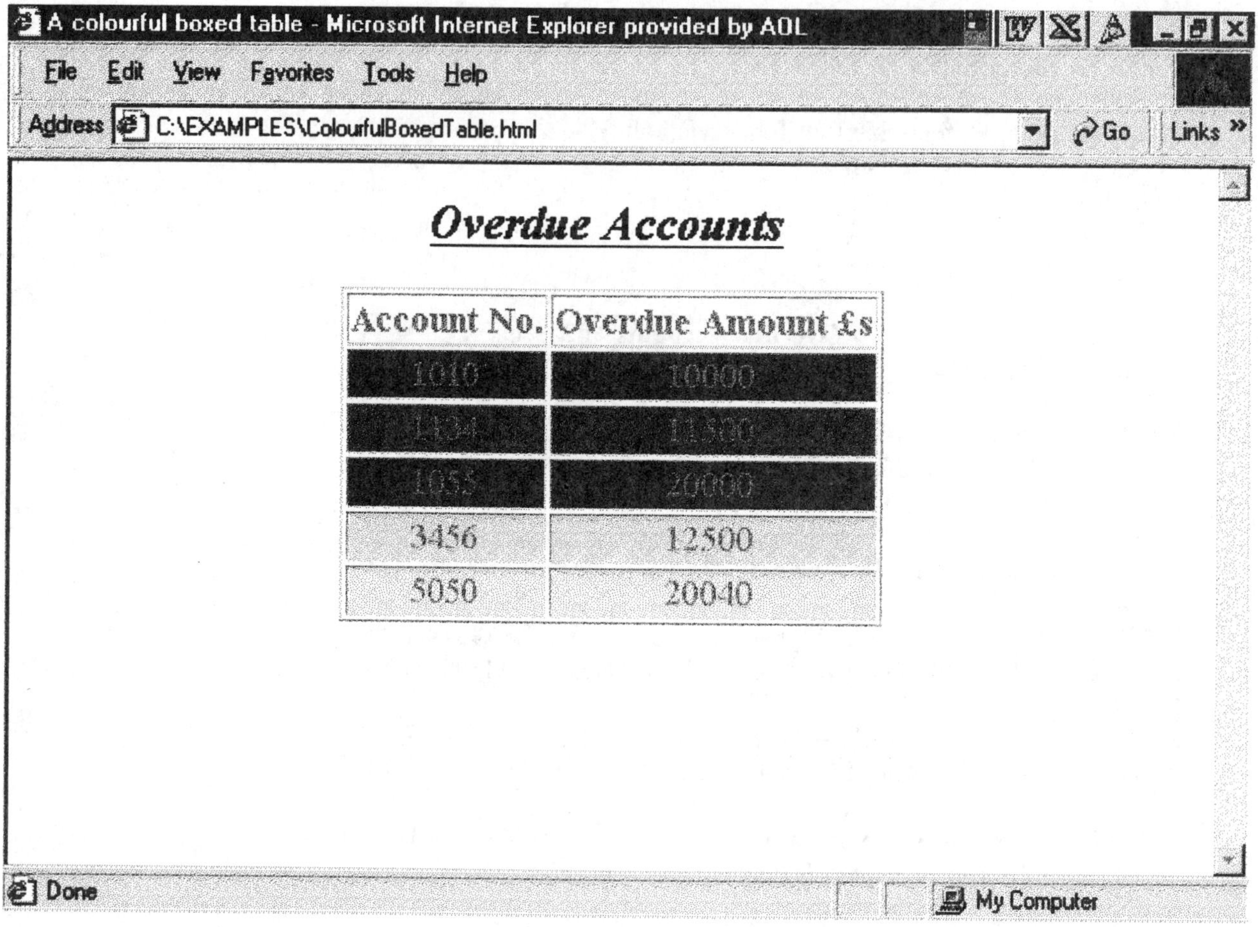

A colourful boxed table - Microsoft Internet Explorer provided by AOL
File   Edit   View   Favorites   Tools   Help
Address 🔲 C:\EXAMPLES\ColourfulBoxedTable.html   ▼   𝒶 Go   Links »

Overdue Accounts

Account No.	Overdue Amount £s
1010	10000
1404	11500
1055	20000
3456	12500
5050	20040

🔲 Done   🖳 My Computer

Diagram 12

These colours are standard colours. You should be able to see them on your colour monitor.

Chapter 7

Including complex tables in your Web page

The purpose of this chapter is to extent the features of tables introduced in the last chapter. Here, you will learn how to construct complex tables.

. Complex(advanced) tables

- Can you divide a table into groups of rows and columns?

- How can you format individual columns in a group of columns?

- Why should you format individual columns in a group of columns as it seems to defeat the objective of creating a group of columns? Is it not so?

- Can you divide the table into sections?

You have learnt that the **COLSPAN** and **ROWSPAN** options let you set the size of cells in tables. You can also group together columns by applying **<COLGROUP.....>** option. You can apply formatting options such as alignment to a group of columns and rows. Within a group of columns, each column can also be formatted by means of **<COL....>** feature.

.What will be the effects of formatting columns and group of columns on a group of rows ?

It will override any formatting set for a group of rows.

The reason for formatting individual columns in a group of columns is practical and simple enough. You have already seen the application of **<BORDER....>** option above. It may be that within a border you wish to create a group of columns in such a way that a distinction between individual columns can be made by means, say, of using different backgrounds.

. A division of a table

A table can be divided into **head**, **body** and **foot**. This division facilitates cells formatting within each section at the same time. Furthermore, a table can have several bodies, but only one head and one foot.

. How is this done?

You can start a new group with **<TBODY... >** tag. This new group can allow you to add new rows.

. What other HTML 4.0 markup tags can be implemented for designing a table containing rows and columns?

The following markup tags can also be used for creating complex tables together with the table options which have been discussed in this chapter.

< SPAN...>	**< WIDTH...>**
• The number of columns that can be grouped together is specified by span.	• The default width of each column in a group of columns is set by this option.
< THEAD... >	**<TFOOT...>**
• Table Header tag - visible when the table body scrolls.	• Table footer tag for setting up the footer - visible when the table body scrolls,

<TBODY...>

• the Body tag for setting up the body

. Alignment in sections of a table

The following alignments are permissible when dividing the table into sections. However, the problem is that these are not yet fully supported by all browsers.

• ***alignment*** - left, center (American spelling), right, justify or char.

General format $\Longrightarrow$ **Align ="alignment"**

- *__verticalalignment__* - top, bottom, middle   General format $\Longrightarrow$ **Valign = bottom**

- *__decimalcharacter__* - for aligning decimal point in figures/data

  General format $\Longrightarrow$ **char ="decimalcharacter"**

- *__decimaloffset__* - Offset in pixels to the decimal position.

  General format $\Longrightarrow$ **charoff ="decimalcharacter"**

. <u>Example 1</u>

The aim of this example is to demonstrate the application of advanced table developing techniques by creating a table for the information shown below.

<u>Sales Invoices 10 June 2000</u>

Customer	Account No.	Sales Order No.	Sales Invoice No.	Total in Pounds Sterling
London Private Property C	1234	A0020	C0101	689.00
The Millennium Stores M	1550	A0021	C0102	1260.76
CWS Heilbronn Deutschland C	2020	A0023	C0104	498.99

Please place in customer column M= monthly settlement. C = cash sales

Your HTML document should include the following requirements:

- The heading of this table should be displayed above the table as it is not part of this table. This heading should be in the centre of the screen (browser's window), and it should be in *italic* style font, size 18, but in black.

- The table should be displayed in the centre of the browser's window. It should have around it a border as thick as at least 5 pixels.

- The table header should be displayed on a silver background.

- The main body of the HTML document should have three groups of data to be created with **<TBODY.. . >.**

  - First group data set starts with **London**. This should be displayed on a fuchsia background.

  - Second group data begins with **The**. It should be on a yellow background.

  - Third group starts with **CWS**. This should be displayed on a cyan (= aqua) colour.

  - You should place the information in the centre of each cell in these three groups.

  - The footer should be on a white background, and aligned in the centre of the table.

The HTML document for this example is shown in diagrams 1 and 1A, and previewed in diagram 2.

<u>HTML code for example 1(cont. in diagram 1A)</u>

```
<html>
<head>
<title>An example of advanced table</title>
<Style type="text/css">
h2{color:black; font-size:18pt;font-style:italic}
body{color:black}
</style>
</head>
<body>
<center>
<u><h2>
        Sales Invoices 10 June 2000
</h2></u>
<Table Border =5 align ="Center">
 <THEAD bgcolor = silver Align = center VAlign = bottom>
<TR>
     <TD> Customer </TD>
     <TD>Account No.</TD>
<TD> Sales Order<BR> No.</TD>
```

<u>Diagram 1</u>

HTML code for example 1 (cont. from diagram 1)

```
<TD> Sales Invoice<BR> No</TD>
      <TD> Total in <BR> Pounds Sterling </TD>
</TR>
<TFOOT bgcolor = White Align = center>
<TR>
<TD COLSPAN = 10> Please place in customer column: M = monthly settlement, C = cash sales
</TD>
</TR>
<TBODY bgcolor = FF00FF>

<TR>
      <TD Align =center><h4>  London Private Property  <BR> C </h4></TD>
      <TD Align =center > <h4> 1234 </h4></TD>
      <TD Align=center ><h4> A0020</h4></TD>
      <TD Align =center ><h4> C0101</h4></TD>
       <TD Align =center ><h4> 689.00</h4> </TD>
</TR>
<TBODY bgcolor = yellow>
<TR>
      <TD Align =center ><h4> The Millennium Stores<BR> M</h4> </TD>
      <TD Align =center ><h4>1550</h4></TD>
      <TD Align =center><h4>A0021</h4></TD>
      <TD Align =center><h4>C0102</h4></TD>
      <TD Align =center><h4>1260.76</h4></TD>
</TR>
<TBODY Bgcolor = cyan>
 <TR>
      <TD Align =center><h4> CWS Heilbronn Deutschland <BR> C</h4></TD>
      <TD Align =center><h4>2020</h4></TD>
      <TD Align =center><h4>A0023</h4></TD>
      <TD Align =center><h4>C0104</h4></TD>
      <TD Align =center><h4>498.99</h4></TD>
</TR>
</Center>
</Table>
</body>
</html>
```

Diagram 1A

.Explanation

- By now, you are familiar with the construction of a table with rows and columns. In the HTML document above, I have identified in bold letters the beginning of segments of the code which set the border and divide the table into its sections namely, the header, footer and body.

- The border is set within the <TABLE ....>. It is then followed by the <THEAD..> for setting up the group of rows which constitutes the head section of the table. Within this section<TR> and <TD> tags are used in order to place data in cells. You have seen this process before.

- It should be noted that the segment of the code for **footer** comes next instead of the body code.

. Why?

The browser lays out the header and the footer first. This way, within these top and lower sections of the table, it can place the data in the main body of the table. The main body of a table can have several bodies, each having its own rows. Thus, the browser does not have to search through all rows for laying out the table structure.

- Each <TBODY...) within <TR> <TD> contains the actual information for filling cells. In this example, there are three sub bodies within the main body, and each sub body has its own data and is formatted separately.

. Grouping columns together & formatting columns individually

You can group a number of columns together. All columns within the group can be formatted simultaneously by means of the group tag **<COLGROUP.... >**.

If you wish, you can within any group format any individual column. This method enables you to identify by using different backgrounds any individual column and a number

. Example 2

The example 2 illustrates the technique of grouping together three columns under the heading:

Outstanding sales accounts as at 30 June 2000

for the data items shown in the shaded area on the next page, below diagram 2. It is continued below diagram 2 due to lack of space here.

An example of advanced table previewed in IE

An example of advanced table - Microsoft Internet Explorer provided by AOL

File   Edit   View   Favorites   Tools   Help

Address C:\EXAMPLES\Advanced TableFirst.html   Go

Sales Invoices 10 June 2000

Customer	Account No.	Sales Order No.	Sales Invoice No	Total in Pounds Sterling
London Private Property C	1234	A0020	C0101	689.00
The Millennium Stores M	1550	A0021	C0102	1260.76
CWS Heilbronn Deutschland C	2020	A0023	C0104	498.99
Please place in customer column: M = monthly settlement, C = cash sales				

Done   My Computer

Diagram 2

Example 2 from the last page continued

You are asked to develop an HTML document in order to generate the required table. The title of the table is outside the scope of the table, but it must be created . The other requirements are given below:-

- Title - use heading level 2, font size *18 italic style* and the text is in black throughout the table. It should be displayed in the centre of the browser's window.

- The table should be surrounded by a thick border whose width should be at least 30 pixels.

- The table header section must be displayed on a silver background, with vertical top alignment.

- The footer section of the table, " To credit control department. Please take appropriate action. Thanking you." to be displayed on a yellow background. You should apply the **span option**, so that the footer fits in the width of the table within the border. The message must be centrally placed in this long footer column.

- The width of columns within the group of columns should be the same for each column, but the width of other columns is to be different for each column.

- All data items within the main body of the table must be written by using level 4 of the heading tag.

- Figures in cells under "Over 3 months" should be centre aligned on a green background.

- Figures in cells under "Total" have to be displayed on a red background, and placed in the centre of each cell.

Outstanding sales accounts as at 30 June 2000						
Customer	Account No.	Outstanding amount £s				Total
		Over 3 months	May	April	March	
London Private Property London SW11	1234	2000.00	00.00	120.50	250.50	2371.00
The Millennium Stores Manchester	1550	1500.00	2450.80	0.00	500.00	4450.80
CWS Heibronn Deutschland	2020	250.00	278.90	4980.00	1026.90	2053.80
To credit control department: Please take appropriate action. Thanking you.						

HTML code for example 2 (cont. in diagram 3A)

```
<html>
<head>
<title Advanced table 2</title>
<Style type="text/css">
h2{color:black; font-size:18pt;font-style:italic}
body{color:black}
</style>
</head>
<body>
<center>
<u>
<h2>
        Outstanding sales accounts as at 30 June 2000
</h2></u>
<Table Border = 30 Align =Center>
                        <Colgroup Span =3 Align = Left>
                        <Col  Width = 30% Bgcolor = White>
                        <Col Width = 10% Bgcolor = White>
                        <Colgroup Span = 4 Width = 60 Align = Center Bgcolor = Aqua>

<THEAD bgcolor = silver Align = center VAlign = top>

<TR>
        <TD Rowspan = 2 Align =center> Customer </TD>
        <TD Rowspan = 2 Align = center> Account No.</TD>
        <TD Colspan =  4 Align = center>Outstanding amount £s </TD>
        <TD Rowspan = 3 Align =center> Total </TD>
</TR>
<TR>
        <TD> Over 3 months</TD>
        <TD>May</TD>
        <TD>April</TD>
        <TD>March</TD>
</TR>
<TFOOT >
<TR>
        <TD COLSPAN =  10 bgcolor = yellow Align = center>
        To credit control department. Please take appropriate action. Thanking you. </TD>
```

Diagram 3

HTML code for example 2 (cont. from diagram 3)

```
</TR>

<TBODY>
<TR>
        <TD Align =center><h4>  London Private Property  <BR> London SW11 </h4></TD>
        <TD Align =center > <h4> 1234 </h4></TD>
        <TD bgcolor = green white Align =center ><h4> 2000.00</h4></TD>
        <TD Align =center ><h4> 0.00</h4></TD>
        <TD Align =center ><h4> 120.50</h4> </TD>
        <TD Align =center><h4>  250.50</h4></TD>
        <TD BGCOLOR = Red Align= center><h4> 2371.00</h4></TD>
</TR>

<TBODY>
<TR>
        <TD Align =center ><h4> The Millennium Stores<BR> Manchester</h4> </TD>
        <TD Align =center ><h4>1550</h4></TD>
        <TD Bgcolor = green Text = white Align =center><h4>1500.00</h4></TD>
        <TD Align =center><h4>2450.80</h4></TD>
        <TD Align =center><h4>0.00</h4></TD>
        <TD Align =center><h4>500.00</h4></TD>
        <TD BGCOLOR = red Align =center><h4>4450.80  </h4></TD>
</TR>

<TBODY>
<TR>
        <TD Align =center><h4> CWS Heilbronn<BR> Deutschland  </h4></TD>
        <TD Align =center><h4>2020</h4></TD>
        <TD bgcolor = green Align =center><h4>250.00</h4></TD>
         <TD Align =center><h4>278.90</h4></TD>
         <TD Align =center><h4>498.00</h4></TD>
         <TD Align =center><h4> 1026.90</h4></TD>
         <TD BGCOLOR = red Align =center><h4> 2053.80 </h4></TD>
</TR> </Center>
</Table>
</body>
</html>
```

Diagram 3A

. Explanation

The HTML document is shown in diagrams 3 and 3A. In these diagrams, the beginning of each section is highlighted, so that you can identify each section to comprehend its working.

- The border is placed within the **<TABLE --.>** tag. It is then followed by the group column code:

<Colgroup Span =3 Align = Left>

- The following segment of the code sets default formats for columns:

<Col Width = 30% Bgcolor = White>
<Col Width = 10% Bgcolor = White>

Here, the width of each column is stated in terms of percentage of the browser window. These two columns are displayed on a white background.

- **<Colgroup Span = 4 Width = 60 Align = Center Bgcolor = Aqua>** - sets 4 columns for the group of columns, together with width, and background colour.

The code between the <TABLE ...> and <COLGROUP SPAN...> provides sufficient information to the browser, which enables it to start arranging the table.

- Within the head section **<THEAD...>** the code is written for overriding the default formats for the column and setting up the rows.

- The next segment of the code is to specify the footer. By now, the browser has all the relevant information to arrange the table without going through the body of the table for finding out how many rows are needed.

- The purpose of the remaining code is to provide the required data in three separate groups **<TBODY...>** together with the alignment, background colour and heading tag levels.

- The document was saved and previewed successfully. See diagram 4.

. Formatting tables with spaces

You can also construct a table with:

- space or distance between the cell content and border by using the option **CELLPADDING**, and

- space or distance between cells using the option **CELLSPACING.**

These distances are stated in pixels. It is to emphasise that different screen resolutions have different fixed pixel widths, and thus your table may not look exactly the same on your machine as it does on my machine or any other machine.

Advanced table 2 previewed in IE

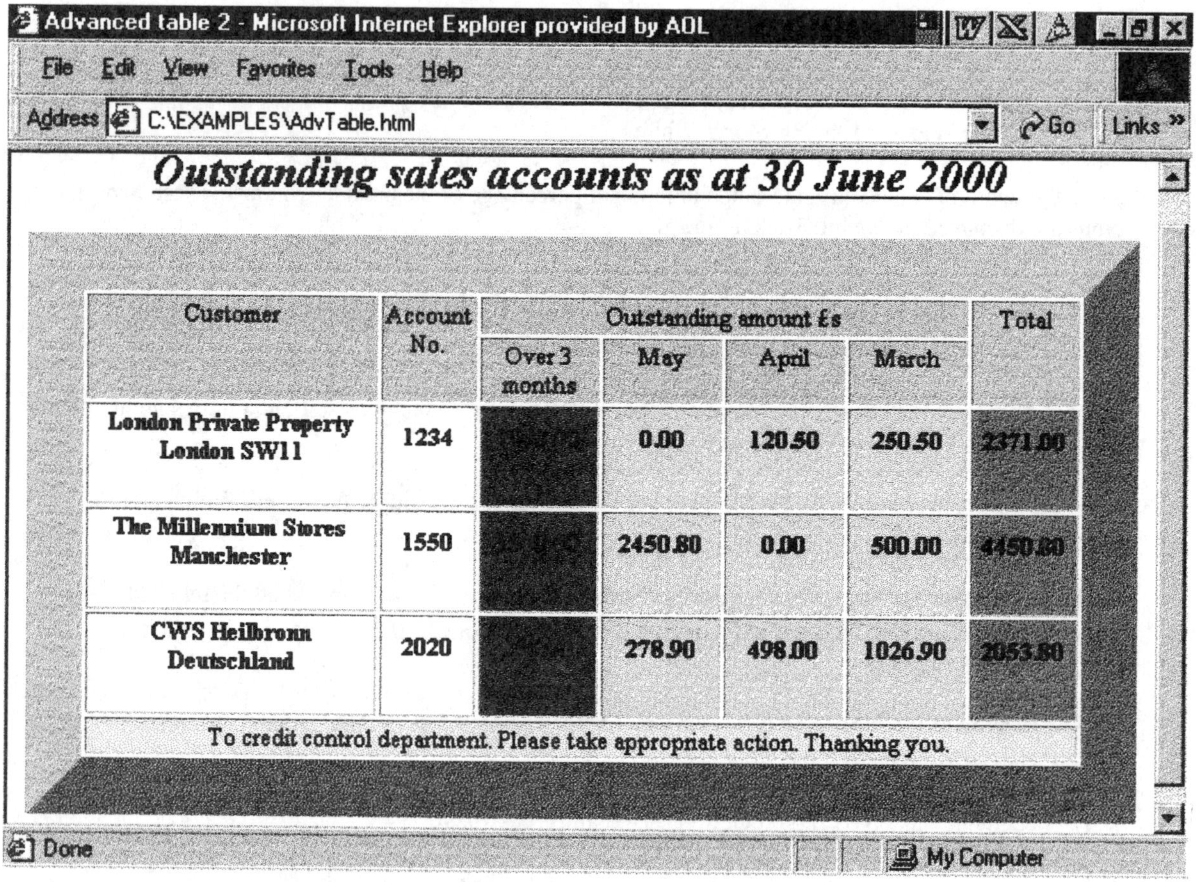

Outstanding sales accounts as at 30 June 2000

Customer	Account No.	Outstanding amount £s				Total
		Over 3 months	May	April	March	
London Private Property London SW11	1234		0.00	120.50	250.50	2371.00
The Millennium Stores Manchester	1550		2450.80	0.00	500.00	4450.80
CWS Heilbronn Deutschland	2020		278.90	498.00	1026.90	2053.80

To credit control department. Please take appropriate action. Thanking you.

Diagram 4

- **How can you create these spaces in a table?**

. Example 3

To illustrate the application of these options, I have amended the HTML document shown in diagrams 1 and 1A. In diagram 1, the code: **<Table Border = 5 align =Center>** has been replace by the code:

<Table Border = 12 align = Center Cellspacing = 10 Cellpadding = 6>

I have also amended diagram 1A, so that the amended HTML document has only two rows of data items to display. The preview showing these amendments is in diagram 5. Now, you can examine the effects of spacing options on the appearance of a table.

Advanced table previewed in IE
with spaces included

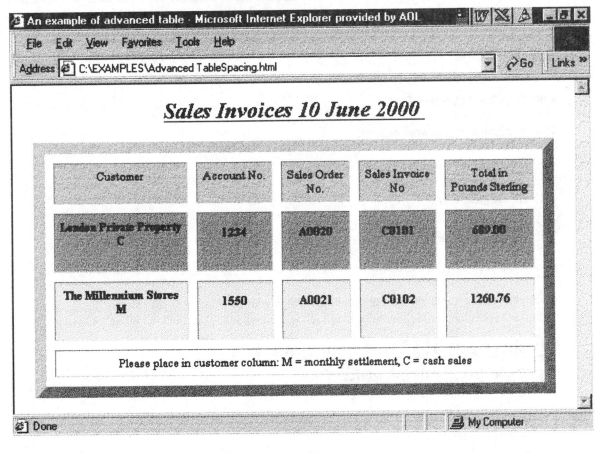

Diagram 5

Chapter 8

Creating documents with links

The purpose of this chapter is to enable you to understand how to incorporate URLs, anchors and links into HTML documents.

In Chapter 1, you were introduced to the fundamental idea of hyperlink. Now, I am going to expand it in order to create and preview a number of HTML documents. A link lets you do the following:

- locate a page at your own site
- move within a page at your own site
- move between the pages at your own site
- locate a page at WWW
- move within a page at WWW
- move between the pages at WWW
- access available resources when are available both at your own site or on the Internet

• Is there any HTML feature that lets you create the desired link?

Yes indeed, you can do so by using the <A> tag. Its general format is shown below.

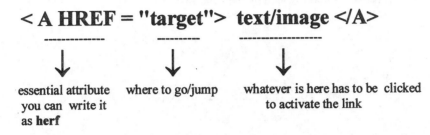

< A HREF = "target"> text/image </A>

↓   ↓   ↓

essential attribute   where to go/jump   whatever is here has to be clicked
you can write it   to activate the link
as **herf**

. How will you link to a Web page ?

You learnt in Chapter 1 that the Uniform Resource Locator, for short **URL** is the key to locating where

a document or any other resource can be found. In addition, it connects to the required resource. Its general format is:

http://domain_name/directory/page

↓   ↓   ↓   ↓

signal to the   the full address of the WWW   sometimes it   the required document
browser for   document to be accessed   is needed, if
creating the link   the document is
                                                    another directory/
                                                    sub-directory

. Is the required document called the home page?

No, you have to first get to the home page. It is like the contents page(s) of a book or the index which enables you to search the location of a document. It is an entry point to any web site. It is also called **index.html**. When you are looking at the home page on your screen, at that time you can make a selection from a number of given selections. Note that for the home page, usually there is no need to write its name. Now, I will show you how to put these ideas into practice.

. Example 1

The purpose of this example is to demonstrate how to create two documents and save them as html files for running on your machine and previewing them locally. One of the HTML files is used to locate a page/ document locally by means of the hyperlink. The shaded area below contains the data for the Book Price list. This list has to be located by the hyperlink.

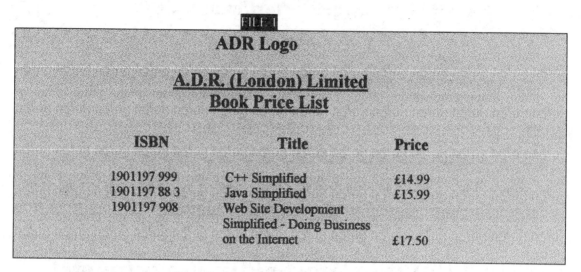

FILE 1

ADR Logo

A.D.R. (London) Limited
Book Price List

ISBN	Title	Price
1901197 999	C++ Simplified	£14.99
1901197 88 3	Java Simplified	£15.99
1901197 908	Web Site Development Simplified - Doing Business on the Internet	£17.50

The information for creating the second html file is given below in the shaded area.

FILE 2

ADR Logo

ADR Publications

Welcome to ADR Web Site

Price List Click here

This files contains the hyperlink **"Click here"** - the text which has to be clicked to locate the price list document/page.

Both Web pages should have borders around them and be colourful in appearance.

. Explanation

The following illustration highlights the relationship of documents created and saved as HTML files for example 1.

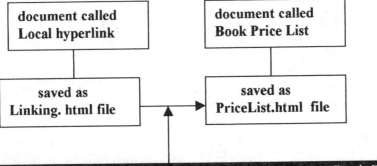

. <u>Diagram 1 -Linking.html file</u>

- This diagram contains the HTML markup code for Linking.html file.

- The flow and structure of this HTML document is very similar to the structures of several
  tables you have seen in the last chapter. However, it has incorporated an image, which is the ADR
  logo. It must appear as the first item, at the top and in the centre of your browser's window. This is an
  image. You can add images to a document, because a browser can handle such images, but they must
  be in either of the following two formats:

. **GIF** - Graphic Image Format, and . **JPG or JPEG** - Joint Photographic Experts Group.

Since Microsoft Paint software cannot handle any of these files, I have used Paint Shop Pro software to
create this file, and then transfer it to Internet Explorer Version 5 supplied with AOL IE version 5.
This topic is dealt with in Chapter 10.

- The following is the segment of the code that will copy this image from **ADRLogo.gif** file.

```
<Center>
            <IMG  SRC="ADRLogo.gif">
```

Note: You do not have to enclose the full name of the source file within " ". It works alright without
these quotation marks. If you wish to use them, you can do so. You are your own boss!

- In order to set this image in the centre of the browser's window , the <Center> tag is placed before
  the image tag.

- This code is analysed below:

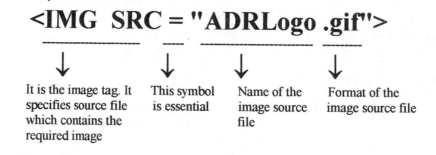

It is the image tag. It specifies source file which contains the required image	This symbol is essential	Name of the image source file	Format of the image source file

- The following segment of the code is put together by using the **anchor tag**. This segment of the code **makes the link**. It is analysed so that you can follow it easily.

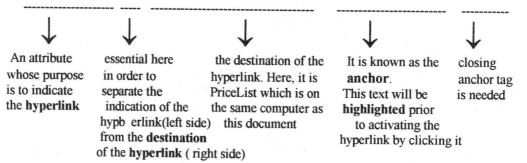

An attribute whose purpose is to indicate the **hyperlink**	essential here in order to separate the indication of the hypb erlink(left side) from the **destination** of the **hyperlink** (right side)	the destination of the hyperlink. Here, it is PriceList which is on the same computer as this document	It is known as the **anchor**. This text will be **highlighted** prior to activating the hyperlink by clicking it	closing anchor tag is needed

Thus, the click on the text " Click here" in the local hyperlink makes the connection by opening the Book Price List page/document. This tag is used to link documents locally. Thus, you can move or jump from one document to another document.

.Which is the other document in this example?

It is the Book Price List which is stored on the same computer as PriceList.html. The code for this file is in **diagram 3**.

The code in this diagram is designed to create the Book Price List. It has all the necessary information described under example 1. The structure of this code is similar to the structure of table design you have learnt in the last chapter. The book price list is linked to document called Local hyperlink (page/s on the same computer). You should experiment with these two documents in order to see how this hyperlink works. Click it and see what happens.

HTML code for Linking.html file

```
<html>
<head>
<title>Local hyperlink</title>
<Style type="text/css">
h1{color:red;font-size = 36; font-style:bold}
h2{color:black;font-size = 28 font-style:italic}
</style></head>
<body>
                        <center><IMG  SRC="ADRLogo.gif">
<Table Border = 15>
<TR>
<TH COLSPAN = 3 BGCOLOR = yellow><h1><U>
     ADR PUBLICATIONS<BR><P></P><P></P>
<h2>Welcome to ADR Web site </u>
<h3>Price Table
                        <A HREF=PriceList.html> Click here
          </A></Center></body></html>
```

Diagram 1

Local Hyperlink ready to be activated previewed in IE

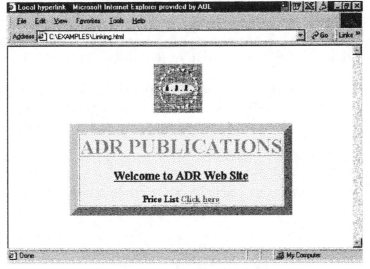

Diagram 2

HTML code for PriceList.html

```
<html>
<head>
<title>Book price list</title>
<Style type="text/css">
body{color:black}
h1{Background Color = cyan}
h2{color:black;font-style:italic}
h3{font-style:bold}
h4{color=red; font-size:12pt; font-style:italic}
</style></head>
<body>
<center>        <IMG  SRC="ADRLogo.gif">
<u><h1>       A.D.R.(London) Limited <BR>Book Price List  </u></h1>
<Table Border = 20 >
<h3>
<TR >
        <TH COLSPAN=4 BGColor =fuchsia> ISBN</TH>
        <TH COLSPAN=6 BGColor=fuchsia>TITLE</TH>
        <TH COLSPAN=4 BGColor= fuchsia> Price in Pounds Sterling</TH>
<TR >
        <TD COLSPAN=4 BGColor =yellow ALIGN=center> 1901197 99 9</TD>
        <TD COLSPAN=6 BGColor=silver Align=center>C++ Simplified</TD>
        <TD COLSPAN=4 BGColor= white ALIGN=center> £14.99 </TD>
<TR>
        <TD COLSPAN=4 BGColor=yellow ALIGN=center>1901197 88 3</TD>
        <TD COLSPAN=6 BGColor=silver Align=center> Java Simplified </TD>
        <TD COLSPAN= 4 BGColor = white Align =center> £15.99 </TD>
<TR>
        <TD COLSPAN=4 BGColor=yellow ALIGN=center> 1901197 80 8</TD>
        <TD COLSPAN =6 BgColor=silver Align=center>
              Web Site Development Simplified - Doing Business on the Internet  </TD>
        <TD COLSPAN =4 BGColor="white" Align="center"> £17.50</TD>
</h3></center></body></html>
```

Diagram 3

- Can you create a further link so that more than two documents linked together? Yes, you can do so. This is discussed soon.

• <u>Chain of links</u>

So far, you have learnt how to create a link between two documents on the same computer. Indeed, you can link more than two documents or pages together. The following example illustrates the technique of linking several pages together.

<u>Hyperlink activated showing Book Price List previewed in IE</u>

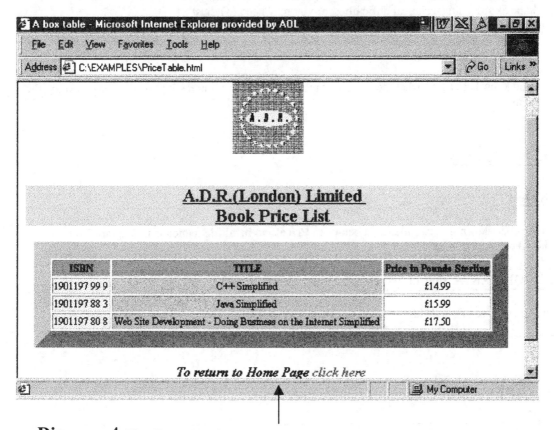

<u>Diagram 4</u> First Home Page has to be created and stored - at present it does not exist

- If you try to activate the link by clicking " Click here", it will not work, and you will not be able to visit the home page. **Why?** The simple answer is that the **Home Page** has not been designed and stored on the same computer. In fact, you will get an error message of which a small part is shown below.

Part of an error message   - screen capture

The page cannot be displayed
The page you are looking for is currently unavailable. The Web site might be experiencing technical difficulties, or you may need to adjust your browser settings.

Well, you know better than what the message says. It is becoming interesting, so you must develop the Home Page.

. __Example 2__

__Task 1__

Add the code shown in the shaded area below to **PriceList. html file,** which is in diagram 3.
It should be after the line:

```
<TD COLSPAN =4 BGColor="white" Align="center"> £17.50</TD>
```

You should place this code just above the last line - closing tags.

```
<h2>

   To return to Home Page
   <A HREF = IndexTable.html>click here</A>
</h2>
```

- The tail end of your file should be as shown below.

```
<TD COLSPAN =4 BGColor="white" Align="center">£17.50</TD></h3>
<h2>
    To return to Home Page
 <A HREF = "IndexTable.html">click here</A>
</h2></Center></body></html>
```

. Note: Browser ignores closing tags.

Saved this amended file as **PriceList . html**, and preview it to test that it has all the requirements for the Book Price List, together with the hyper link created with this anchor tag.

Task 2

To design a Home Page which will include the following information for your Web site visitors. This home page must be within a border, and also be colourful.

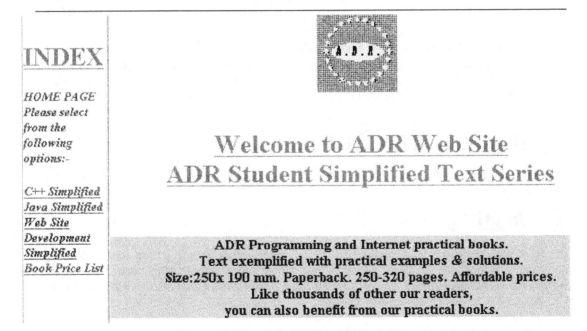

Home Page Layout

. Explanation

The task 2 of this example is somewhat more demanding as you have to create the following HTML files listed below.

	Web page	HTML file
1	Home Page	IndexTable. html
2	C++ Simplified	C++. html
3	Java Simplified	Java++. html
4	Web Site Development Simplified	Web. html
5	Book Price List	PriceList . html

- You have already met **PriceList . html file** in example 1. Thus you do not have to design and save it again. The other four files must be designed and saved, so that this Web Site development can be tested locally first, prior to its public viewing. These files are discussed below, separately first, and then the role of each file is demonstrated as part of this Web site.

. Creating the Home Page

The HTML file shown in diagram 5 below is designed to create the home page by using the given information/data.

. Explanation

The technique for drawing a table can also be used for a **page layout**. By using table drawing tools, the home page is divided into two areas (columns), one for the index or table of contents, and the other area for related information. See data above. The table is surrounded by a border which is 3 pixels wide, and some standard colours are also applied.

- Since there are four documents which can be visited through this home page, you must create four relevant hyperlinks by implementing the **anchor HTML tag** for creating each separate hyper link. The segment of the code shown below generates these required links:

Please read on at the end of diagram 5.

HTML document for the Home Page

```
<HTML>
<HEAD>
<TITLE< Creating table of contents </TITLE>
<STYLE TYPE="text/css">
h1{color=red;font-size=20pt;font-style:bold}
h2{color= green; font-size= 10pt;font-style:italic}
h3{color=black ;font-size=11pt;font-bold:italic;background Color=aqua }
</STYLE></HEAD>
<Table Border =3>
<BODY>
 <TR>
<TD>
<u><h1>
        INDEX
</u>
<h2> HOME PAGE <BR>
     Please select from the following options:-<BR>
<P>
  <A HREF="C++.html"> C++ Simplified </A><BR>
  <A HREF="Java.html"> Java Simplified</A><BR>
  <A HREF="WEb.html"> Web Site Development Simplified </A><BR>
  <A HREF="PriceTable.html"> Book Price List</A> <BR>
  </P>
</TD>
<TD>
<Center>
        <IMG  SRC="ADRLogo.gif">
<h1><u>
     Welcome to ADR Web Site<BR> ADR Student Simplified Text Series</u><h1><BR>
<h3>
        ADR Programming and Internet practical books.<BR>
        Text exemplified with practical  examples & solutions.<BR>
        Size:250x 190 mm. Paperback. 250-320 pages.
        Affordable prices.<BR> Like thousands of other our readers,<BR>
        you can also benefit from our practical books.
 </h3><Center></TD></BODY></HTML>
```

Diagram 5

Repeat: The Browser ignores closing tags. I do not always include them - it works without Them.

```
<A HREF="C++.html"> C++ Simplified </A><BR>
  <A HREF="Java.html"> Java Simplified</A><BR>
  <A HREF="WEb.html"> Web Site Development Simplified </A><BR>
  <A HREF="PriceTable.html"> Book Price List</A> <BR>
```

The coded data will be displayed on the left side of the browser window (home page).

- The other part of the table for this home page, must contain the ADR logo and related information. All this is to be aligned centrally. The segment of the code, which is below the segment of the code listed above, performs this task. You have seen similar codes in example 1.

- The preview is shown in diagram 6. So far, through this home page, you can only visit Book Price List, because this is the only page for which an HTML file called PriceList.html has been created and stored on my machine.

• <u>What do links look like?</u>

Usually, links appear <u>**underlined**</u> and in two different colours. **Unvisited link** is in a **blue** colour, and **Visited link** is in a **purple** colour. It is possible to re-set the colour of the link.

Your layout does not have to be in this format(as in diagram 6), but the advantage of placing the information in a table surrounded by a border catches the visitor's eye. The above screen capture does not show the whole border. If you preview this home page, you will be able to see the whole border around the table.

Task 3

The next requirement is to write the page markup code for **C++. html file**. The information which will form this web page is shown below in the shaded area. The HTML code is listed in diagram 7 and its preview is shown in diagram 8. Information for building **C++. html** file is shown in a box below and on the next page(because of lack of space here) in a box.

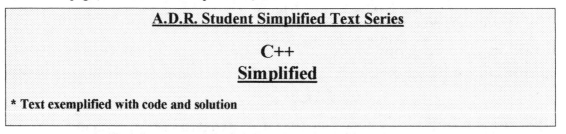

<u>A.D.R. Student Simplified Text Series</u>

C++
<u>**Simplified**</u>

* Text exemplified with code and solution

* **Learn fast through practical examples**
* **Gain confidence in your C++ programming skills**
* **Explore Java and compare it with C++**

For
Students and Beginners
By
Adam Shaw

Size: 249 x190 mm   Pages: 309 Paperback   Published: 1998   Second Edition

A.D.R. (London) Limited

Home Page previewed in IE

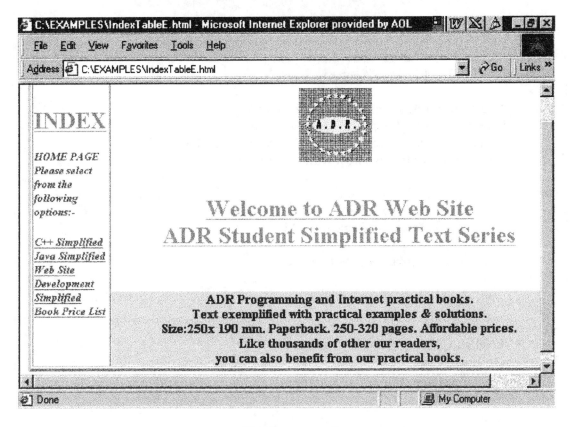

Diagram 6

HTML document for C++ Simplified page

```
<html>
<head>
<title> Learn to program in C++</Title>
<style type ="text/css">
Body {background:yellow; border-width:20}
h1 {color:red; font-size:26;  font-style:bold}
h2{color:black}
h3{color:red; Font-size=12; Font-style=bold }
</style></head>
<body>
<center><h2><u>


        A.D.R. Student Simplified Text Series </u></h2>


<h1 align = center> C++ <BR>
<u> Simplified<BR></h1></u></center>
<h3>
        * Text exemplified with code and solution<BR>
        * Learn fast through practical examples    <BR>
        * Gain confidence in your C++ programming skills <BR>
        * Explore Java and compare it with C++ <BR>


<center>
                        For <BR>
                Students and Beginners<BR>
                        By<BR>
                Adam Shaw</h3>
<h2>
            Size: 249x190mm  Pages: 309 Paperback      Published: 1998 Second Edition
<BR>
<u >
  A.D.R. (London) Limited<BR></u></center>
To return to Home Page
<A HREF ="IndexTable.html">Click here</A>
</h2></body></html>
```

Diagram 7

Learn to program in C++ previewed in IE

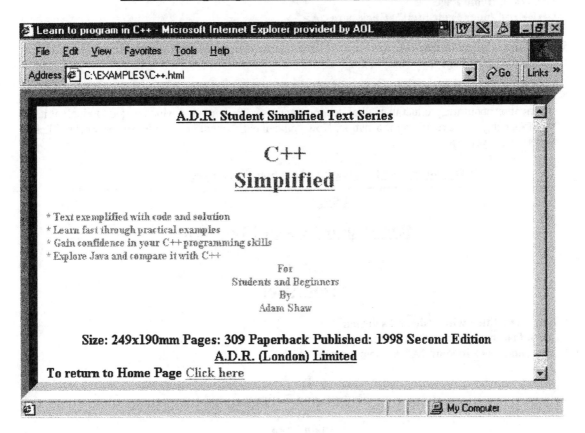

Diagram 8

. Explanation - Diagram 7

The page has to be surrounded by a border equivalent to the width of 20 pixels. It will affect the whole page. For this purpose, its code is written within the style sheet rules segment of the code.

Body {background:yellow; border-width:20}

↑

essential here - note its form

There are other applications of border attributes which are discussed elsewhere in the book. At the end of the C++ information markup code, you should write the following code.

> **To return to Home Page**
> `<A HREF ="IndexTable.html">Click here</A>`

Without this segment of the code, there will be no association between the page created by this HTML code and the Home Page. It creates the link.

- This page does not have an image to display, since the purpose of its design is to give sufficient information about the product instead of generating a visual presentation which is good to look at it, but does not give the required information. Now you can experiment how the hyperlink works. Click and see what you get.

Data/Information for creating Java Simplified page

> **Logo**
>
> **A.D.R. Student Simplified Text Series**
>
> ## Java
> ## Simplified
>
> *** Text exemplified with code and solution**
> *** Learn fast through practical examples**
> *** Gain confidence in your JAVA programming skills**
>
> **For**
> **Students and Beginners**
> **By**
> **Adam Shaw**
>
> **Size: 249x190 mm   Pages: 314 Paperback   Published: 1999**
>
> # A.D.R. (London) Limited

.Diagrams 9-10

The information required for creating a Web page called Java Simplified is shown above in the box. The HTML markup code for this page is in diagram 9. This code is similar to the other codes in this chapter. The preview is shown in diagram 10. For this page, I have included an image, which is the ADR Logo. It has taken a considerable space at the top of the page. The browser window has a limited space, and thus you have to scroll the page to see all the information.

It is a good idea to design a page which can be fitted on the screen, and the viewer is able to read the whole page without scrolling it up and down or from side to side in order to view it. For the purpose of proving that all HTML files discussed in this book have been tested for their accuracy and reliability, I have included screen captures for all examples. This screen capture does not have the top, the bottom and the sides of the browser's window. Why? It is simply because the screen was captured when the full screen option **(View → Full screen)** was selected in order to have the full page shown and captured. If you do so, your screen is full with the required page only. This is what you see in diagram 10.

HTML file for Java Simplified page

```
<html>
<head>
<title> Learn to program in Java</Title>
<style type ="text/css">
Body{background: yellow}
h1 {color:red font-size:20; font-style:bold}
h2{color:black}
h3{color:red}
</style></head>
<body><center> <IMG  SRC="ADRLogo.gif">
<h2><u>A.D.R. Student Simplified Text Series</u></h2>
<h1>Java <BR>
<u>Simplified<BR></h1></u> </center>
<h3>
            * Text exemplified with code and solution<BR>
            * Learn fast through practical examples    <BR>
            * Gain confidence in your JAVA programming skills <BR>
<center> For <BR> Students and Beginners<BR> By<BR> Adam Shaw<BR>

        Size: 249x190 mm   Pages: 314  Paperback    Published: 1999 <BR>
<h2 align = center><u>
                A.D.R.(London)Limited<Br>
                To return to Home Page
    <A HREF="IndexTable.html"> - Click here</A>
</Center></u></h2></body></html>
```

Diagram 9

Page Java Simplified previewed in IE

A.D.R. Student Simplified Text Series

Java
Simplified

* Text exemplified with code and solution
* Learn fast through practical examples
* Gain confidence in your JAVA programming skills

For
Students and Beginners
By
Adam Shaw
Size: 249x190 mm Pages: 314 Paperback Published: 1999

A.D.R.(London)Limited
To return to Home Page - Click here

Diagram 10

Task 4

In order to complete the second example, one more HTML file namely **Web . html** must be designed. For the construction of this file, the necessary information is given on the next page. In diagram 11, the required HTML code is listed, and diagram 12 contains the preview for this page. The HTML file for this page follows the pattern of the previous file. This page contains less descriptive information. This is reflected in the screen capture, as the whole page in the browser window has been captured for your information. Now, the whole example has been fully completed. It is entirely your decision what to do next. It is suggested that you experiment with these files on your system. Run the Home Page, and select any of these pages, and from any of these pages return to the Home Page. This way, you can learn more, and design your own home page for your own web site.

Information/data for Web Site DevelopmentPage

A.D.R. Student Simplified Text Series

Web Site Development

Simplified

* Build a cost-effective Web Site yourself

Daniel Lancaster

Size: 249x190 mm   Pages: 300 Paperback   Published 2000

A.D.R. (London) Limited

Page Web Site Development previewed in IE

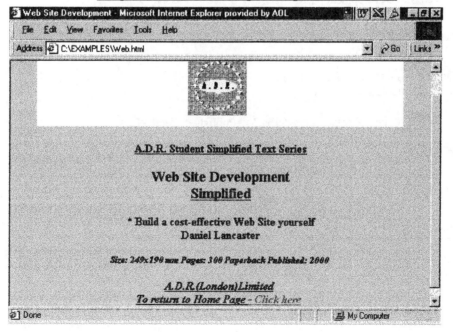

Diagram 12 (Diagram 11 is on the next page due to lack of space to fit it here)

HTML document for Web.html file

```
<html>
<head>
<title> Web Site Development</Title>
<style type ="text/css">
Body{background: lime}
h1 {color:red font-size:20; font-style:bold}
h2{color:black}
h3{color:blue font-size:16;font-style:italic}
</style>
</head>
<body>
<center>
            <IMG  SRC="ADRLogo.gif">
<h2><u>
            A.D.R. Student Simplified Text Series </u></h2>
<h1>
               Web Site Development <BR>
<u>
              Simplified<BR>
</h1></u>
<h2>
          * Build a cost-effective Web Site yourself<BR>
                Daniel Lancaster <BR>
<h3>
          Size: 249x190 mm   Pages: 300 Paperback    Published: 2000 <BR>

<h2 align = center><u>
                A.D.R.(London)Limited<Br>

                To return to Home Page
                <A HREF="IndexTable.html"> - Click here</A>
</Center></u></h2></body></html>
```

Diagram 11

Two- way communication

From the Home Page, you can select any page which is linked to it, and from the selected page, you can always return to the Home Page. This process can be repeated. It is just like a two-way communication between the Home Page and documents which are linked to it as visualised below in sketch 1.

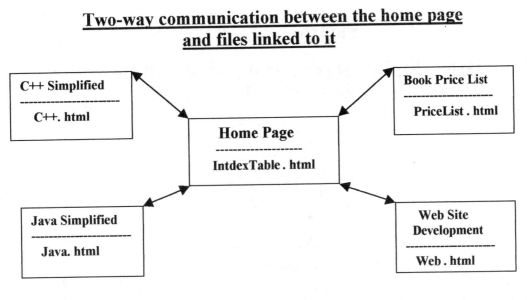

Two-way communication between the home page and files linked to it

Sketch 1

. How do you navigate the document for the required information?

Certainly, you can jump to a particular place in the same document. In this chapter, it has already been suggested that you should attempt to keep your page short and precise so that it can be fitted and viewed by the visitor without any unnecessary scrolling up and down or from side to side.

Indeed, sometimes, it may not be possible to fit the information on a single page, and the document must have more than one page. For such documents, it is desirable that the designer has created some links which can enable the Web site visitors to find easily the required information.

. Links within a page

Here, the idea is to create some links, which can facilitate jumps to some target positions in the same document. The HTML attribute called **NAME** is used with the **<A...> and </A> tags** to point to each target position in the same document. A target position is in fact an **anchor**, which is embedded in the document. For instance, if you have five target positions in a document, you can place them (their 5 names), at the beginning of a page, in the form of a simple **list**. In order to jump to these anchors or destination or the targets (call them what is easy for you to understand), you should also <u>anchor the list itself</u>. If you do so, it will assist the visitor to your Web Site to select any of these targets as many times as one wishes. This process is depicted in Sketch 2 on the next page so that you can visualise it.

Sketch 2

A sketch showing the relationship of four anchors embedded in the document called Brochure

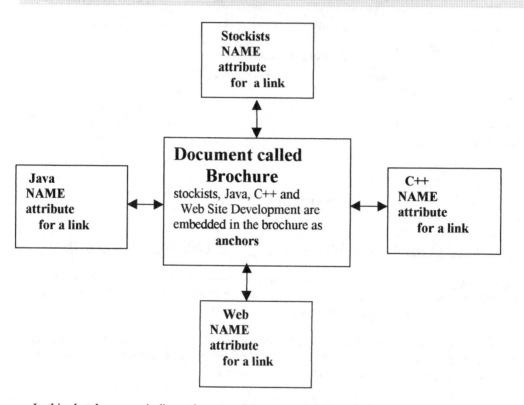

- In this sketch, arrows indicate that any of these targets in the list can be re-visited. It does not mean here two-way communication, but repetition of links. In this example:

- C++ , Java, Web and Stockists are links. These links are put together at the beginning of the page, as a simple list.

- This simple list containing C++, Java, Web and Stockists names is also **anchored**. **Why?** The idea is to provide the visitor with an opportunity of selecting any of these links or repeating the same link for information held under these names in the brochure.

. Example 3

The aim of this example is to demonstrate how to build some links within a page. A Web page is to be created by using the information shown below in the shaded area. It is a summary of a brochure called **Challenging the Future** for on-line sales. The idea is to enable visitors to select randomly, and as many times as one wishes to choose any of the four topics listed at the beginning of the page. You should run it on your system and preview it to test that its design meets all requirements.

Data/Information for the Web page called Challenging the Future

Brochure
Challenging the future
Contents

C++ Simplified 2nd edition
* Second edition published 1998
* UK Price £14.99 + P & P £2.50
* Overseas Price £14.99 + P & P £4.00
* ISBN 1901197 999

Java Simplified
* Published 1999
* UK Price £15.99 + P & P £2.50
* Overseas Price £15.99 + P & P £4.00
* ISBN 1901197 883

Web Site Development
* Published 2000
* UK Price £17.50 + P & P £2.50
* Overseas Price £ 17.50 + P & P £4.00
* ISBN 1901197 808

Stockists
A branch of Waterstone's near you
Blackwell's Branches
Hodges Figgis Ireland
YBP Library Services New Hampshire

. Explanation

. The HTML code for this example is shown in diagrams 13 and 13A.

. to create a hyperlink within a page, you must name the destination/**anchor** by means of the **NAME** attribute within the anchor tag. The following segment of the code named the destination/anchor as **start**.

<A NAME = start>

anchor tag same as for links	signifies a specific marked place in the document	essential symbol to separate attribute from marked place - name	specific place/spot in the document. I call it start as it is a marker for the beginning of the page. You can call it anything you like

The marker will **not** be displayed. You can place it anywhere you like. For instance, it can be at the top of a page, or a sub-heading, or the beginning of a paragraph or an image.

- In the following code, **start** is the anchor on the heading

```
<A NAME =start> <center><h1><u>Brochure <BR> Challenging the Future<BR>
                              Contents</u></h1></center></A>
```

This example has four options. You have to create four anchors by implementing this <NAME> tag - one for each option. In addition, one has to be to returned to the top page heading. So, five such lines are required.

- In this case, the link's anchor is "Brochure Challenging the Future" to which a direct jump can be made. **How?** You can jump directly by means of the following segment of the code.

* Go to <A HREF = # start> top of page </h3></A>

$\uparrow$

crosshatch is an essential prefix before the name to make the link to the anchor.

It creates a link. Thus, to link to an anchor , the **URL** is the anchor name, prefixed by # as shown above. There are four such lines of code in this example. **Why?**

- **This way, you can jump from any of the four options to the top of the page, " Brochure ...".**

- Now, study the whole code and try it on your machine. This technique is commonly used to jump to the top of the document, or an index or a list. In order to demonstrate its application, you need to have a long page. Since in this book, HTML features discussed are fully tested, and proof is given in the form of previews, I have tested it and provided the proof. You can see it in diagrams 14 & 14A. Due to its size, it was not possible to capture all of it in one screen capture. However, it provides you with proof that the technique is invaluable. It is commonly used on the Internet.

- Links can be held in a contents list. In this example, such a list contains four options. This list is shown at the top of the page. See diagram 14. This list is also anchored. This way, the visitor is able to return to the list in order to select another option.

- When you try it on your system, you will be able to jump to any of the topics and return to the beginning of the page.

- It is best to design a page to fit it in a single screen. If you cannot do so, you must include a means of navigating within the document. Take care!

HTML code for links within a page (cont. in diagram 13A)

```
<HTML>
<HEAD>
<TITLE< Links within a page </TITLE>
<TITLE< Links within a page </TITLE>
<STYLE TYPE="text/css">
h1{color= red font-size = 30pt; font-style:bold}
h2{color= blue; font-size= 14pt;font-style:italic}
h3{color= black ;font-size=10pt;font-bold:italic; background:white}
</STYLE>
<BODY>
        <A NAME =start> <center><h1><u>Brochure <BR>
                        Challenging the Future<BR> Contents</u></h1></center></A>

<h2>        Please select any of the following topics:-</h2>
<h3>
                                        * C++ Simplified
        <A HREF=# C++> C++ <BR></A>
                                * Java Simplified
        <A HREF=#Java> Java    <BR></A>
                                        * Web Site Development Simplified
        <A HREF=#Web> Web Site <BR></A>
                                * Stockists
        <A HREF=#Stock> Stock <BR></A>
</h3>
        <A NAME =C++><h2>C++ Simplified for students & beginners</h2></A>
<h3> * Second edition published 1998<BR>
        * UK Price £14.99 + P & P £2.50<BR>
        * Overseas Price £14.99 + P & P £4.00<BR>
        * ISBN 190 1197 999<BR>
        * Go to <A HREF =#start> top of  page </h3></A>
<A NAME = Java><h2>Java Simplified for students & beginners</h2></A>
<h3> * Published 1999<BR>
        * UK Price £15.99 + P & P £2.50<BR>
        * Overseas Price £14.99 + P & P £4.00<BR>
        * ISBN 190 1197 883<BR>
        *Go to <A HREF =#start> Top of  page</h3></A>
 <A name=Web><h2>Web Site Development Simplified</h2></A>
<h3> * Published 2000<BR>
```

Diagram 13

HTML code for links within a page (cont. from diagram 13)

```
        * UK Price 17.50 + P & P £2.50<BR>
        * Overseas Price £17.50 + P & P £4.00<BR>
        * ISBN 190 1197 808<BR>
        * Go to <A HREF =#start> top of  page </h3></A>
        <A name=Stock><h2>Stockists</h2></A>
<h3>    * A brach of Waterstone's near you<BR>
        * Blackweell's Branches<BR>
        * Hodges Figgis Ireland<BR>
        * YBP Library Services New Hampshire USA<BR>
        *Go to <A HREF =#start> Top of  page </h3></A></BODY></HTML>
```

Diagram 13A

Preview showing links within a page

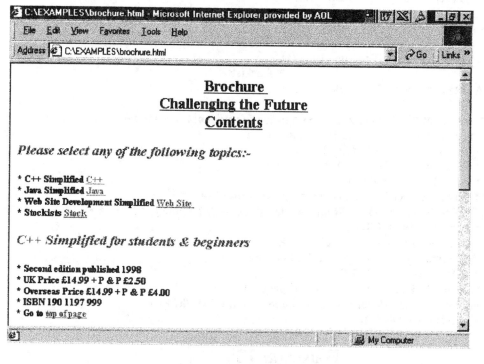

Diagram 14

Preview showing links within a page

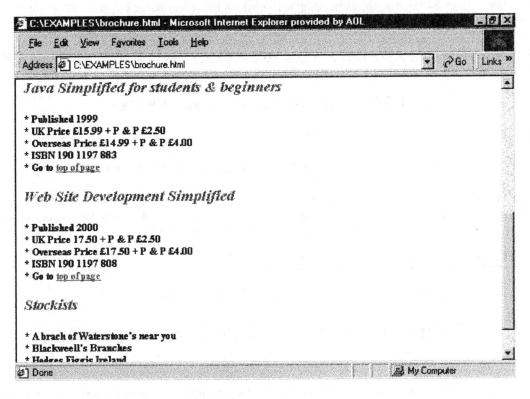

Diagram 14 A

. URLs - Universal Resource Locators

Up to now you have learnt how to create hyperlinks to local documents by means of anchors and links. The hyperlink is the coloured and underlined text which you can click to go to a file, or a destination in a file. It can also be an image or a graphic. The creation of these hyperlinks involves HREF and NAME attributes with the anchor tags <A...>text</A>.

In HTML language, the hyperlinks which you have learnt so far, are known as **Relative URLs**. Documents containing relative URLs are on the same computer as the parent document. In order to link to other pages on the same site, the relative path name within the HREF attribute in the <A> tag looks like:

<A HREF = C++.html > C++ Simplified</A>

The relative links do not involve the inclusion of such information as the address type(see below) and Internet host name /service provider. The browser thinks that all links are relative to the current page, and thus it looks for them on the same computer on which the parent document is stored. If not found, an error message is printed.

On the other hand, a link to a page across the Web, is possible when you use an **Absolute URL** within the HREF attribute in the <A> tag. It looks like:

< A HREF =http: // www.javasoft.com>JDK</A>

It is the full or the absolute URL. It will link you to:

It will link you to Javasoft so that you can get Java Development Kit from this site.

Most people seem to think **http is** the only URL, and that URLs always have the same format. It is true to say that the most used address type for the URL is http, as it is for the Web. Some other address types also form part of URLs. In Table 1, seven such address types are listed.

. How can you create an URL?

The following is a general URL format, when using an ISP's Web server.

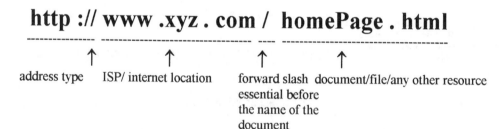

You can make it your own URL by substituting your own information as shown below.

http:// www . MyName . com / Index . html

Index . html file contains the home page.

. Will it work, if, after the forward slash, the home page file is omitted?

Yes, without specifying the home page file, you can still access the home page. This is because both the server and the browser search for the home page file first.

Address Types

Type	Nature
http://	Hypertext Transfer Protocol - it links to a Web Site, and returns a Web page.
https://	As above, but it has security features. It is more protective for the financial services, such as money transfers with both debit and credit cards.
ftp://	File transfer Protocol . You can also write as FTP. It is used for copying files across the WWW. It works fine, if you create links to some files stored on some public sites. On the other hand, if you let other people download files from your site, you have to install on your FTP software/server on your system.
gopher://	An old system, which is still useful, mainly in the academic world. Once, it was the only search tool which existed for users.
file://	It is a file link within your own system. This part of the address has an additional forward slash.
localhost://	Local Web server - for information from your own server.
Mailto:	This address form does not use **://** instead, it has: which are followed by an e-mail address as its URL.

Table 1

• Some examples of known URLs - http links

• Microsoft Developer Network Web Site - http:// msdn.microsoft.com/developer/

• The World Wide Web Consortium's Home Page - http:// www3.org/

• Javasoft for obtaining the Java Development Kit:- http:// www.javasoft.com

• Yahoo! UK & Ireland Web Site: http:// ww.yahoo.co.uk

It is an important Web Site for you, if you are looking for some ISP companies in the UK. The full URL for accessing the list of ISP providers at **Yahoo** is as follows:

http ; // www.yahoo.co.uk / Business_and_Economy/Companies/ Internet Services / Internet providers/

- In order to link to other Internet resources, you have to replace the **http address** with that of the required site. For instance, a **Linking to Gopher Site** looks like this:

gopher : // gopher.well.sf.ca.us/11/outbound/Yanoff

• How can you create links within your documents in order to access resources across the Web and other specialist sites?

So far so good, but the whole idea is to create links with URLs across the Web, so that you can link to any other site on the World Wide Web. Indeed, the Internet is a vast library on-line. You can get information in the form of documents, pictures, sounds, and so on. All kinds of information are published on the Internet. It is possible to download, free of charge, files of your interest from these sites on your system. For instance, you can download files from the specialist sites known as FTP sites. FTP stands for File Transfer Protocol). The following example aims to demonstrate how to create such links.

• Links across the Web

• Example 4

The HTML code shown in diagram 15 illustrates the construction of five URLs for creating links across the Web. One link is to the specialist site, and the other two links are to two local files.

Web Sites links	Specialist Sites link	Local links
http:// www.w3.org/TR/REC-html40/		unorderedList.html
http://www.waterstones/co.uk /		C++.html
http://www.yahoo.co.uk/		
http://msdn.microsoft.com/developer/		
http://www.javasoft.com /		
	gopher://gopher.well.sf.ca.us/ 11/outbound/Yanoff	

• Explanation

The URLs constructed for the Web call an HTTP server directly. The technique of creating a hyperlink containing these URLs involves <A> tag with the **HREF** attribute. You have already seen these in action a number of times in this chapter. The gopher is an old protocol. It also uses the URL, but its access method is different. The HTML code in diagram 15 is pretty straightforward. However, it is important to learn that the URL is part of the HREF attribute.

HTML code for example 4

```
<html>
<head>
<title>URLs links across the Web</Title>
<style type ="text/css">
Body {background: white ; border-width:20}
h1 {color:red; font-size:26;  font-style:bold}
h2{color:blue}
h3{color:black; Font-size=12; Font-style=bold }
</style>
</head>
<body>
<center><h1><u>Some Examples of URLs
<h2>You can click any of the following links to make a connection.</u></center>
<UL type = "circle">
<h3>
    <LI> World Wide Web Consortium
        <A HREF=http://www.w3.org/TR/REC-html40/>HTML 4.0 Specification</A></LI>
    <LI>Yahoo UK & Ireland
        <A HREF=http://www.yahoo.co.uk/>Yahoo</A></LI>
    <LI> Waterstone's Booksellers
        <A HREF=http://www.waterstones.co.uk/>Waterstone's</A></LI>
    <LI> Microsoft Developer Network
        <A HREF =http://msdn.microsoft.com/developer/> Microsoft</A></LI>
    <LI> Java Develoment Kit
        <A HREF = >JDK</A></LI>
        < <LI> Gopher Site
        <A HREF =gopher://gopher.well.sf.ca.us/11/outbound/Yanoff>Yanoff </A/</LI>

<p></P> <center><h1> <u> Also Two Local Links</u></h1></center>
    <LI> A local file
        <A HREF = unorderedList.html> Unordered list</A></LI>
    <LI> Another local file
        <A HREF = C++.html> C++  Simplified</A></LI>
</h3></UL><body><html>
```

Diagram 15

In diagram 16, you can see the preview of the document created by the above HTML code. You can click any of these URLs to access any of these sites, including two local files. In fact, you can also open these files, if you have already stored all HTML documents, which are discussed so far in this book. If you have done so, then they are local to you. Try any of these links.

URL's links across the Web page previewed in IE

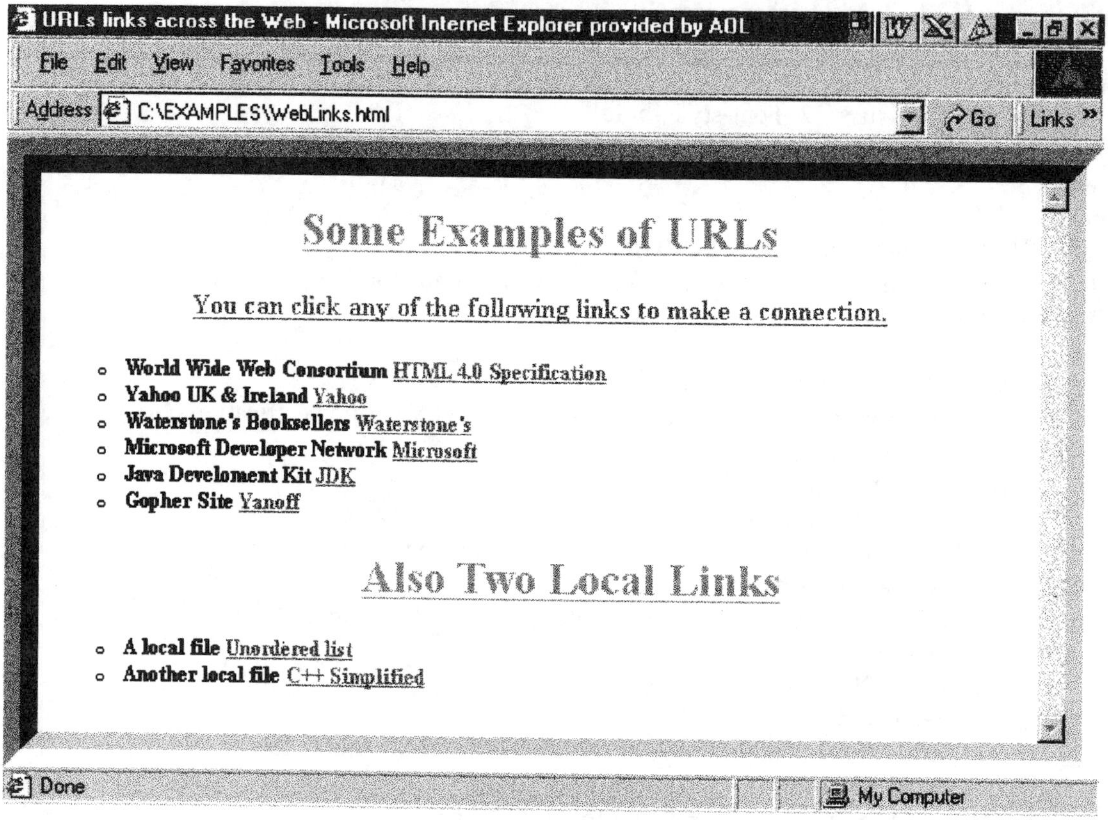

Diagram 16

- ## Gopher Root Directory displayed by the IE

In diagram 17, you can examine a screen capture showing you the working of one of the links shown in diagram 16. Gopher sites are not as popular as they used to be before the arrival of the Web. Even so, they can give you some invaluable information. In fact, you can also access a list of Gopher sites through the Yahoo Web site.

Diagrams 17 and 18 are screen captures of two clicked hyperlinks

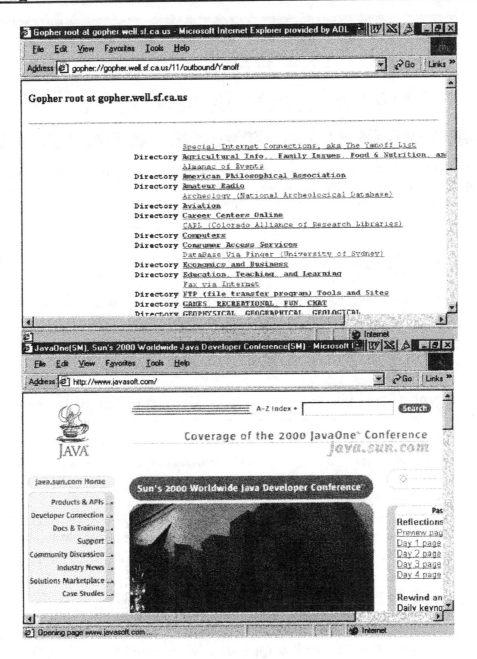

Diagrams 17 and 18

Chapter 9

Frames in your documents (1)

The purpose of this chapter is to enable you to understand the nature of frames, and how to construct them in order to include them in your documents. You should be able to construct both simple frames and nested framesets for a complex layout.

. What are frames?

The techniue of framing enables you to divide the browser window into a number of sub- windows. Each sub-section of the browser window is then a frame. This frame is independent and it is also interactive.   You can design these frames in such a way that you can either restrict the viewer to have some degree of control over these windows or no control at all. You can classify frames as static and dynamic types, each type having its own characteristics as identified below.

Static type of frames	Dynamic type of frames
. Always visible	. Response to user's simple actions
. contents do not change	. User can change their contents by
. useful for table of contents navigational tools	a simple action such as clicking the hyperlink
. for things which must remain visible	. User should have a large work area allocated for this type as this is where the action takes place

. Are frames highly desirable for presentation?

• The inclusion of frames in your HTML document can lead to better presentation. But, if you include too many frames, you will not have a big enough working area which will defeat the purpose of having frames.

- The display of several frames at a time can lead to smaller frames, which may not be user-friendly.

- Frames which look good on a larger screen do not impress the viewers who have smaller screens. One should remember this at the time of designing documents with frames.

- The static type frames used for navigational purposes can result in the reduction of links in and out of pages. This is useful.

It may be that frames are highly desirable as layout and navigation tools for a specific task, but the inclusion of them in documents should be considered carefully, so that the presentation of information and the effectiveness of the document are not hindered by their presence.

. How can you create frames ?

Firstly, it is desirable that you understand the basic frames terminology, so that it becomes easier for you to follow how to construct frames.

- In order to define a frame in an HTML document, you must implement the following two tags.

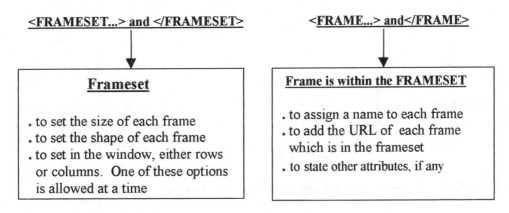

<FRAMESET...> and </FRAMESET>

Frameset

. to set the size of each frame
. to set the shape of each frame
. to set in the window, either rows
  or columns. One of these options
  is allowed at a time

<FRAME...> and</FRAME>

Frame is within the FRAMESET

. to assign a name to each frame
. to add the URL of each frame
  which is in the frameset
. to state other attributes, if any

. What is a frameset?

The frameset consists of all frames within a document and their definitons. Its prime function is to arrange pages and their connection to each other. It contains no information itself for the user. It is just another HTML text file.

. <u>What is a frameset container?</u>

A frameset is defined within the frameset tags as shown above. A defined frameset is called <FRAMESET> container.

. <u>Example 1 - frames definition</u>

A <FRAMESET> can take any of the two attributes as outlined above. In this example, the frames definition takes **COLS** as its attribute. It will divide the browser window into two equal vertical divisions.

. <u>Explanation</u>

In order to create two frames and display some information in these frames, you require three html files which are shown below in illustration 1.

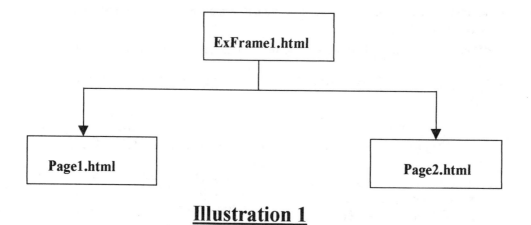

<u>Illustration 1</u>

- The code for ExFrame.html is in diagram 1. Its main features are explained below:-

- **<FRAMESET Cols = 50%, 50%>** - this frameset container divides the browser window into two equal halves. The attribute COLS/Cols results in vertical division or two columns as required.

- Two pages which should be displayed in these two frames must be created. If these pages do not exist, you will not be able to see anything in these frames, and thus the frameset will not work at all.

- **Page1. html** file is shown in diagram 1A . **Page2. html** is in diagram 1B. The codes for these two files are simple to follow.

- Back to diagram 1 - Now, you know well that the defined frameset has to call on these two HTML files, so that it can display the required two pages in these two frames.

• How do you make the connection between these two files with the frameset?

This is achieved by implementing HTML attribute called **SRC** or **scr**. Its purpose is to refer to an external resource. Its general format is shown below.

$$< Frame\ SRC\ =\ "url">$$

```
----------------      ------------   -----      ---------
     ↑                     ↑          ↑             ↑
  frameset             attribute   essential   location of the file - this can be
  container           for linking              any URL or local html file
                   external resources          " " optional. It works without them
```

- For displaying page 1, the frameset will call on page1.html file, when the following code is executed.

<FRAME SRC = page1.html>

• Can a <FRAMESET ...> have more than one SRC attribute? No!

Only one SRC attribute is allowed for each frame in the <FRAMESET...>. This is the reason for the following code for the second page to be displayed in frame2/window 2.

<FRAME SRC = page2.html>

- </FRAMESET> tag is essential in order to close the frameset container. When it is met, the frameset container is created.

- Diagram 2 contains the preview . You can see it has worked successfully. All three HTML files/documents have been linked together and generated the requireed two frames containing two pages in them.

• What is the reason for not having <BODY> and </<BODY> tags in the HTML file for creating a frameset container?

These are not allowed here. It means that you cannot apply any attributes associated with these tags. For instance, you cannot create colourful backgrounds for frameset pages. However, a page which is external to the frameset and apperars in it, can have body attributes.

• Is it possible to define frames dimensions by means of pixel values instead of percentage widths and heights of the browser window?

You can define frame dimensions by means of pixel values. However, there is one serious drawback which is due to the fact that you do not know the display size of your viewer's monitor. For instance, the width of your frame can be bigger than the width of the viewer's window. In that case, your frame will not fit into the screen of the viewer. It is not all too bleak; if, for instance, you know the height of an image in pixels. In such a case, it is advantageous to specify frame dimensions in pixels. If you do so, the image will be displayed where you want in the viewer's screen, irrespective of the display dimensions of the viewer's monitor.

HTML code for creating two frames/ windows

```
<html>
<head>
<title>An example of creating two frames</Title>
</head>
<FRAMESET Cols = 50%,50%>
<FRAME SRC = page1.html>
<FRAME SRC =  page2.html>
</FRAMESET></html>
```

Diagram 1

HTML code for page 1

```
<html>
<head>
<title> This is frame 1</title>
</head>
<body><center>
<h2><u>It occupies 50% space of browser window. <BR>
     The browser window is divided equally and vertically.
<P></P><P></P>This is page 1.</u></h2></body></html>
```

Diagram 1A

HTML code for page 2

```
<html>
<head>
<title> This is frame 2</title>
</head>
<body><center>
<h2><u>
        It also occupies 50% space of browser window. <BR>
        The browser window is divided equally and vertically.
<P></P><P></P>
        This is page 2.</u></h2></body></html>
```

Diagram 1B

An example of creating two frames previewed in IE

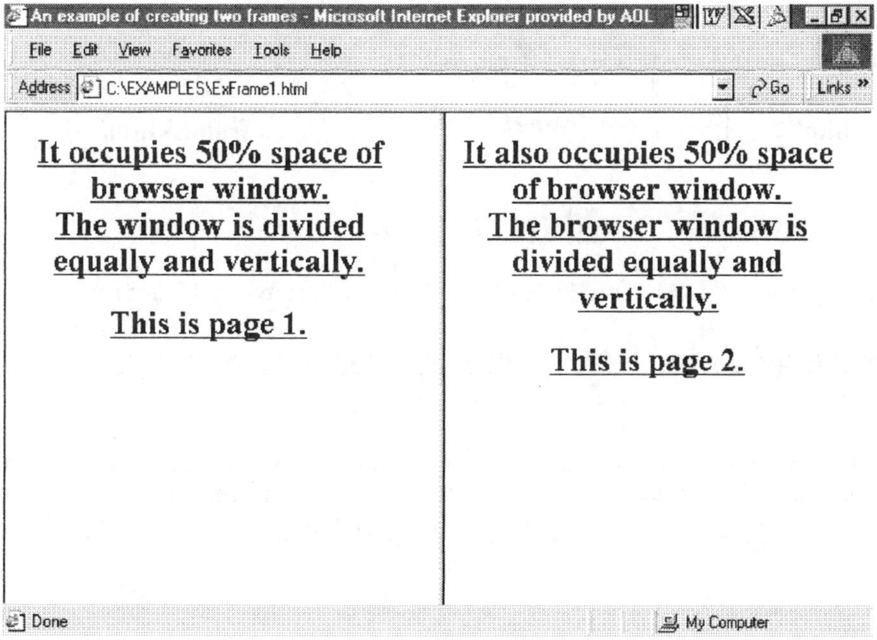

Diagram 2

. <u>Example 2</u>

The aim of this example is to demonstrate how to create three frames horizontally and display three external pages in threse frames. The sizes of top and middle frames equal to 25% each of the browser window, and the remaining 50% is to be allocated to the bottom frame.

. <u>Explanation</u>

Yes, you are right, you need to create four separate HTML files for this example. The relationship of these files is depicted below in illustration 2.

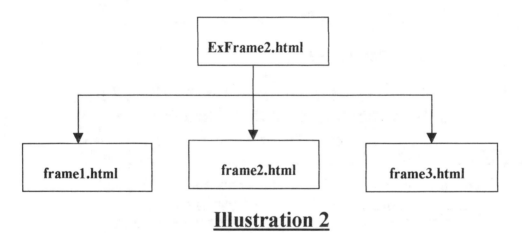

<u>Illustration 2</u>

● The code for **ExFrame2.html** is listed in diagram 3. It ceates three required frames only.

● <u>What are the differences between this code and the one which is shown in diagram 1?</u>

The code in diagram 3 is for creating three frames not two frames. Furthermore, frames are to br drawn horizontally not vertically. Because of these basic differences, the frame container differs. It is coded as

<FRAMESET ROWS = 25%, 25%, 50%>

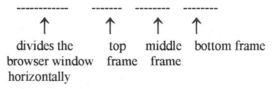

divides the   top   middle   bottom frame
browser window   frame   frame
horizontally

• The <FRAMESET...> has to call on three external files which are shown in the above illustration.

• Three separate files containging HTML code for three separate pages are listed in diagrams 3A, 3B and 3C. These are ordinary HTML files containing codes which by now you are familiar with.

HTML code for creating three frames

```
<html><head>
<title>An example of creating three frames</Title></head>
<FRAMESET  ROWS = 25%,25%,50%>
<FRAME SRC = frame1.html>
<FRAME SRC = frame2.html>
<FRAME SRC = frame3.html>
</FRAMESET></html>
```

Diagram 3

HTML code for frame 1

```
<html>
<head>
<title> This is frame 1</title></head>
<body>
<center><u>This is frame 1</body></html>
```

Diagram 3A

HTML code for frame 2

```
<html>
<head>
<title> This is frame 2</title></head>
<body><center><u>
    This is frame 2 >/U></body></html>
```

Diagram 3B

HTML code for frame 3

```
<html>
<head>
<title> This is frame 3</title>
</head>
<body><center><u>
    This is frame 3</U></body></html>
```

Diagram 3C

An example of creating three frames previewed in IE

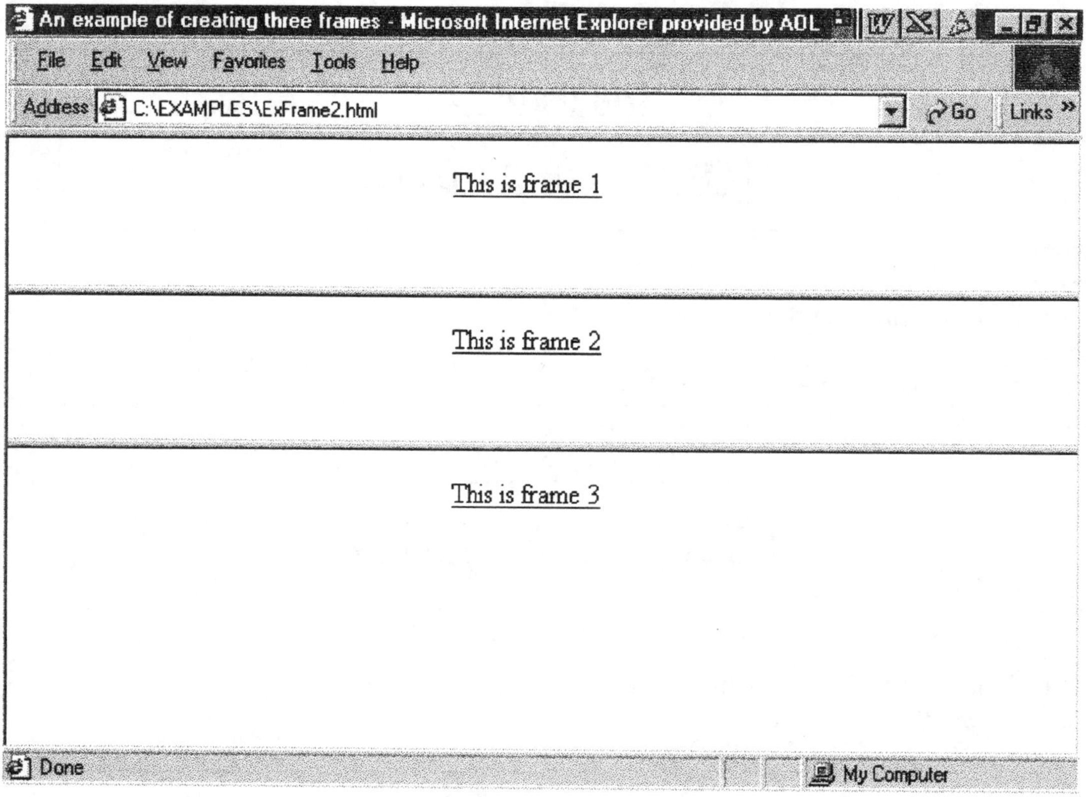

Diagram 4

. Nested Framesets

So far, you have seen simple frames. For a complex layout , you have to create nested framesets.

A frameset inside another frameset is called a nested frameset. For instance, if you divide the window into two rows, and then divide one row into two columns. The divisions into two columns of one of these rows is a nested frameset. You may have to create even more complex frames. The following example demonstrate the technique involves in creating such complex frames.

. Example 3

The purpose of this example is to create three frames by dividing the browser window horizontally into two sections. The top section will display **Heading**, and the lower section is to be further divided vertically into two unequal sections namely, left and right. The left section will display **Contents**, and the right section will be called **Work Area**.

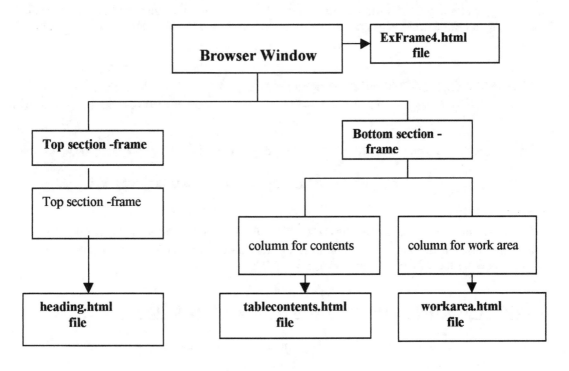

Illustration 3

. Explanation

The above illustration attempts to highlight the required divisions of the browser window and html documents to be created for the completion of this example.

- The HTML file in diagram 5 contains the code for setting up the main frameset and nested frameset in it. The first step is to create the row structure for setting up the nested frameset. In this diagram, it is achieved by the following segment of the code:

<FRAMESET ROWS = 20%,*%> ⟶ sets two rows of unequal width 20% and 80%.
                                   *% means the remaining area which is 80% here

<FRAME SRC = heading.html> ⟶ declares the file which will be loaded into the top row

It sets the main frameset, but it will not perform its task without the html file which contains the html for the bottom row. Therefore, this has to be immediately followed by the following segment of the code:

<FRAMESET COLS = 20%,60%> ⟶ sets the nested frameset for two columns of unequal
                                  width as required. Here, the left column is 20% and 60%
                                  for the right column

<FRAME SRC = tablecontents.html> ⟶ This file's contents will be displayed in the left column

<FRAME SRC = workarea.html> ⟶ This file's contents will be displayed in the right column

- Of course, you can appreciate that this HTML file will not work properly without the other three html files listed in diagram 5. To demonstrate how this nested frameset technique operates, I have listed codes for these files in diagrams 5A, 5B and 5C.

. How does the browser interpret all these files ?

- The browser reads the file which sets the framesets. For this example, it is **ExFrame4.html**. It is the top or master file.

- When it reads the row definition and looks for the **SRC** - an external resource, it finds the file which is on the same line as the SRC. This file contains the Heading. It is then loaded into the top row.

- The browser searches for another html file for loading it into the remaining area of the browser window which is 80% for the bottom row, but on the next line, it finds another frameset definition. This frameset is the nested frameset. In accordance with this frameset, it creates two columns as per given sizes.

- Next, it reads the line which refers to SRC. - the external file. It reads its contents and loads it into the left column. It sees another reference to another SRC. It then loads this file's contents into the left column .

- It reads the next lines in this sequence of lines. It finds two </FRAMESET> lines, meaning the end of the framesets. The process of frameset's creation and loading the contents of all files into the appropriate frames ends here successfully. You can see the result in diagram 6.

. Can you define a frameset for just one column or one row ?

It is not possible to set up a frameset for just one column or a row. Thus, the following codes:
< FRAMESET = COLS = 100%>   and   <FRAMESET = ROWS = 100%> will result, in both cases, displaying blank pages. You must set up a frameset for at lease two columns or two rows.

HTML code for creating two frame containers/framesets

```
<html>
<head>
<title>Labelling frames</Title></head>

<FRAMESET  ROWS = 20%,*%>
<FRAME SRC = heading.html>
<FRAMESET COLS = 20%,60%>
<FRAME SRC =tablecontents.html>
<FRAME SRC = workarea.html>
</FRAMESET>
</FRAMESET></head></html>
```

Diagram 5

HTML code for heading

```
<html>
<head>
<title> Heading</title></head>
<body>
<h2><u>
 Heading</u></h2>
</body></html>
```

Diagram 5A

HTML code for Index

```
<html>
<head>
<title> Table of contents  </title>
</head>
<body>
<h2><u>
 Contents</u></h2></body></html>
```

Diagram 5B

HTML code for Work Area

```
<html>
<head>
<title> Work Area</title>
</head>
<body>
<h2><u>
   Work Area </u></h2>
</body></html>
```

Diagram 5C

. When should you use frames?

Frames are fine if you do not have more than three rows or columns, and would like to the advantage of control features associated with frames.

. How about tables in place of frames?

Use tables if you have more than three rows and columns of static type data. Anyway, it will not be a good idea to use frames for so many rows and columns that the browser window is too crowded, and has too little space for things to happen in one of the frames.

Labelling frames previewed in IE

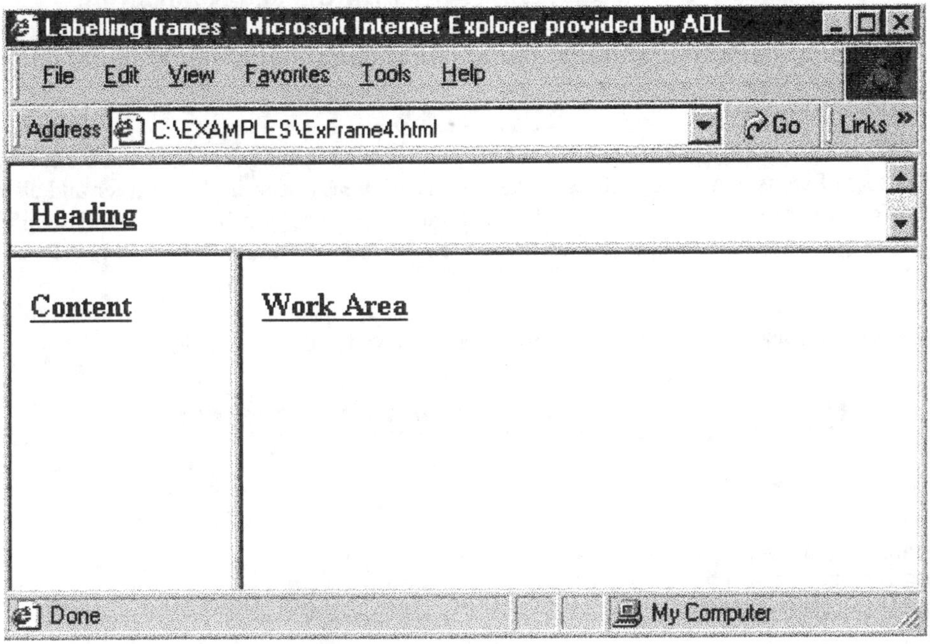

Diagram 6

. Is it possible to control the appearance of a frame?

You can change the appearance of a frame's default look and behaviour by means of using some of the **<FRAME> attributes**. You might have noticed that frames have silver edges. Furthermore, when the page is too big to fit into the window, frames automatically include scroll bars. All frames are also re-sizeable You can make use of some of the following frame attributes to control the appearance and behaviour of frames. The problem is that these control mechanisms will not work on all browsers. Remember that all HTML 4.0 features are not supported by all older browsers and many other browsers.

. Example 4

The purpose of this example is to demonstrate how to apply some of the attributes listed in table 1 below. The browser window is to be divided into two columns of the same size. The appearance of the presentation is to be controlled in such a way that the user cannot resize the layout, no scroll bars are to be added to the frames, margins to be set to 10 pixels , and the border of 20 pixels in yellow to be drawn between these two frames. The further requirement is to display in these two columns/frames, the contents of two html files. These files are called **Moscow.html** and **Rome.html**.

. Explanation

Three HTML files for the completion of this example are shown in diagrams 7, 7A and 7B. The construction of these files is pretty much the same as you have already seen in this chapter and elsewhere in this book. However, the declaration of the required frames attributes is made within the <FRAME...> tag. I have declared border colour in <FRAMESET...> tag, but it could have been made in the <FRAME...> tag.

The preview of the frames created together with pages displayed is in diagram 8.

HTML code for setting up the frameset

```
<html>
<head>
<title>Frame Attributes</Title></head>
<FRAMESET COLS = 50%,50% border =20 bordercolor = yellow>
<FRAME SRC = Moscow.html>
<FRAME Scrolling = no noresize  marginwidth = 10 marginheight=10
 SRC = Rome.html>
</FRAMESET></html>
```

Diagram 7

HTML code for Moscow.html file

```
<HTML><HEAD>
<TITLE> Moscow </TITLE></HEAD>
 <BODY><center><u><h1>MOSCOW </h1></u></center>
 <h2>Capital of the  Russian Federation.<BR>
        It is on the river Moskva.<BR>Population about 9 million.</body></html>
```

Diagram 7A

HTML code for Rome.html file

```
<HTML><HEAD>
<TITLE> ROME </TITLE></HEAD>
<BODY><center><u><h1> ROME</h1></u></center>
 <h2>Capital of Italy.<BR> It is on the river Tiber.<BR>
            Population about 3 million. </body></html>
```

Diagram 7B

Frame Attributes previewed in IE

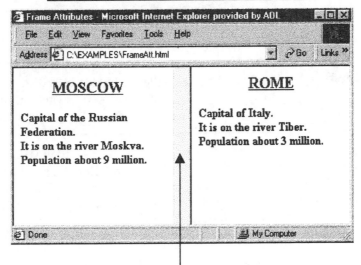

Diagram 8   **Frame Border** between two frames in yellow.

Frame Attributes

Attribute	Function
. noresize	It implies that the frame cannot be re-sized. But, you can re-size a frame by dragging its edges to a place where you want. It should be set within the <FRAME...> tag. In fact, in practical terms, it has no effect, as you can always re-size the frame by dragging its edges to where you want.
. scrolling = yes, no, auto	" **auto**" scrolling is by default as mentioned above. If it is undesirable, just say so, by "**no**". It should be set within the <FRAME...> tag.
. marginwidth = "value"	to control the margin of text or graphics image in a frame. Margin value must be in pixel, and that the smallest margin width is one pixel. It should be set within the <FRAME...> tag. You can set marginwidth marginheight attributes in pixels. marginheight controls upper and lower margins of a frame.
. frameborder = 0,1	This can either be hidden or shown. **frameborder** ="**0**" switch off the border. **frameborder** ="**1**" switch on the border.
. bordercolor =	You can set it inside the <FRAMESET...> tag or <FRAME...> tag. Borders within a < frameset...> must be of the same colour. You can have vertical border of one colour and the horizontal border of a different colour.

Table 1

.Your logo in a frame

If you have a logo for your business or for your own personal use, you can easily place it in a frame. You can place it where you think it suits you. It does not have to be in the left or right corner. The choice is yours! You are the boss!

.Example 5

It is aimed at creating an HTML file which will place your company logo in a particular place of your choice, together with the company's address. Other requirements are discussed below.

.Explanation

The first requirement is the creation of a file which contains the logo. This requires a GIF type file called **ADRLogo. gif**. This file was created by Serif graphics software and then converted to GIF type by the Paint Shop Pro graphics software in order to incorporate it in HTML documents. The following segment of the code is in diagram 9A, which holds the logo as an image in the html file.

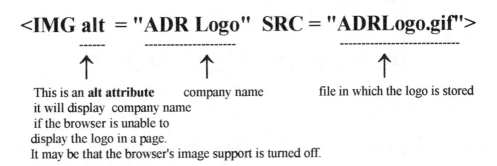

$$\text{<IMG alt = "ADR Logo" SRC = "ADRLogo.gif">}$$

This is an **alt attribute**   company name   file in which the logo is stored
it will display company name
if the browser is unable to
display the logo in a page.
It may be that the browser's image support is turned off.

- It is also required to display the company's address. You can have both address and the logo stored in the same file, but I have stored the logo in a different file , so that it can be copied on to other pages without the address.

- It is also required to use the <FRAME...> attributes in order to display the page without the frame border, restrict the user from resizing the window (but the user can still find a way to change it), and include no scrolling bars. Without the frame border and scrolling bars, it looks as it is one frame.

- The next requirement is to divide the browser window into two rows. The upper row/frame contains the logo . The upper frame, where the logo is placed, is sized 110 pixels.

. Why is it in pixels?

This way, the height is precisely measured. The logo will always have this fixed frame area, and the remaining browser window area will be for the lower frame. You have to make sure that the frame is high enough for your logo. Furthermore, if the frame is just big enough to accommodate the logo, it is highly likely that scroll bars will appear. If you do not want them , just include **scrolling = no** as shown in diagram 9.

HTML code for setting up the frameset for example 5

```
<html>
<head>
<title>A frame with ADR Logo</title>
</head>
  <Frameset  frameborder = "0"  noresize rows = "110,*" >
        <Frame src = "ADRLogo.html" SCROLLING ="no">
        <Frame src = ADR.html>
  </frameset></html>
```

Diagram 9

HTML code for ADRLogo.html file

```
<html><head>
<title> ADR Logo</title>
</head><body>
  <IMG alt ="ADR Logo"  SRC = "ADRLogo.gif"></body></html>
```

Diagram 9A

HTML code for ADR.html address file

```
<html><head>
<title> ADR Logo</title>
</head><body>
  <H1> A.D.R.(London) Limited Bridlington UK</body></html>
```

Diagram 9B

A frame with ADR Logo previewed in IE

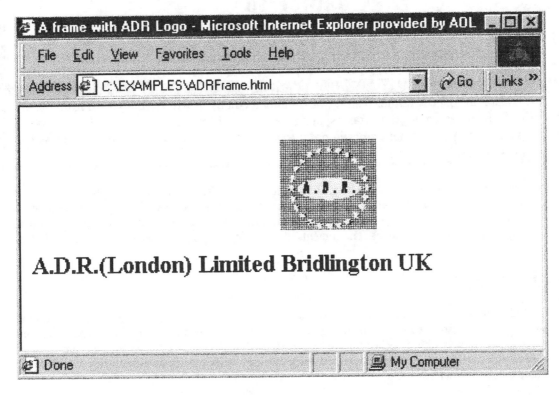

Diagram 10

. A word of warning!

Older browsers cannot handle frames. More about frames in the next chapter.

Chapter 10

Dynamic frames in your documents (2)

This chapter introduces further features of framing methods. It will enable you to learn the skills of naming and navigating frames, and making use of frames in your html documents. You should be able to create frames in order to load contents into existing windows, into new windows and floating frames.

In the last chapter you have learnt the basics of how to construct frames. The statistic type of frames are not suitable for all kinds of purposes. Such frames do not give the user the opportunity to select information by clicking the hyperlinks. The following examples are designed to demonstrate how to construct and use **dynamic frames.** The contents of such frames change in response to user's action.

. Example 1

The task is to design two frames, each of which will have its own page to display. Each frame must have a hyperlink associated with its own page, and its contents. When the user clicks a hyperlink in any of these two frames, the associated page information should be loaded into the relevant **current window** in which the hyperlink is clicked. If the user clicks both hyperlinks in both pages, each frame should display its own page in it

. Explanation   Illustration 1

The illustration 1 shows the required html files and their relationship for this example.

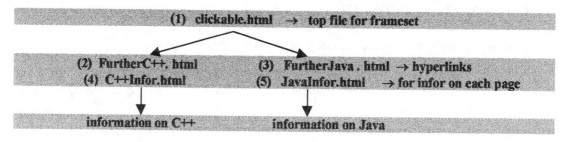

- Illustration 2 expands the relationship of files shown in illustration 1. You can see what happens when the user activates any of the two hyperlinks

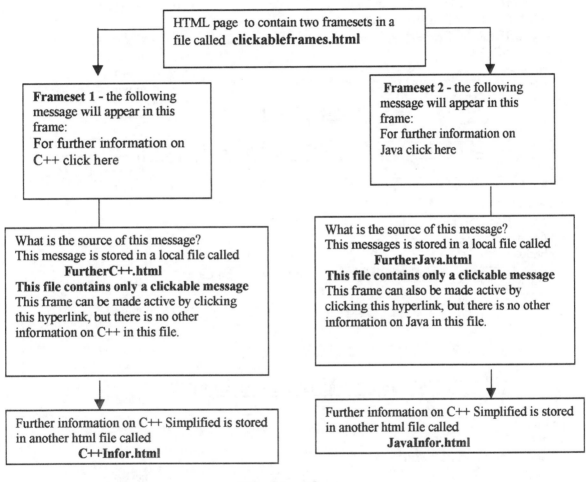

Illustration

- The HTML files are listed in diagrams 1, 1A, 1B,1C and 1D.

HTML code for setting up the main frameset for this example

```
<html>
<head>
<title>Clickable frames</Title></head>
<FRAMESET  COLS = 50%,50%>
<FRAME SRC = FurtherC++.html>
<FRAME SRC = FurtherJava.html>
</FRAMESET>
</html>
```

Diagram 1

HTML code for making frame 1 active

```
<html>
<head>
<title> This is frame 1</title>
</head>
<body>
   <A HREF = C++.html><h2> For further information on C++
   click here
   </h2></A></body></html>
```

Diagram 1A

HTML code for making frame 2 active

```
<html>
<head>
<title> This is frame 2</title>
</head>
<body>
   <A HREF = Java.html><h2> For further information on C++ click here
   </h2> </A></body></html>
```

Diagram 1B

HTML code for C++ Infor.html file

```
<HTML><HEAD>
<TITLE< C++ Simplified </TITLE>
<BODY>
<center> <u><h1>  C++ Simplified</h1></u></center><BR>
<h3>Chapter 1   Introduction to C++ Programming <BR>
Chapter 2   C++ Program Structure<BR> Chapter 3   Conditions Testing ( 1 ) <BR>
Chapter 4   Conditions Testing ( 2 )<BR> Chapter 5   Functions<BR>
Chapter 6   Arrays  <BR> Chapter 7   Pointers  <BR>
Chapter 8   Character Strings<BR> Chapter 9   Mixed Data Structure <BR>
Chapter 10 File Processing <BR> Chapter 11 Object Oriented Programming<BR>
Chapter 12 Suggested Programs & Solutions <BR>Chapter 13 Glossary of Terms<BR>
Chapter 14 Exploring Java  <BR> Index</body></html>
```

Diagram 1C

HTML code for Java Infor.html file

```
<HTML><HEAD>
<TITLE< Java Chapters </TITLE></HEAD>
<BODY>
<center> <u><h1>  JAVA Simplified</h1></U></center><BR>
<h3>
Chapter 1  Towards Understanding Java Language <BR>
Chapter 2  Java Application Program Development  <BR>
Chapter 3  Fundamental Concepts & Applications  <BR>
Chapter 4  Arrays Data Type  <BR>Chapter 5  Conditions Testing  <BR>
Chapter 6  Working with objects and classes <BR>
Chapter 7  Applets Basic understanding <BR> Chapter 8  Fonts and colours <BR>
Chapter 9  The graphical user interface - UGI<BR>  Chapter 10  Event Handling <BR>
Chapter 11  Drawing Shapes  <BR> Chapter 12  Drawing Shapes using 2D Graphics<BR>
Chapter 13  Animation and Threads <BR> Chapter 14  Exception Handling <BR>
Chapter 15  Suggested Solutions <BR> Glossary of Terms  <BR>
Index   <BR> </body></html>
```

Diagram 1D

. How does it work?

The simpliest explanation of the process of linking all these files together in the way it is desired is as follows:-

• The browser first reads the file shown in diagram 1 - setting up the frameset.

• It sees the frameset tag in which it finds column defintion. It divides the window of the browser into two equal sections - two frames.

• In the sequence of lines, it goes to the next line and discovers the SRC which is a reference to an external resource. In this case, it is an html file called **FurtherC++.html**. It reads this file. This file has an URL and some clickable text. Thus, it places this text as underlined in the left frame.

• Having obeyed the instruction, it proceeds to the next line of code. Here, it meets another SRC, which refers to another html file called **FurtherJava.html**. It reads it and finds out that it has an URL and some text as well. Once again, it obeys the instruction, and it displays in the right column or frame, the relevant text for hyperlink.

• Finally, it reads the next line, which happens to be the closing tag for the frameset. Now, it can do nothing else except finish its task.

• Now, both frames are active/dynamic - ready to interact with the user. You can see the preview of this process in diagram 2. See diagrams 2 & 2A. **It works!**

. What can happen next?

The above process has set up two windows showing two pages with their hyperlinks underlined. Now, you, the user, can click any of these hyperlinks or both of them if you wish. If you click the hyperlink in the left frame, it will load the contents of the **C++.html** file into the left frame. The code for this file is shown in diagram 1C. If you click the hyperlink text in the other frame, it will make a connection with the **Java.html** file. The code for this file is in diagram 1D.

Now, you should be able to understand and appreciate the reason for creating all these files for this example.

. Are there any disadvantages in loading pages into the current windows?

There are two drawbacks with this method. These are outlined below:-

- As soon as you click the link, the page is loaded with the required information. Thus, the clicked link is no longer visible. You cannot re-click it.

- If there waas more than one link, you can only click one of them, because of the reason given above.

. How can you improve this situation?

There is another technique which involves the loading of pages into different windows. This technique is discussed next.

Clickable frames showing frames with their clickable hyperlinks previewed in IE

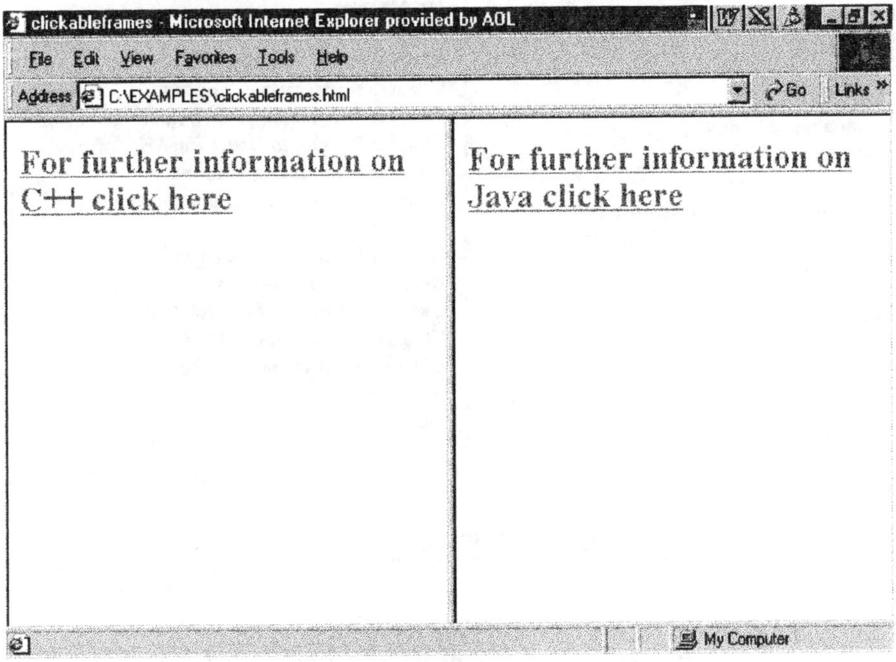

Diagram 2

Clickable frames previewed with both pages' contents loaded into the current windows

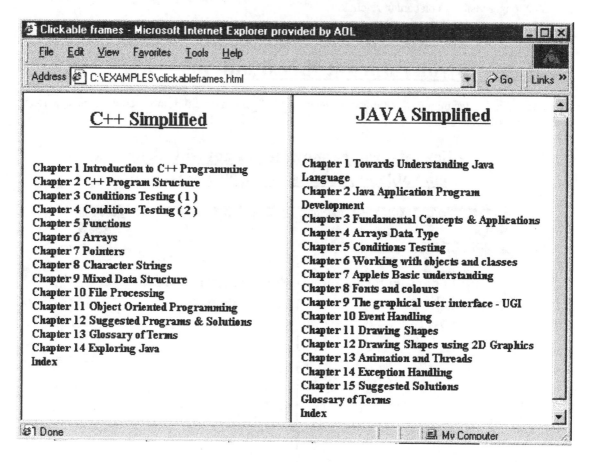

Diagram 2A

- ## Loading a page into a different window

- ## Example 2

The prime aim of this example is to demonstrate the application of frames. In order to do so, it is required to divide the browser window into two unequal rows. The top row will hold the company logo at all times. Thus, it is a static frame. Divide the bottom row into two unequal columns namely left and right. Place in the left column the **Index** for allowing the user to select any of the four options by clicking the appropriate hyper link. The right column is the dynamic frame, where the selected page will be displayed. Its contents should change when another choice is made in the index frame.

. Explanation

The HTML code for creating the nested frameset is given in diagram 3. Illustration 2 is drawn to show the links between html files and the **GIF** type file needed for the company logo. Total number of files for this example = 8. This illustration will help you to understand their relationship.

. The process of executing the file containing framesets and its associated files

- The explanation given for the last example is very relevant to this example. Like the previous example, the HTML file for setting up the nested frameset is listed in diagram 3 . It is pretty much the same, except that here you have to place the company logo in the top frame by **naming** the frame. The **NAME attribute** is placed within the <FRAME ...>tag. By using this attribute, you can name each frame within the frameset.

- As you have seen in the previous example, the browser reads first the file which contains frameset. It finds a line of code which requires the setting up of two rows 30% and 70%. Thus, it divides the area of the browser window accordingly to create two frames.

- It sees the next line of code which contains name attribute and refers to an external resource. This happens to be the file containing ADR logo. Now, **ADRLogo.gif** is opened and its content, the logo is placed in the first row, which is the top frame.

- This file has already been mentioned in this book before. The following segment of the code places this graphics image, in the top frame:

< FRAME NAME = SRC = IMG SRC="ADRLogo.gif">

In this case, name is not given as top, bottom, left or right, to specify the windows, but the external resource (SRC) which is the ADR logo. Anyway, this logo is placed in the top window, which is the only window created so far.

Illustration 2

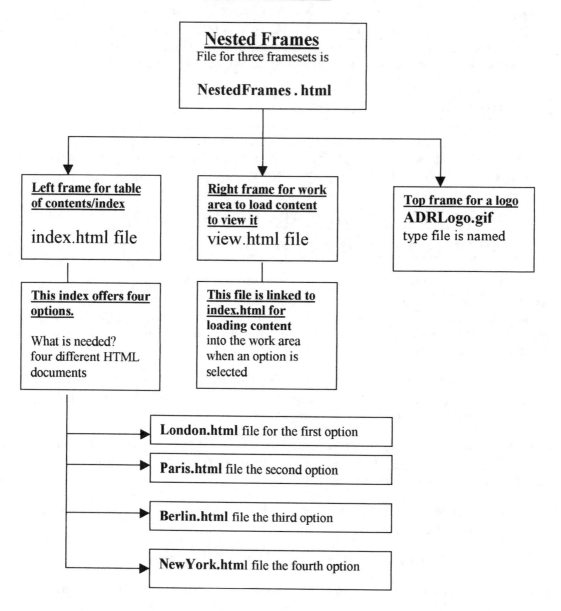

Nested Frames
File for three framesets is

NestedFrames . html

Left frame for table of contents/index

index.html file

Right frame for work area to load content to view it
view.html file

Top frame for a logo
ADRLogo.gif
type file is named

This index offers four options.

What is needed?
four different HTML documents

This file is linked to index.html for loading content into the work area when an option is selected

London.html file for the first option

Paris.html file the second option

Berlin.html file the third option

NewYork.html file the fourth option

- After this action is performed, it goes on to read the next line of code. This time, it finds a **nested frameset**, which requires the division of the remaining space of the browser window in to 30% and 70%. These are columns.

- Having created these columns, it reads the next line, on which it finds a reference to another SRC which is an html file: **index.html** to be red and its content to be displayed in the frame named **"left"**.

- This file is listed in diagram 3A. This is in fact an index. This sets the index for 4 hyperlinks. When any of these links is clicked, it sends the content of the relevant file into the named frame. Where? See below.

- It reads the next line of code. It is another reference to another SRC called: **view.html**. This file is shown in diagram 3B. This has <u>no</u> contents of its own, but it is linked to the **index.html** in order to receive the contents of the page clicked in the index. It receives this in its own frame named: **right**. To emphasise the point again, when the user clicks any of the 4 hyperlinks, its content is loaded into the right window. This right window is that **different window**, created just for viewing the content of the page clicked in another (left) window.

- To complete this process of executing the file **NestedFrames.html**, the browser finds two </FRAMESET...> in this file, and ends this process. At this stage, the browser window is divided into three frames. Top frame displays the logo, and the left window displays hyperlinks, ready for the interaction, and sending the clicked page to the right window which plays a dynamic role of displaying different pages as required.

. <u>What roles do other files play?</u>

The HTML files shown in diagrams 3C, 3D, 3E and 3F are source files. These files have stored the contents of the hyperlinks pages namely, **London, Paris**, **Berlin** and **New York** cities. These files have hyperlinks in the index.html file. For instance, when London hyperlink in the Index is clicked, the following segment of the code sends its content to the right window for displaying. This method applies to other links as well.

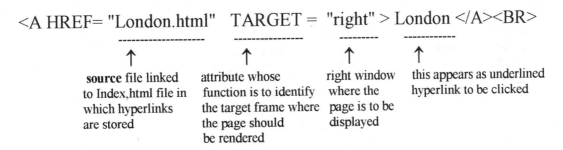

- Diagrams 4 and 4A show previews of frames created and the page London displayed. You are now able to load any of the hyperlinks pages into a different window. Go back to the index and select any of the pages as many times as you wish. Thus, the **TARGET** tag has helped to improve greatly, the working of the windows and hyperlinks.

HTML code for NestedFrames.html file

```
<html><head>
<title>Nested frames</Title>
</head>
        <FRAMESET ROWS = 30%,70%>
        <FRAME NAME = SRC = IMG SRC="ADRLogo.gif">
       <FRAMESET  COLS = 30%,70%>
        <FRAME SRC = "index.html" NAME  ="left">
       <FRAME SRC =  "view.html"  NAME = "right"></FRAMESET></FRAMESET></html>
```

Diagram 3

HTML code for Index.html file

```
<HTML><HEAD>
<TITLE< Creating table of contents </TITLE>
<STYLE TYPE="text/css">
h1{color=red;font-size=20pt;font-style:bold}
h2{color= green; font-size= 14pt;font-style:italic ; background:aqua}
h3{color=black ;font-size=11pt;font-bold:italic;background Color=aqua }
</STYLE></HEAD>
<Table Border =3>
<BODY>
 <TR><TD><center> <u><h1>INDEX</u>
<h2> Please select from the following options:- <BR>
<h3>
    <A HREF= "London.html"  TARGET = "right"  > London </A><BR>
   <A HREF= "Paris.html"   TARGET = "right"> Paris</A><BR>
  <A HREF= "Berlin.html"  TARGET = "right"> Berlin </A><BR>
  <A HREF= "NewYork.html" TARGET =  "right" > New York</A>
</center> </TD><TR></body></html>
```

Diagram 3A

HTML code for view.html file

```
<html>
<head>
<title> This is view area</title></head>
<body>
    <A HREF = index.html > </A></h2></A></body></html>
```

Diagram 3B

HTML code for London.html file

```
<HTML>
<HEAD>
<TITLE< Creating table of contents </TITLE>
<STYLE TYPE="text/css">
h1{color=red;font-size=20pt;font-style:bold}
h2{color= green; font-size= 14pt;font-style:italic ; background:aqua}
h3{color=black ;font-size=11pt;font-bold:italic;background:yellow }
</STYLE></HEAD>
<Table Border =3>
<BODY>
<TR><TD>
<center><u><h1>London

 <h2>  Capital of England and the United Kingdom</u><BR>
<h3>
   It is on the River Thames. Its metropolitan area, Greater London, has an area
   of 1580 sq km. Population about 7 million. The population of its metropolitan area is
   about 9 million. London has buildings in all styles of English architecture since the 11th
   century.<BR>

   <p></P> The Hyde Park, Kensington Gardens, Regents' Park and St James's Park are
   situated  in the centre of  London.<BR>  They are charming throughout the year.
 </center> </body></html>
```

Diagram 3C

HTML code for Berlin.html file

```
<HTML><HEAD>
<TITLE< Creating table of contents </TITLE>
<STYLE TYPE="text/css">
h1{color=red;font-size=20pt;font-style:bold}
h2{color= green; font-size= 14pt;font-style:italic ; background:aqua}
h3{color=black ;font-size=11pt;font-bold:italic;background:yellow }
</STYLE></HEAD>
<Table Border =3>
<BODY>
<TR><TD><center><u>
<h1>Berlin
 <h2>Capital of the Federal Republic of Germany</u><BR>
<h3>
    Population about 4 million. Berlin has more trees lining the streets
    and more pubs<BR>than any other city between the Atlantic and the Ural  Mountains.
</center> </TD><TR></body></html>
```

Diagram 3D

HTML code for Paris.html file

```
<HTML><HEAD>
<TITLE< Creating table of contents </TITLE>
<STYLE TYPE="text/css">
h1{color=red;font-size=20pt;font-style:bold}
h2{color= green; font-size= 14pt;font-style:italic ; background:aqua}
h3{color=black ;font-size=11pt;font-bold:italic;background:yellow }
</STYLE></HEAD>
<Table Border =3>
<BODY>
<TR><TD><center><u>
<h1>Paris
 <h2>Capital of France</u><BR>
<h3>
 Paris is on the River Seine. Population: 9,400, 000. <BR> The River Seine is spanned by 32 bridges.
The oldest bridge is the Pont Neuf 1578. It has many attractive landmarks. The Eiffel Tower built for
the 1889 Paris Exhibition stands in the Champ de Mars.<BR> It is 320 m/1,050 ft high and made of
iron. </center></TD><TR></body></html>
```

Diagram 3E

HTML code for NewYork.html file

```
<HTML>
<HEAD>
<TITLE< Creating table of contents </TITLE>
<STYLE TYPE="text/css">
h1{color=red;font-size=20pt;font-style:bold}
h2{color= green; font-size= 14pt;font-style:italic ; background:aqua}
h3{color=black ;font-size=11pt;font-bold:italic;background:yellow }
</STYLE></HEAD>
<Table Border =3>
<BODY>
<TR><TD><center><u>
<h1>NEW York City
<h2>Largest City in the USA</u><BR>
<h3>
Population about 9 million. It is also known as the Big Apple.<BR>
It was the capital of the USA 1785-89. <BR>The largest power failure in history took place
9 Nov 1965,<BR> blocking out all New York City as well as parts of other states and
parts of Canada.
</center></TD><TR></body></html>
```

Diagram 3F

ADRLogo.gif file is not re-produced here. You have to incorporate your own logo/image.

. BASE target

In diagram 3A you can see that the attribute target is used four times, as there are four links(pages) targeted in the frame named right. For each page, you must write the TARGET attribute. In order to save time typing in the same target, and to avoid possible typing errors, you can set a **BASE TARGET** in the <head> section of HTML document. Its general format is shown below:

<BASE TARGET = " frame name "> for example:

<BASE TARGET = RIGHT>, where RIGHT is the name of the target frame in which the hyperlink page will be sent. Example 3 fully illustrates its use.

Nested frames previewed in IE

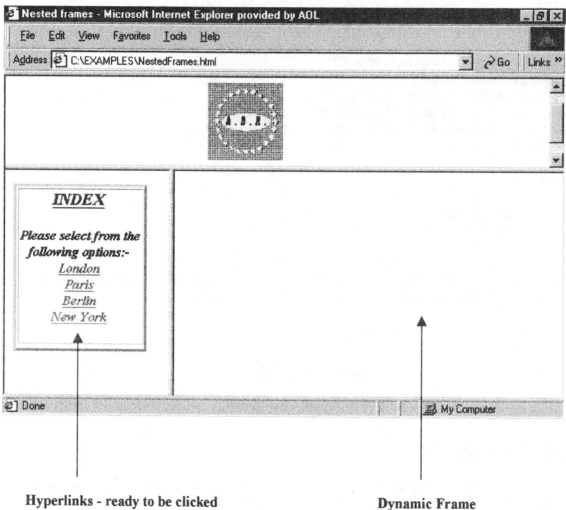

Hyperlinks - ready to be clicked

Dynamic Frame
the result of your click will appear
in this frame

Diagram 4

I clicked London. In response to my action, the information on London displayed in the right frame.
You can see this result in diagram 4A on the next page.

Nested frames shown with Lonodon
hyperlink page atcivated in the IE

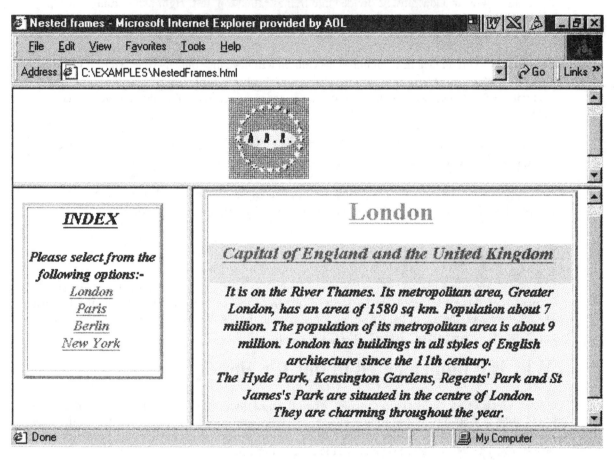

Diagram 4A

- ## Applying the BASE tag with the target attribute

- ## Example 3

Here, the idea is to demonstrate the application of the base tag together with the target attribute in order to improve html page design, eliminate possible typographical errors, and speed up the process of developing html documents. Furthermore, it shows you how to set up a four-window frameset.

Thus, the browser window must be divided into frames called **top**, **left**, **right** and **bottom**. The top frame will be **static** (row). Thus, it will contain the title of a book. The user will not be able to change the contents of this frame.

- The left frame will, in fact, be a column. This column will have the contents page. Thus, it will have **three hyperlinks** for information on three chapters of this book displayed in the top window. The user will be able to interact with these hyperlinks in order to view the information on any of these pages.

- The **bottom frame** will be another row. The bottom frame will display sales information. The user will not be allowed to alter this information (**static frame**).

- In the right frame, the result of a hyperlink clicked will appear. It will be a dynamic frame, as you will be allowed to change its contents by clicking another hyperlink in the left window.

. Explanation

The above illustration has listed altogether eight html files for the completion of this example. The construction of these files does not basically differ from the construction of files in the last two examples. However, the use of the BASE tag together with the TARGET attribute is introduced for the first time in file: **contents. html**, shown in diagram 5A.

. Why is it implemented in this file alone ?

The links which a user clicks are in this file. When the user clicks a hyperlink in the left window, the relevant page is displayed in the right window. For this reason alone, you should include the **base target tag** together with the **target** attribute in this file. It should be declared in the head section as shown below. The following is a segment of the code in this file.

\<BASE Target = right\>

```
        ------------        ----------
             ↑                   ↑
```

Specify the window   the name of the target window is **right** in which
where all three links   all links in the contents page will be loaded in it when
listed in the Contents   they are clicked individually. Each time the right
will be displayed   window will have the content of the page clicked.

An illustration showing the relationship of HTML files required for example 3

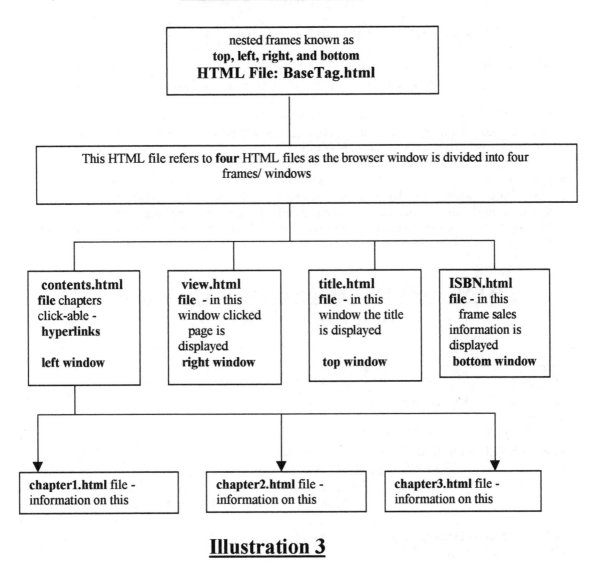

Illustration 3

. **Is the name right coded in the main frameset file?**

Yes, it is. The following segment of the code is from **BaseTag.html** file. Here, the name **right** is defined for the frame to which the contents of the said file will be sent.

<FRAME SRC = view.html NAME = right>

- The other html files are similar to the files of the last example. The process of reading or executing the file containing framesets and associated files is the same process as discussed under example 2.

- It is suggested that you key in all html files, which are shown in diagrams 5, and 5A to 5F in your own machine, and learn by experience. If you do so, you will be able not only to appreciate how it works, but to develop your practical skills further .

- You will find this technique invaluable, when there are many linked pages to be displayed in the same named window. It may be that there are just a few linked pages, which should be sent to another named frame. In such cases, you must change the specified target to the new target (window name) where the linked page or pages are to be displayed. This is much easier than typing the target name many times for a much longer file than the one you have seen in this chapter.

HTML code for setting up nested framesets
(BaseTag.html file)

```
<html>
<head>
<title>Base Tag Application</Title>
</head>
<FRAMESET ROWS = 20%,60%,*%>
<FRAME SRC = title.html NAME = top>
                <FRAMESET  COLS = 30%,70%>
                        <FRAME SRC = contents.html NAME  =left>
                        <FRAME SRC =  view.html  NAME = right>
                </FRAMESET>
<FRAME SRC = ISBN.html NAME = bottom >
</FRAMESET></html>
```

Diagram 5

The contents.html for creating the contents page - hyperlinks are stored in it

```
<HTML>
<HEAD>
<TITL Contents </TITLE>
<Table Border =3>
<BASE  Target = right>
</HEAD>
<BODY>
<TR><TD>
<center><u>
<h2>Contents</u>
<h3>
                    Chapter 1<BR>Chapter 2<BR>Chapter  3<BR>
                <u>Please select any of the following chapters:-</u><BR>

<A HREF = chapter1.html>chapter 1<BR> </A>
<A HREF = chapter2.html> chapter 2 <BR></A>
<A HREF = chapter3.html> chapter 3 </A>

</h3> </center></TD><TR></body></html>
```

Diagram 5A

The title.html file for storing book title (top frame)

```
<HTML>
<HEAD>
<TITLE< Title </TITLE>
<STYLE TYPE="text/css">
h1{color=white;font-size=24pt;font-style:bold;background:blue }
</STYLE></HEAD>
<BODY>
<center><u><h1> Web Site Development Simplified</u><BR>
 <h2>Daniel Lancaster </center></body></html>
```

Diagram 5B

The isbn.html file for displaying sales information (bottom frame)

```
<HTML>
<HEAD>
<TITLE< Distribution </TITLE>
<STYLE TYPE="text/css">
h2{color=white;font-size=10pt;font-style:bold;background:blue }
</STYLE></HEAD>
<BODY>
<h2>
 ISBN: 1901197 808 Price: £17.50  Add P&P UK orders £2.50. Overseas orders
  £4.00  <BR> Cheque should be sent with your order to:-<BR>
  <center><u> A.D.R.(London) Limited</u><BR>
 24 St. Alban Road Bridlington YO16 7 SS England</center></h2>
     <A HREF = BaseTage.html></A>
</body></html>
```

Diagram 5C

Information on Chapter 1 file: chapter1.html

```
<HTML><HEAD>
<TITLE< Chapter 1 </TITLE>
<STYLE TYPE="text/css">
h2{color = white;font-size =14pt;font-style:bold;background:blue}
</STYLE>
<Table Border =3>
</HEAD>
<BODY>
<TR><TD>
<h2>
The chapter introduces you to some essential ideas necessary to understand
 the World Wide Web, the Internet and related services required to be
 on-line. It lays the foundation towards the understanding of the next chapter and beyond.
</TD></TR)</body></html>
```

Diagram 5D

view.html file for loading the clicked page into a different window

```
<html>
<head>
<title> This is view area</title></head>
<body>
        <A HREF = index.html > </A>
</body></html>
```

Diagram 5E

Information on Chapter 2 file: chapter2.html

```
<HTML>
<HEAD>
<TITLE< Chapter 2 </TITLE>
<STYLE TYPE="text/css">
h2{color=white;font-size=14pt;font-style:bold;background:blue}
</STYLE>
<Table Border =3>
</HEAD>
<BODY>
<TR>
<TD>
<h2>
        The purpose of this chapter is to enable you to acquire the basic knowledge and
        skills of using HTML in order to create your first , simple Web page.
        You will also learn how to use some of the essential tools, which are part
        and parcel of your Windows 98 software.
</TD></TR)
</body></html>
```

Diagram 5F

Information on Chapter 3 file: chapter3.html

```
<HTML>
<HEAD>
<TITLE> Chapter 3 </TITLE>
<STYLE TYPE="text/css">
h2{color=white;font-size=14pt;font-style:bold;background:blue }
</STYLE>
<Table Border =3>
</HEAD>
<BODY>
<TR><TD>
<h2>
   This chapter lays the foundation of understanding and using HTML basic style sheets. It
   demonstrates the application of essential techniques for creating headings, line breaks,
   text alignment and character formatting with different text formatting tags. You should be
   able to apply these tools when developing your web site.</TD></TR)

</body></html>
```

Diagram 5G

. Using frames

By now you have learnt how to create both simple and complex frames. You should be able to include dynamic frame(s) in your HTML document, place them on the screen, and allow the user to have some degree of control over these frames. For instance, let the viewer use mouse pointer to select any of the items in one of the windows, and view it in another window without affecting the rest of the display on the screen. You can have in your document both simple static and simple dynamic frames.

One should remember that windows and their contents can only be helpful to both your business and visitors to your web site, provoding they are simple and easy to navigate. Too many frames and too much information on the screen do no good in keeping the visitor interested. In fact, if you visit some of the web sites of some well known organisations, you will find out how annoying their web sites can be. You can spend considerable time, energy and money (charges) in just trying to find and click the correct hyperlink. Often, you have to scroll several screens for the same page. They are really difficult to navigate. **They are designed by "experts"**.

Base Tag Application document previewed in IE

Top window

It has a navigation bar. It enables you to adjust the display in it. You can have in it what you want.
You do not always use it for a company logo or some banner. The navigation bar is added automatically, if the area of the window for the display is merely big enough to hold it. If it is too big, the navigation bar is not usually added automatically.

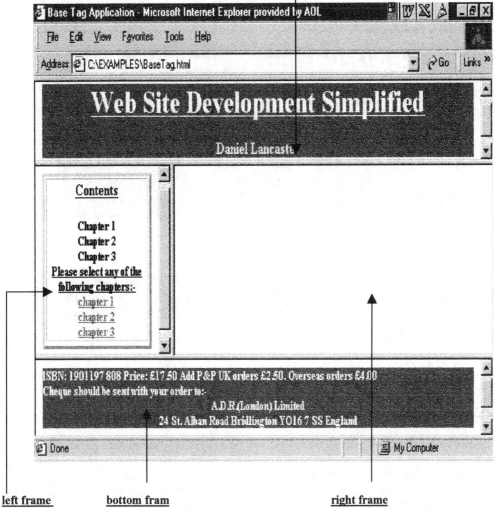

left frame
It is here that an
action takes place
when any of the hyperlinks are
clicked. None of them is clicked yet

bottom fram
This frame can also be made dynamic

right frame
This is where for this example
the hyperlinked pages are displayed
when clicked in the contents page in the left frame

Diagram 6

Base Tag Application document previewed in IE

In this preview you can see some information on Chapter 1 displayed in the right window. It is the result of clicking chapter 1 in the contents page in the left window. You can also see the selected option has a box drawn around it. You can also revisit any of the options as many times as you wish without losing the conents page. **This is the advantage of using the TARGET attribute.**

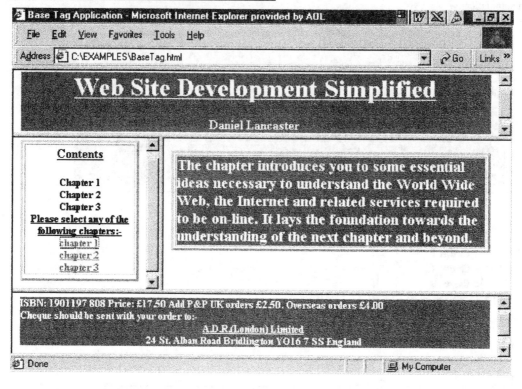

Diagram 6A

. Summary

You should aim at simplicity, and include frames only, if you think that a user can navigate these frames without any frustration, be successful in getting the correct information, and, eventually, do business with you. Try not to insert frames just for the sake of making use of them. Use them only, if you can design simple and easy to navigate frames. Finally, it is strongly suggested that you should sketch your scheme for frames to identify all links, contents of all relevant files and their HTML versions. This will help you to design HTML documents with frames for your site.

Chapter 11
Forms for on-line application

The purpose of this chapter is to enable you to understand the nature of HTML forms in order to incorporate some of them in your web pages for collecting information for a variety of reasons. You should be able to create some forms by using a number of form design elements, and include them in your HTML documents. The user should be able to fill the form, and send it to your web site server by using Common Gateway Interface (**CGI**) scripts, and eventually return it to you.

.Introduction

The good news is that forms tags have been in existence since HTML 2.0. These tags are now standard tags across all browsers. Thus, it is highly likely that your web site visitors will be able to make use of your forms. The most common type of forms is fill-in. Its prime purpose is to collect user input information for whatever purpose you wish to do so. In fact, in business management, form design for a good response is a specialist field. An efficient form design, which meets the proposed form's objective, requires planning and answers to some of the following basic questions:

- What is the purpose of the proposed form?

- What sort of information should be collected?

- For what purpose is the information needed?

- Who is likely to complete the form?

- What sort of precise and concise information will the respondent be able to provide without any hesitation?

- How and when will the collected information become meaningful, and useful?

It will not serve any useful purpose if you just include form filling in your web pages without the careful planning and consideration of your requirements and the users' perceived responses.

Depending on the nature of your business, and the answers to such questions above, the format of the form will emerge for on-line business. You may consider modifying your current business form or converting them into your html format, if you think that these forms are still relevant for on-line business.

• Some essential features

First of all, it is vitally important to know the following essential features of form design techniques:-

- **The <FORM...> tag** is at the heart of form design in the same way as the **<TABLE...> tag** is for designing tables. It takes two mandatory attributes namely, ACTION and METHOD.

- **A fine distinction** between the mandatory attribute **ACTION** and **METHOD** is illustrated below.

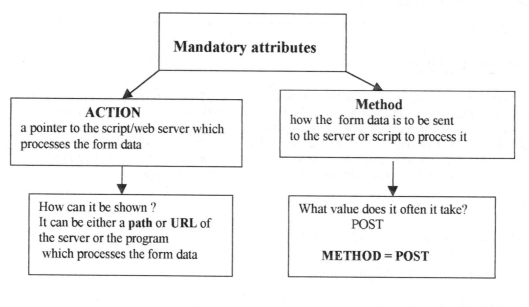

Illustration 1

- **Form elements** - By an element it means some sort of standard space on the screen in which the user can enter or select the data on your form. For instance, the **text filed** is an element. It is the most common element for entering any type of input. Some other elements are listed below in tables 1 and 1A. Soon, you will be able to include them in your html documents. Be patient!

. <u>How can you create an element which goes on a form?</u>

Some of the elements, for instance, the text filed can be created with the **<INPUT...>** tag. Some elements, such as **BUTTONS** can be created by both the **<INPUT... >** tags and **<BUTTON... >** tag. In table 1, you can find more information on each element and the tag or tags are used for creating each element.

- **The <INPUT> tag** collects the data, saves it and then whenever it is required, sends the collected data/information to you.

. <u>How is the information given on the form identified?</u>

There are two attributes namely, **NAME** and **VALUE** which are used with the <INPUT...> tag.

<u>NAME   attribute</u>

Each and every element is
allocated a NAME - this way
all questions can be identified
individually.

<u>VALUE attribute</u>

To identify which user response belongs to
which question, each answer is considered
as a value for the relevant question.

- The format in which these attributes are returned is always in pairs: **NAME = VALUE**

<u>Some form design elements</u>   <u>(cont. on table 1A)</u>

Element name	Nature	Tag used for creating an element
. **Buttons**	A form should have a minimum of one button. This button is known as **SUBMIT**. What is its purpose? The submit button sends the data back to you	. <INPUT...> tag OR . <BUTTON...> tag
	There is another useful button called **RESET** It is very useful, as it lets the user clears the response so that he/she can re-enter it - change of mind allowed!	

<u>Table 1</u>

Some form design elements (cont. from table 1)

Element name	Nature	Tag used for creating an element
. **Radio buttons**	A number of radio buttons can be put together as a group, but you are allowed to select just one of the **predefined choices** at a time. . When you create a group, you can assign it a particular **NAME** of your choice, but different **VALUES**. Reason for it → . Unselected buttons → called inactive → no value returned and thus ignored	. <INPUT TYPE = RADIO...> in this tag, you have to include NAME and VALUE for a group otherwise, default value is returned . NAME = VALUE → a pair . to match answers to relevant questions
. **Checkboxes**	Useful for selecting several choices from a list of **predefined choices.** . A checkbox can be **checked** by the the user. This is useful for simple yes/no type responses.	. <INPUT TYPE = CHECKBOX...> . NAME = VALUE as for radio buttons OR . default value →**on** for the checked box
. **drop-down menus and scrollbarboxes/bars**	. For multiple choices . User must press CTRL+ mouse. . An option can be "selected" first to encourage the user to choose it as his/her answer. . When size is given with multiple choice, no scroll bar appears. . For a single choice, scroll bar is displayed, so that a choice can be made.	. <SELECT MULTIPLE SIZE ="no."> and </SELECT> This pair of tags is essential for options. it lets you select a number of options. Or the user can select the whole list. The option tag is . <OPTION VALUE = "name" > . <OPTION SELECTED>**LONDON** is the name already selected , but the user can change it. . for choosing just a single option from an <OPTION>Birmingham, where Birmingham is the option

Table 1A

Some form design elements (cont. from table 1A)

. **Text field**	. Use for entering a single line text.	. <INPUT TYPE = "text" NAME="name" Size = "no".. >
		. Closing tag is not essential
	. It is the most applied element. . This is the most versatile element and it can take a number of options → . Useful for many user entries.	. It can take the following attributes: . NAME . VALUE . SIZE . MAXLENGTH
. **Text area**	. Gives the user the choice to enter several lines of text. You can fix its size in terms of rows & columns. . Anyway, it is still limited to what a user's browser can display. . It is commonly used.	. <TEXTAREA NAME ="name" COLS ="no." ROWS = "no."> </TEXTAREA> - a pair of tags is essential. . the column **width** is one character . the default size = 20 column by 2 rows . Maximum size cannot be specified
. **FIELDSET**	. use it to set a group of fields to treat it collectively. . Useful for grouping related items on a form.	. <FIELDSET><LEGEND ALIGN =".."> some form element(s) ---</FIELDSET> . ALIGN can be "top",bottom", "left" or "right".

Table 1B

. How do you create a form?

The construction of a form in HTML takes the same format as any other types of pages. The following examples are intended to demonstrate the design of forms by implementing the elements described in tables 1, 1A and 1B. Before proceeding any further, I must add that these elements are not the only one which are available for form designs, but they are sufficient for creating simple to complex HTML forms for collecting information for processing by using the Common Gateway Interface(CGI). More about CGI later on.

<u>**Advance Warning**</u>

Once again, I have used both lower and upper case letters. You can see that all my HTML files have been tested successfully. Furthermore, sometimes, I have placed some requirements within the" ". In fact, you can miss out these double quotation marks, if you wish.

In the shaded area of all HTML codes in this chapter, there is the code for setting up the page layout. You have seen this kind of layout before on numerous occasions.

. **Example 1**

The purpose is to design a simple form using the **text field element**. The form is to be filled in by the user, by entering his/her name in a one-line box. This is to be followed by his/her address in three simple boxes, each will have only one line of text.

At the end of the address, the user must write the ISBN number of the free booklet available from you. Since the form has to be processed using the CGI, the user must be given the opportunity to send it off to the server, by simply clicking the **Submit button**. The submit button is to be labelled as, "Send it now!".

. **Explanation**

The HTML code for this example is listed in diagram 1.

• The following line contains the HTML code for setting up the initial requirements to get feedback from a form. **ACTION** specifies the program or CGI script which will process the filled in form. Here, it is "URL" (see below). **Method** specifies which HTTP method will be used to submit the form with data for processing. here, it is **POST**.

<form ACTION = "URL" method = "POST">
```
             ------------
                  ↑
```

It is usually the name of the program (CGI script)at your ISP /Web server which processes the form.

I have tested this and other HTML codes locally in the Internet Explorer. For this purpose, it is sufficient to write as above.

- It is emphasised again that when you have to set up your web site, you must find out from your ISP firm the full URL of the **CGI script**/program to be used for form feedback purposes. You must also discuss with your ISP firm, if they offer any programs which can make feedback from the form easier and present it in a meaningful format. It may be that you are expecting a large number of forms, and therefore, it is worth sorting out from the start, if there is any likely text tidying up to do, when the form feedback is returned to you, and how to achieve it.

- The next line contains the code for setting up a heading:" Please enter your full name: ", and to create a text box, size 40 characters long. It can contain 40 characters. There is no mention of rows and size, as it is going to have only one line of text in it. This is achieved by the following segment of the code:

Please enter your full name:
                    <input type = text Name ="name" size = "40">

- The rest of the code, except the code for creating the submit button, follows this pattern to create other text fields.

- **<input type = submit value = "send it now!">** this line is for creating the submit button. There is no need to include in this input tag the NAME attribute.

- Diagram 2 shows the preview of this simple form. No data has yet been entered by the user.

- Diagram 2A, you can examine the whole form together with data entered in all text fields. It has worked, as it was successfully tested and previewed in the IE.

- ## What happened when the submit button "send it now!" was clicked?

You know that the full URL of the program/script which should process this form was not given, except the word "URL". This is not a workable URL, and thus the IE generated an error message. The part of the message is shown below. The message may not make any sense, but you do know the reason for this failure.

HTML code for example 1

```
<html>
<head>
<title> A Simple Form </title>
<STYLE TYPE="text/css">
h2{color = black; font-size =14pt; font-style:bold;background:aqua}
h3{color = black; font-size =12pt; font-style:italic;background:aqua}
</style></head>
<body><center><u><h2>
Please help us to help you by sending your completed form to us
  </h2></u><BR>
<h3>
<form ACTION = "URL" method = "POST">
 <P> Please enter your full name:
                       <input type = text Name ="name" size = "40">
  <P> Please enter your address below:</P>
                      <input type = text  Name = "add1"    size = "30">
 <p>                  <input type = text  Name = "add2"    size = "30">
 <p>                  <input type = text  Name = "add3"    size = "30">
<P> Please enter the ISBN number of a free booklet you wish us to supply you. <BR>
                     <input type = text   Name ="isbn"    size ="12"><BR>
                     <input type = submit  value = "send it now!">
</form></center></body></html>
```

Diagram 1

Diagrams 2 & 2A are on the next page due to lack of sufficient space here.

. Example 2 - text area

The purpose of this example is to design a **Book Search Form**. The form should begin with its heading," Book Search Form". The user should be able:

- to enter in a text area the ISBN, book title, author, publisher and publication year;

- to enter his/her own name, telephone number together with address for a reply; and

continued after diagram 2A

Diagrams 2 & 2A showing a blank form and filled in form previewed in IE

- to submit it to a bookseller (yourself) for a book search.

This example requires the implementation of two form design elements namely, the text field and text area. This way, you can put into practice what you already know about text fields, and learn how to create a text area. It is advisable to sketch the desired format of the proposed form on a piece of paper, so that you can refine it, before you generate the HTML code for creating, storing and testing it.

HTML code for example 2

```
<html>
<head>
<title> A form with a text area & text field </title>
<style TYPE="text/css">
h1{color = black; font-size =14pt; font-style:bold;background:aqua}
h2{color = black; font-size =12pt; font-style:italic;background:white}
</style></head>
<body><center><u><h1>
                        Book Search Form
<h2> Please supply as much information as you can and send it right away</u>
                                <FORM  ACTION =" URL" METHOD = POST>
<P> Please enter ISBN, book title, author, publisher and publication year below:-<B>
                <TextAREA  NAME = request COLS= 70 ROWS = 5></TEXTAREA>
<P>
   Name:
                        <input type = text Name ="name" size = "40">
        Telephone:
                        <input type = text Name ="name" size = "16"></BR>
  <h1>
  Your address:
                        <input type =  text Name ="add1" size = "30">
                <input type= text   Name = "add2"    size = "30"><BR>
                <input type = text   Name ="add3"       size = "60"></h1>
<center> <input type = submit value = "send it now!"> </center>
</form></body></html>
```

Diagram 3

. Explanation

The HTML code for this example is shown in diagram 3. It is similar to the code for the last example, but it demonstrates how to design a document by using not only text fields, but also text area. Its page layout also shows you how to make it not only attractive, but also practical by applying other features of HTML. The segment of the code which creates the text area is shown below:

<TEXTAREA NAME = request COLS = 70 ROWS = 5> </TEXTAREA>

Here, the name attribute defines the name for this element as request. COLS specifies the width of the text area. In this case, it can accommodate 70 characters. ROWS specifies the number of rows. Here, the 70 characters can be entered on five lines. However, in practice, the user can type as much as he or she wishes.

- In diagram 4, you can see the result of the code in diagram 3. The Search Book Form is ready to be filled in by the user. If the user clicks the "send it now!" submit button, he/she will encounter the same problem which has been discussed already - the effect of not writing the full URL for ACTION. Once again, it is suggested that you analyse this form's design and experiment with this code in order to improve your practical skills.

Book Search Form previewed in IE - ready to be filled in

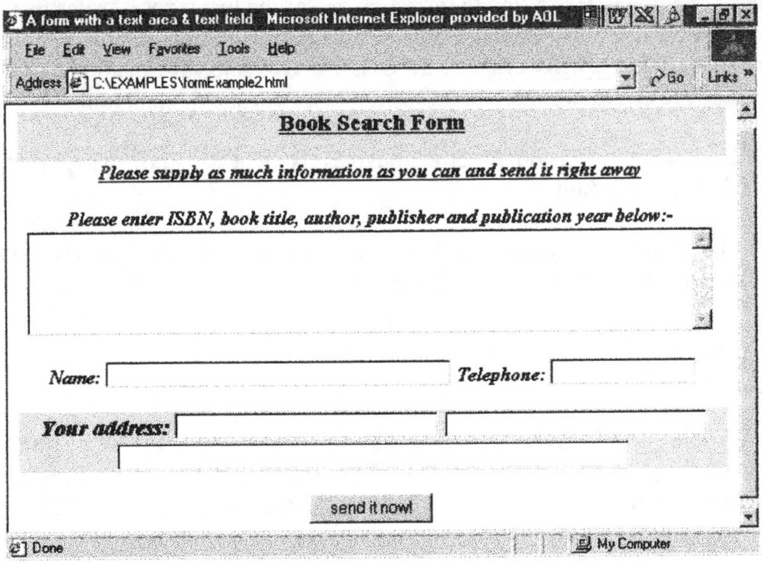

Diagram 4

. <u>Text area</u>

Although the size is specified with COLS and ROWS, the user can enter as much text as one wishes. In fact, you can see **a scrollbar**, which can let you scroll and see the text which is entered beyond the size set. You can carry on typing all night if you wish, but the text which will appear in it, it will be only equivalent to the amount of text the user's browser can display.

Usually, the text within the text area is formatted in the fixed format. Some browsers allow text wrapping in text areas, but some others scroll to the right. My browser allows scrolling within the text area.

. <u>Check boxes and Radio buttons</u>
. <u>Example 3</u>

Here, the idea is to demonstrate how you can design a form in order to present the user with some **pre-defined choices.** You can make use of checkboxes and radio buttons to achieve this objective.

Your task is to create :

<u>Credit Control Information Request Form</u>

In the **<u>first section</u>** of this form, the user is asked to tick/click one of the two types of sales namely, retail and wholesale. In the **<u>second section</u>**, the user is given five ranges of credit limits. The user can only apply for one range only. In the **<u>third section</u>**, the user is asked to select the method of account settlement. He/she can click one of the two methods of settlement - cheque or bank transfer.

The user must also send the full name and address of the business, so that you know who has applied for the credit limit on the business account.

Finally, the user is given the opportunity to send this form for action by you. This has to be done by means of the submit button, which is labelled as "send it now!".

. <u>Explanation</u>

The HTML code for this whole task is listed in diagrams 5 & 5A. Besides other HTML features implemented in order to layout the page and its background colour, it shows how to create pre-defined choices by means of check boxes and radio buttons. Now, examine the following segments of the code:

- **<input type = Checkbox Name = sales Value = Retail> Retail**

In this code, within the <input ..>tag, name attribute is called sales. It is the name given to the group of two check boxes. The other check box is for the Wholesale.

• How about the value which has to be passed to CGI script?

Retail is the value which will be passed to CGI script. It is the value of the check box.

This line will create a check box. The check box for the other option wholesale is created in the same way. See the diagram 5. Next to the check box, the word **Retail** will be displayed, as it comes after the <input...> tag as shown above.

- **<input type = checkbox Name credit Value = credit>£1000**

Where, **credit** is the name of this particular group of five check boxes for five different credit limits. **Value** is the value of the check box which will be passed to the CGI script for processing it.

- The code for the other four credit limits in this group works in the same way.

- **Radio buttons** - for the selection of one of the two options namely, by cheque and by bank transfer, a group of two radio buttons is created. The code for By Cheque method is shown below:

<input type = Radio Name =payment Value = settlement>By Cheque

Its structure is much the same as creating the check box, except that you have to substitute Radio for the check box. It operates like the check box code. The result of this code is shown in diagram 6.

HTML code for example 3 (cont. in diagram 5A)

```
<html>
<head>
<title> A form with checkboxes & radio buttons </title>
<style type="text/css">
h1{color = black; font-size =16pt; font-style:bold;background:aqua}
h2{color = black; font-size =12pt; font-style:bold;background:aqua}
</style></head>
<body><center><u><h1>
            Credit Control Information Request Form </h1></u></center><BR>
<h2><form ACTION = URL method = POST>
     <P> Sales type - Please tick one type of sales:- <BR>
```

Diagram 5

HTML code for example 3 (cont. from diagram 5A)

```
<center>
        <input type = Checkbox Name = sales Value = Retail> Retail
        <input type = Checkbox Name = sales Value  = Wholesale > Wholesale</center><BR>
     Wholesale credit limit request - Please tick one item only:-<BR>
        <input type = checkbox Name credit Value = credit>£1000
        <input type = checkbox Name credit Value = credit>£1500
        <input type = checkbox Name credit Value = credit>£2000
        <input type = checkbox Name credit Value = credit>£2500
        <input type = checkbox Name credit Value = credit>Max £3000<BR>
Method of settlement - Please select one method:-<BR>
        <input type = Radio Name =payment Value = settlement>By Cheque
        <input type = Radio Name =payment Value = settlement>By Bank Transfer
<p> Please enter your business's full name and address: <BR>
        <Textarea Name = address COLS = 55 ROWS  = 5></Textarea>
        <input type = submit value = "send it now!"></form></center></body></html>
```

Diagram 5A

Credit control request form previewed in IE (ready for completion)

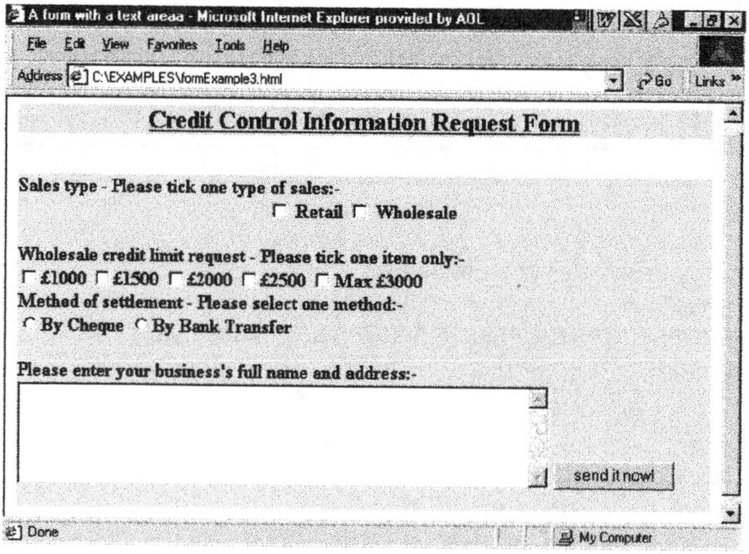

Diagram 6

. Making drop-down menus and scrollboxes

These are two other features of form design techniques for multiple choices offered to the respondent on a form to select the appropriate response(s). This requires the implementation of two markup tags known as <SELECT> and <OPTION>. Once again, I shall demonstrate their application by means of the solved example below.

. Example 4

Design a form for your local chess club which is organising a Chess 2000 Tournament to be held in a number of places in the UK. It invites anyone who wishes to travel with the club to watch this chess competition. Your local club has also made travelling arrangements by air, train, car and coach. You can travel to as many places as you wish, but only by one mode of travel. Design an appropriate form for this purpose. The form should have a heading, and also the respondent/ user should be able to submit it.

. Explanation

HTML code for example 4 (cont. in diagram 7A)

```
<html>
<head>
<title> Drop-down menus & scrollboxes </title>
<style type="text/css">
h1{color = black; font-size =16pt; font-style:bold;background:aqua}
h2{color = black; font-size =12pt; font-style:bold;background:aqua}
</style></head>
<body><center><u><h1>Chess  2000 Tournament </h1></u></center><BR>
<h2>
<FORM ACTION = "URL"   METHOD = "POST">
  Select one or more places to travel for Year 2000 Chess Competition in the UK:-<BR>
        For making several selections, press CTRL key with the mouse.
    <center>
            <Select Multiple Size =6>
```

Diagram 7

HTML code for example 4 (cont. from diagram 7)

```
<Option value =Lond >  London
            <Option value = Man> Manchester
            <Option value = Ed> Edinburgh
            <Option value =Leeds>Leeds
            <Option value =Bir> Birmingham
            <Option value =Card > Cardiff
</Select></center>
            Mode of travel - please select only one travel mode:-<BR>
            <select name = journey>
            <option > By air
            <option>By car
            <option>By train
            <option> By coach
</Select>
     <Select>   <Option Disabled> Please write below your telephone number and fax
number (if any)</Select>
  <P><center>
            <Textarea  name = com   COLS = 50  ROWS= 2 ></Textarea>
 <p><input type = submit value = "send it now!">
</form></body></html>
```

Diagram 7 A

- The structure of this HTML file in diagrams 7 & 7A does not vary greatly from the structure of the code for the previous example. However, the difference lies in the implementation of <SELECT> and <OPTION> tags as follows:-

< Select Multiple Size = 6 >

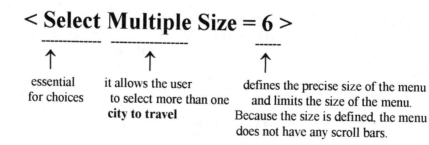

| essential for choices | it allows the user to select more than one **city to travel** | defines the precise size of the menu and limits the size of the menu. Because the size is defined, the menu does not have any scroll bars. |

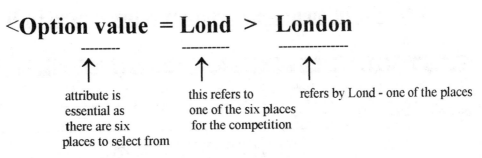

The other five lines of options for places to visit follow the same pattern - each line of code defines a different vale, because of different cities.

- If you want to suggest a particular city for this Chess tournament, you can pre-select it for the user.

. How can you do it?

The result of the code shown below will show London pre-selected. However, the user can change it. See Table 1A.

<Option value =Lond selected>   London

- Once all options are coded for the menu, it is vitally important to close the select process by placing the </SELECT> tag at the end of a group of options.

- It is also required to allow the user to select only one mode of travel. For this purpose, another <SELECT> and <OPTION> process begins with:

<select name = journey>.

Here, name attribute is essential. It is given the value/name journey.

- This line of code is followed by four lines of options available. The first one is: <option > By air this will create BY air in the menu. This line is then followed by other remaining three options. The </SELECT> tag must be placed at the end of this process.

You can see the result of this whole code in diagram 8, which shows the form ready to be filled in by you. You can only do so, if you run this code on your system.

. Field Grouping

This is another useful feature of form design. It can enable you to group together some related items of data, which can be dealt with collectively. The example 5 is designed to demonstrate this aspect, which requires the implementation of <FIELDSET> and <LEGEND> tags.

Drop-down menus & scrollboxes previewed in IE

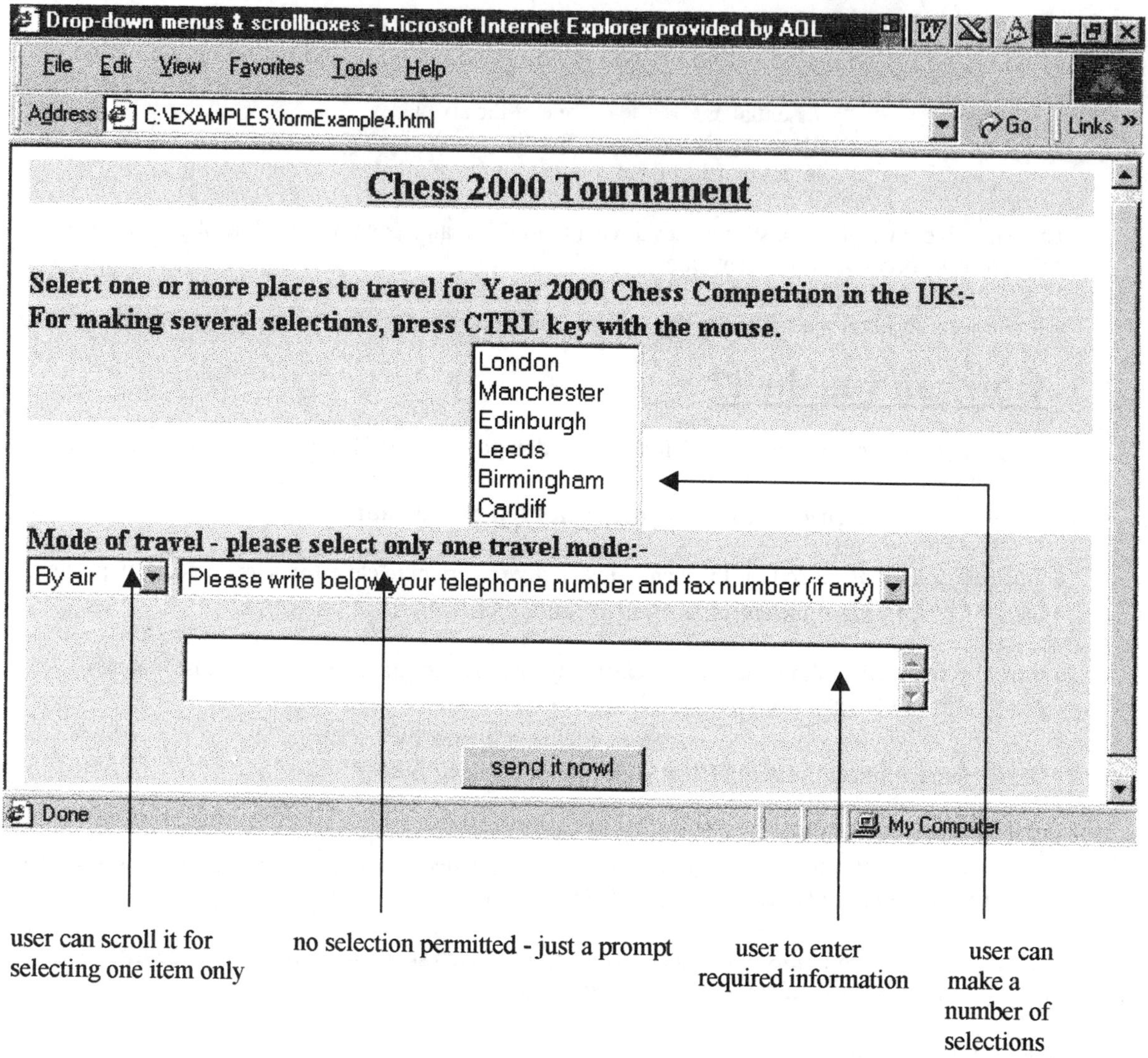

Diagram 8

. Example 5

The idea is to design a goods despatch note. This document must have appropriate headings, so that it can be differentiated from other business documents. You must divide the form into some distinguishable sections, for the sake of not only ease, but also practicality of information given on the form.

. Explanation

The HTML code for this example is in diagram 9, and its result is in diagram 10. If you examine first diagram 10, you can see the design of the form. Besides the page layout and headings necessary, the form has two groups.

The first group consists of heading and relevant **text fields** of different **sizes**.

Account No.   Customer: Address: Telephone:

The other group, just below this, group has the following headings.

Product code: Quantity: Standard   Express

Standard has next to it a radio button. Similarly, **Express** has a radio button next to it.

. These are the two groups for which you have to implement two sets of **fieldsets.** In the first fieldset, you have to create the heading of this document, and place it in the centre of the form. To achieve this the <LEGEND> tag is used within the <FIELDSET> as follows:-

```
<Fieldset>
        <Legend Align = center> Despatch Note
    </Legend>
```

- This code is then followed by four lines of code for four text fields. At the end of the last line, it is essential to close the fieldset by means of </FIELDSET>.

- Code for the second group is within <FIELDSET> and </FIELDSET> without the LEGEND tag. **WHY?** Well, the legend tag is used for alignment which is not needed for the second group.

- Now, it is suggested that you key in the code shown in diagram 9, and preview it in your browser to analyse its structure and flow, and improve your practical skills.

HTML code for example 5

```
<html>
<head>
<title> Fieldset </title>
<style type="text/css">
h1{color = black; font-size =16pt; font-style:bold;background:aqua}
h2{color = black; font-size =12pt; font-style:bold;background:aqua}
</style></head>
<body><center><u><h1>Sales Order<BR>
<h2>
<FORM ACTION = "URL"   METHOD = "POST">
<Fieldset>
          <Legend Align = center> Despatch Note
            </Legend>
        <P> Account No.
          <input type = text size= 5>
            Customer:
            <input type = text size = 40></p>
  Address:
                        <input type = text size = 30>
      Telephone:
                      <input type = text size = 20><BR>
                      <input type = text size = 50>
                      <input type = text size = 30></fieldset>
<fieldset>
        Product code: <input type = text size = 12>
        Quantity:       <input type = text size = 4>
        <input type = radio name = del value = st > Standard
        <input type = radio name = del value = ex> Express</Fieldset>
<P><center> Any delivery instructions
              <Textarea  name = com   COLS = 80  ROWS = 2> </Textarea>
<p><input type = submit value = "send it now!"> <input type =RESET>
</form></body></html>
```

Diagram 9

Fieldset previewed in IE

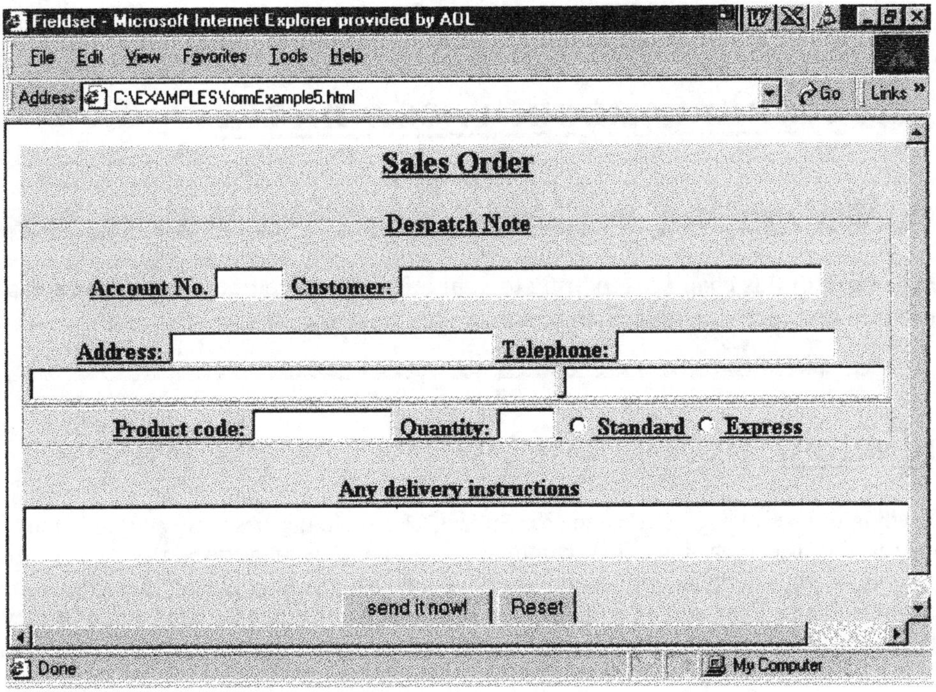

Diagram 10

Summary
The following are some suggestions for your consideration when designing a form:
. Design your proposed form first on a piece of paper.
. Examine questions critically.
. Make it simple and short.
. Tell the user the purpose of asking for the information.
. If possible, make it just big enough to fit into no more than two windows.
. User should be able to change his/her mind, and re-enter the data - include submit and resubmit buttons.
. There are many good ideas on form designing techniques in management related books.
If necessary, visit a good library for one or two books on this topic. It will pay you in the long run!

Chapter 12

Thinking about E-commerce

The prime objective of this chapter is to bring to your attention some of the important areas which you should consider when planning to set up your business on-line.

.Introduction

Buying and selling on the Internet is E-commerce. In fact, electronic business transactions started between businesses a considerably long time before the advent and popularity of the buzz word E-commerce, and its methods of doing business on-line. I assume that you have already deducted from 'E' the word electronic. The Web and Web pages for business advertisement have spread the ever-increasing use of E-commerce across the world. The media has taken a great interest in spreading the E-commerce to such an extent that the E-commerce revolution has a strong grip on all kinds of large to small businesses, consumers at large, and has been transforming the fast selling and buying aspects of both businesses and individuals. The new era of on-line marketing, selling, buying and general shopping has already begun. With the availability of Digital TV, E-commerce can take place in every home.

.Is E-commerce essential for any business?

The straightforward frank answer is no. Why? Simply because not all small businesses, such as a local corner shop or a small retailer will benefit from the investment in setting up the E-commerce facility for its local customers, and passing public which may stop to purchase something. The size of business is not the deciding factor for installing facilities for E-commerce in a firm, but the firm's business strategy governs the choice of moving on to on-line trade. For instance, if a small business wants to trade nationally or globally, and has a new business plan for E-commerce, such a business has an opportunity to launch a business on the Internet, and possibly in the long run increase its sales and profitability.

It should be emphasised that setting up E-commerce facilities are within the financial bounds and human resources of many small businesses, but one should first search for answers to the following basic questions. It may be that your business has a number of products or services or both to sell. You have to find the answer to:

. <u>What should we market on the Internet?</u>

You must also explore the following areas:

• <u>What are the likely short and long term benefits arising from an investment in E-commerce?</u>

Of course, a general answer to this essential question will not satisfy all businesses, but at the same time, it can provide a base upon which relevant questions concerning E-commerce for a particular business can be raised. The other important question concerning marketing is:

• <u>What are we trying to achieve from marketing on the Internet?</u>

It may be that your marketing strategy for doing business on the Internet includes any or all of the following aims:

- to increase your current share of the national market

- to expand your sales both nationally and internationally

- to enter the on-line market first time, hoping to increase sales beyond one's imagination and make a fortune in a short space of time

- to support your present sales

- to build your new brand image

It should be remembered that E-commerce is in the process of evolving, and thus your marketing strategy should be flexible enough to be successful. It is also highly desirable to examine the following considerations:

- <u>In what ways E-commerce can influence other functions of your business and staff.</u>

- <u>What does E-commerce mean to other areas of your business?</u>

Think in terms of:

- staff training and job satisfaction
- finance
- buying
- distribution
- production if you make things
- other aspects of your business
- legality and data protection
- The other area one should search is competition.

Another area one should research is the competition. It may be highly desirable for you to search for the answers for the following questions:

. <u>Competitors</u>

. <u>How will your competitors react to your on-line presence?</u>

Explore it in terms of your **share** of on-line market:

- how you can build it - expanding your market
- how you can maintain it - not to lose customers
- how you can protect it - guard your business against unhealty competition

You should also give careful consideration to:

- <u>How can you notify your existing customers about your entry into the on-line market?</u>

- <u>Are your regular current customers Internet-literate to a desired level?</u>

- <u>How can you stimulate the interest of your current customers to visit your Web site?</u>

. <u>Stimulate interest in your Web site</u>

In order to maintain the interest of your existing customers in your business, it is essential to provide them with sufficient information about your Web site. This will not only help your existing customers, but also will help your business to keep them interested in doing business with your company.

Just informing people about your **URL** may not be enough. Think how you can enable your current customers to understand the purpose of your Web site, how best and with the minimum waste of time successfully interact with your Web site, and continue doing business with your firm.

It is a fact that many people, when they are on-line, do not have the time or the desire to learn how to get the required information or place an order for buying your goods or services. They want to do business with you rather than learn about your Web site at their expense while on-line. It may be that your present customers are not Internet-literate to the desired level in order to be able to easily follow for instance, your ordering and payment systems. It may be that in your kind of trade E-commerce is not so widespread, and that customers lack the experience of buying on the Internet.

Therefore, to help your business, you must send them in advance some helpful information as concise as possible on how to make the best use of your Web site. Remember that all business Web site visitors are not Internet Wizards. Keep it as simple as possible. Hopefully, this will generate interest in your Web site off-line, and indeed, enable potential customers to buy from you on-line, providing they have an access to the Net.

Now-a-days, it is an acceptable practice to have customer loyalty bonuses, an attractive range of discount levels, special offers, free gifts, etc. It may be that you already offer such goodies to your current customers. It is worth offering such benefits to your Web site visitors, so that they re-visit your Web site and buy from you.

• Support a customer on-line

• How can we support a customer on-line?

Another important area to consider carefully is customer support on the Internet. Having supplied the goods or services to customers on-line, it is essential to retain their interest in your products, services, or both. In fact, on-line trade brings customers and suppliers much closer than the traditional means of trade. It is due to the fact that both parties can contact each other more frequently, faster than ever, and comparatively cheaper. Furthermore, distance is no problem. Of course, one expects that an existing business already has a customer relations policy in operation. You may refine it or amend it to suit your business and prospective customers on the Net. You can implement it on with the view to evaluating it and re-designing it as your E-commerce experience grows. Be flexible in your approach, and follow the principle of learning by doing!

One big advantage of the Net is that it can create instant interaction between the customer and supplier. It means that you can support your customers on your Web site, or by means of a mailing list or newsgroup. You can provide an opportunity for your customers to ask questions, which you can answer. You can also communicate by means of e-mail, if a customer prefers. You can conduct customer surveys. All these and similar activities are two-way communication, and thus you can have a captive audience for your business success.

.Concise and precise information

- ## How much information should you put about your firm on the Web site?

- ## How much information should you give to prospective customers on-line about your products or services or both?

It is recommended to provide the Web site visitors with precise factual information about your business. There is no point in boring your prospective customers with a long history of your company profile, supported with photos of several key members of staff. In fact, a Web site with lots of photos of a factory, shops, offices and individuals can distract the attention of visitors. Your visitors may find it in their way when searching what they made a visit to your Web site for. A visitor is looking for some sort of product, service or advice/information. Thus, he/she has a specific need to satisfy. It is, certainly, a problem solving activity for his/her personal need or on behalf of a business. Here, their prime goal is to find a solution rather than learn about your business in some depth. Indeed, you want visitors to trade with your company.

Therefore, you should highlight some present unique features of your business, so those visitors stay with your Web site, and eventually, place an order. Most certainly, the whole idea is to win orders. Thus, it is suggested that you think hard about your business information that can stimulate the interest of visitors in whatever you wish to sell. Remember that a business is a unique entity. You should think how best you could exploit this uniqueness on-line to achieve your objectives of going on the Internet.

There are two schools of thoughts concerning how much information you should give away about merchandise, service or whatever you wish to sell on the Net. One school of thought believes in giving ample information, so those visitors learn enough about products or services. This may make them trust you and buy from you. It may be that your prospective customers do not require all that information right away, but find it useful when needed, and thus return to your Web site more than once, and buy from you. Think how philosophy fits into your current practice.

The other school of thought thinks just the opposite. It persuades its followers to just highlight some good points about the merchandise or service.

Here, it is suggested to stimulate visitors' interest in your products/ services, not by promising what is not entirely feasible in terms of benefits arising to customers by doing business with you, but good value for what they will pay for it. This should enable visitors to decide whether to place an order or not. There is no point in creating an erroneous impression, as such a sales technique will not work in the long run on the Net. Think in terms of winning a share of a wider market by creating some trust in your company and its products/ services, and maintaining this trust for continued success on the Internet. After all, first, you have to build your reputation on the Internet as a reliable company, with whom it is worth trading for quality products, services, or both. One should do all what can be done truthfully to create your firm's new image on-line, and benefit from it in the long run. It is worth trying!

It is fine to list prices in your own country's currency for the national market, but not for E-commerce world-wide. Prices in US Dollars are more likely to be acceptable on the Net. If you think your prospective customers are in Europe, it is then practical to include prices in EU currency. Think which currencies are most suited for your type of business, and work out prices in these currencies, if you can. I would most certainly include prices in US Dollars. It is worth mentioning here, that due to differences of exchange rates, your product may be more expensive in other countries. Thus, try not to compete on-line on price levels. It is quality and reliability which attract prospective customers.

It is important to clearly highlight postage and packing charges or shipping rates, if any, in the chosen currencies.

It is a well-known fact that the Net's strength is that it can facilitate masses of information for any kind of business. So, if you do not provide visitors with the right amount of relevant information, the visitor can easily switch to another Web site, and never again return to your Web site. In fact, usually, one can get a lot more information from a Web site than you can hope to obtain from a brochure. This point should be born in mind when designing the Web site. A Web site full of graphics is also undesirable, unless your Web site is for young people, and those who are involved with graphics, and you want to impress them. Someone who is looking for product or service on the Net during business hours has no time to admire your graphics presentation. They want to solve their problems, and thus your Web site should help them by its business substance, not just its graphical presentation, no matter how colourful and attractive it appears on the screen.

. Money from customers on-line

. How should you collect your money from customers on-line?

What's the point of selling on the Net, if you are not able to collect your money promptly, and without paying too much fee/commission to any other organisation that assists you to collect your money from customers. Yes indeed, like off-line trade, you must consider offering your prospective customers a variety of ways of paying you for whatever they wish to purchase from you. If you are a small business, going first time on the Net, with small working capital, and doubtful about your sales, if any on the Net, let alone multiplying your current sales over night, it is highly desirable that you research into the available methods of payment offered by a growing number of companies who provide transaction processing across the Net. You may find their service rather costly.

Certainly, it is attractive to customers, if they can pay by a method that is convenient to them, but **in no way, it is suggested in this book** that you should set up an expensive method of payments from customers, and without knowing enough about the background of some selected transaction processing firms in terms of their business reliability, security and guarantee that your money will be safe.

. Transaction processing/payment service providers

A transaction processing company has a computerised payment system, which operates over the

Internet. When a buyer (or surfer) visits a particular Web site and buys some thing, the buyer can make a payment on-line by using a credit or debit card via the transaction processing company. The transaction processing company clears the card transaction instantly, and at the same time, the cardholder's account is debited accordingly.

This type of business is growing quickly. Some of them conform to the UK based banks **Merchant Service Security Guidelines**, but it does not mean that these banks approve of them. If you wish to use the services of any transaction processing firms, I suggest that you should carefully examine written sales literature of some transaction processing firms, compare, and contrast the following chargeable items:

- **set-up charges** - cost of setting up for you customers' payments system.

- **monthly minimum charges** - charges for the benefit of having a link to their system.

- **unauthorised transaction charges** - a charge if the customer's bankers refused to pay.

- **authorised transaction charges** - a charge when the customer's bankers agreed to pay.

- **bureau merchants charges** - if you do not have a merchant status - it means that your business does not accept any credit cards. In this case, you can use the payment service provider's own internet transaction processing for which you must pay an additional charge.

- **credit or debit cardholder's address verification (AVS)** - It may be that a transaction processing firm is offering service of checking that the address given by the buyer on-line is the same as held by the bank that has issued the card to the buyer. It may be that the buyer is not the card holder, and that the cardholder is not even aware of this transaction over the Net. You have to pay for this service in addition to transaction processing charges. It may be necessary for your business to make such a check, but evaluate it in terms of cost-benefit analysis over a 12 months period, and its effects on your annual profit.

- **merchant status** - if you are a retailer, it is likely that you accept some credit cards, and already know how much per year it costs your business. If you go on the Net and still accept payment by this mode, you have to add this charge to your calculation of likely expenses against the profit.

- **technical support** - find out if there are likely charges for help and advice when most needed.

- **any other hidden charges** - examine small print. For instance:

- **too many currencies -** Your business may not require as many as are on offer. In that case, there is no need to pay for the service your business is unlikely to benefit from, if you are not seeking to do business beyond the UK. It may be that you require only one additional currency for the EU market, and no more. Think!

Chapter 13

Your Web pages for public vieweing

Now, you have designed the home page and pages linked to it, the next stage is to put them on the Internet. To do so, you need to include Meta information in your document and upload pages to the HTTP server at your Internet Service Provider. Furthermore, to get some benefits from your hard work, time and financial investment, you must promote your Web pages. In order to keep it up-date, you must also maintain it on a regular basis.The prime aim of this chapter is to equip you with necessary information to achieve your objectives and run your Web site successfully.

. **Meta Information**

In order to make a computer understand your Web pages, you have to add some additional information. This additional information is known as Meta information. So, you have to implement <META> tag. The meta information is vitally important for the following reasons:

- It tells the visiting search engine that you wish to appear (become visible) when your site is listed;

- it highlights some of your keywords which identify your site and make your site visible to anyone searching for these keywords. Here, some keywords create a summary of your site's content. It is a short paragraph or just a few words to describe your site.

- This information is also used by the Internet directories, if you register your URL with them.

It is worth knowing that most search engines have **crawlers**. Their task is to go around the Web and search for new sites. When a crawler finds a new home page, it copies its title and keywords. For these reasons, it is highly desirable that you include well thought out meta information. Meta information is not shown in your pages when someone is viewing your document.

The Meta information is placed in the <HEAD> section of the HTML document.

• <u>Where do you add meta information in your HTML documents?</u>

The meta information is added by using the <META> tag in the <HEAD> section of an HTML page. The following examples are designed to illustrate the construction of the meta information and place the meta tag in the head section of a Web page.

• <u>Example 1</u>

<u>Coded meta information for example 1</u>

```
<HTML>
      <HEAD>
            <META http-equiv="description" content "We specialise in brain surgery at your
                  home anywhere in the UK.">

            < META http-equiv ="keywords" content =" brain surgery,  low-cost,
                  recovery within seven days guaranteed , brilliant brain promised">

      </HEAD>

        <BODY>

        -----
          </BODY>
</HTML>
```

<u>Illustration 1</u>

• <u>Explanation</u>

In this example, the **http-equiv** and **content** are attributes. These attributes enable you to add keywords to your documents. These keywords will be recognised by the visiting search engine. The search engine will then record them for your site on the Web. This way, your information is passed to a server who requested information by means of the search engine.

• <u>Example 2</u>

It may be that you change your page on a regular basis. For instance, you may have monthly new offers. In this case, you can add to your meta information an expiry date as shown below.

Coded meta information for example 2

```
<HTML>
        <HEAD>
                <META http-equiv ="EXPIRES" contents = " Mon 31 JUly 2000 00:00:GMT" >

        </HEAD>
```

Illustration 2

Not all search engines are keen on meta information, however, it is in your own interest to include it.

.Availability of your Web pages

Well done! You have designed your Web pages, tested them on your machine in the Internet Explorer or another browser successfully and also added meta information. You did all these things to put them on the Net in order to achieve your aims on the Web. Now, you should be asking yourself the following question:

.Can these pages work together as my Web site?

The simple answer is that if you have organised them in one folder, they will be available to a visitor. On the other hand, if you have placed them in different folders, they can still be available to visitors without any fuss whatsoever, providing you have stored files within these folders in the same structure of folders on the server.

It is in your own interest to make sure that your folder or folders do not contain any other unwanted files. **Why?** Well, you do not want other people to know your other files which may be stored at various stages of page development or may not even be associated with the development of your pages. Furthermore, they take up space for nothing. Just remove these unwanted files when finalising the content of the folder(s).

.Is there any recommended method for creating a structure of a Web site?

I cannot list any universally agreed and practised rules on this aspect. However, I can strongly emphasise the **'simplicity rule'** of organising files. In accordance with this rule, it is suggested that you devise a structure of your site which reflects the line of file linkage and flow of information stored within them as depicted below in sketch 1.

Documents/files structure for your Web site

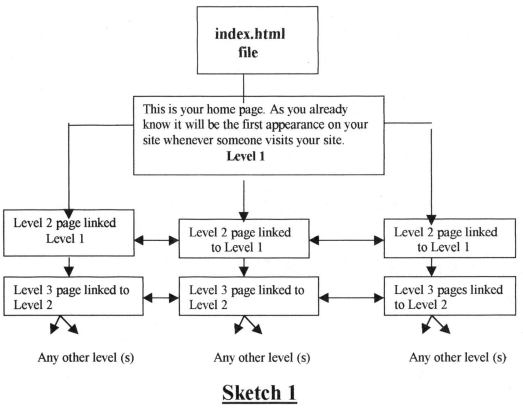

Sketch 1

The ↔ means sideways link.

It is better to keep it as simple as possible. This can be done, if you organise your site without the up and down links which are not shown in this sketch. If you have a few pages to link, then do so without building any sideways links. A small number of files, say 20-25, you can store in one folder and manage them without any difficulties. It is a good idea that you consult your ISP company for advice on this aspect and any other requirements, such as any information which they want you to add to your home page, or give the home page or its file by any other names. You should find out all about these matters prior to entering any binding contract with an ISP firm.

• Copying your pages to a Web server

Since you have developed your Web pages without using any text editor and any Web site management package such as FrontPage Microsoft package, you have to use FTP (File Transfer Protocol) to copy the pages yourself to your ISP's server or Web-serving computer. Indeed, this is an established method of transferring files across the Internet.

Your ISP firm should advise you on the precise method of how to achieve this objective without any serious problems arising during the transfer of files. You should also get from your ISP any passwords which are required for your use. It is highly likely that your SIP firm will include in their service package uploading of pages via FTP or some other software such as Microsoft FrontPage publishing wizard.

• Can I upload Web pages via the browser?

The answer is no. A browser can download a file using FTP. For uploading files to an HTTP server (ISP computer for simplicity) it is suggested to go for WS-FTP software. It is an excellent and low cost software. I suggest that before you invest any money, you should ask your ISP if they have it on their server for you to use it for copying your file onto their system. My guess is that it is most likely your ISP firm have this package for uploading files and have included its use in their service contract.

• Uploading by means of the WS-FTP

As you have developed your pages with Windows 95/98, the WS-FTP package is most suitable for uploading your pages to the HTTP server. It is comparatively low cost, but there is no need to buy it unless you need it on a regular basis. It manages file transfer smoothly. You can get it at:

http://www.ipswitch.com/

It has graphical interface, and thus it is easy to use. Before you try to get a copy of it, speak to your ISP firm as they must assist you with the upload as part of the service contract.

Without the correct and efficient uploading of your pages on to the server of your ISP, the Web site will not work as desired. It is therefore, once again emphasised, that you talk to your ISP before purchasing any software of any kind for this purpose. They must assist you in this matter without any additional cost to you.

• How and where can I announce my Web site ?

There are a large number of search engines on the Web where you can announce the creation of your own Web site. It is a good idea to let more than one serach engine have information about your site.

. On-line forms

Many search engines have **on-line forms**. You can on-line fill some of these forms in order to submit details of your Web site. Of course, it is rather important that your site appears in the most relevant categories.

. Meta tag

The other method for promoting your site is through the incorporation of **meta tag** into your Web pages. This is already outlined above. The following is a list of some sites where you can announce your new site:

. How to Announce Your New Web Site

This is a very useful service for advice at: **http://www.ep.com/fag/webannounce.html**

. Submit IT

There is a free service for you known as **Submit It** at: **http://www.submit-it.com**
They will submit your site to all major search engines. Try them without any hesitation!

. Web rings

There are many thousands of sites of common interest which are linked to each other to form Web rings. You can find more information about these Web rings and lists of sites of your interest at:

http:// www.webring.com

. Link Exchange

It is similar to Web rings. If you join it, you will be able to take part in advertising free of charge banner advertisements on each other's site. Contact them at: **http:// www. linkexchange.com**

. FreeLinks

It is a free web site promotion at: **http:// www.freelinks.com**

It has access to search engines, databases and directories where it can list your site free of charge.

. PostMaster

It is a well known service for which you must pay. It can list your site to about 350 search engines. You have to fill in the on-line form first. It is easy to follow. Contact them at:

http://www.netcreations.com/postmaster/

. Register It

They will register your site with some 400 search engines. They will help you with meta tags and marketing tips to get your web site noticed by your customers. You can contact them at:

http://www.register-it.com

Of course, you will pay for their service.

. Webpageregister.com

It is an American service for submitting your web site but they will charge you. They can submit your site to 1000 plus search engines for prices starting from $29. The good point is that they will submit your site to major search engines: AltaVista, AOL, HotBot, Planet Search and Yahoo!. It is a good idea to use their service. The most important search engine is Yahoo!. From this site you can order a program called **'Yahoo! submit'**. This program will keep resubmitting your site to Yahoo until is registered.

. How can I promote my business ?

. In order to learn about your competitors on-line, you can visit DejaNews at:
www.dejanews.com
Knowing about your competitors' strategies can help you to design your own strategy.

. Find out about **Content services** at AOL, CompuServe and Microsoft Network. They may prove benefical to your business. You have to pay for these services, but there is a free trial period. Take them on on this basis, and evaluate them from your business point of view, and decide accordingly.

. **aol at: http://www.alo.com/**
. **CompuServe at: http://compuserve.com/**

. You can explore the possibility of joining some **on-line mailing lists**. In Chapter 1, I have listed two important mailing list sites, namely List-Link and Liszt. In addition:

. Adland at: http://softfornet.com/adland/list.asp

If you are a small business, suffer from a lack of capital and are looking for some marketing opportunites, try this list. It has comparatively small subscribers, but it can be helpful for your marketing solutions. At least, you can discuss your concerns with them.

. Email Promote at: http://www.emailpromote.listbot.com
It is a free list. You can join it by E-mail. Send it to:

badkes@ sunline.net

There is no harm trying it free of charge to promote your business activities.

. Euro-Business at: http://www.cgtd.com/global/euro/euro.htm

If you wish to explore oportunites in Europe and are searching for some useful marketing information, try them. It is a useful source of information for those who are planning to expand business in Europe.

. GB Internet Marketing at: subscribe@digitalnation.co.uk

If you are UK based, it is a useful source of information. It deals with matters relating to the Internet marketing. In order to join them, just send them a blank E-mail.

. Home Based Business Marketing at:

HBBM-L-Request@InternetWantads.com

It is another useful source of information on marketing aspects for anyone running a business from home. To join them, send the E-mail message: SUBSCRIBE HBBM-L .

. Retailer New Digest at: http://RetailerNews.com./

It is for retail businesses. You may be one of them. If so, you can subscribe to it.

. Women-Talk-Business at:
http://listhost.net:81/guest/RemoteListSummary/WTB

It is open to all, but it is primarly for women. It deals with all aspects of business.

. There are business directories on-line. I list a few below for your information:

. BigYellow Pages at : http:// www.bigyellow.com/

It lists about 11 million businesses in the USA.It even allows you to add your own name and business to it. Since it has a FAQs (Frequently Asked Question) you may find it hepful.

. 192.com at: http://www.192.com/

It is the UK White pages for the UK. It is a very useful source of information. You can purchase on-line from them lists for your business. It has some 20 million residents of the UK who are not listed in the telephone directory. There is a wealth of information for you to tap into.

. ASKALEX at: http://askalex.co.uk/

It has some 1.8 million UK companies listed. It offers a tremendious source of information. A business can buy advertisement space, and personal advertisements are free of charge. It is so popular that about 10,000 searches per hour are made Find our more about it.

. Business Database at : http://www.ypbd.co.uk

It lists about 1.7 million UK based businesses. In fact, it is the business database from Yellow Pages. They claim to be the leader in this area. It costs to advertise for generating sales. It can work for you. Explore it with an open mind!

. Global Trade Center at: http://tradezone.com

If you are a manufacturer, importer or exporter, this site can be very helpful for your business. Besides other information, you can get free import and export trade leads. Not bad!

. Internet pages at : http://the-internet-pages.co.uk

Here, you can find businesses throughout the UK. It claims to cover all kinds of businesses.

. Japan yellow pages at: http:// www.yellowpage-jp.com/

If you are seeking business links with Japan, you can try this source of information.

. UKpages at:http://ukpages.co.uk/

It lists businesses in the UK and provides hot links to Web sites. You can register your Web site with them free of charge. They can list you in four different categories without any charge. So, go for it. For any information on UK try:

. Yahoo! at: http:// www.yahoo.co.uk/business_and_Economy/

They are the world leader in this area. The UK branch of this American company covers everything you want to know for your business. It is worth paying it visit. Millions of people use it everyday.

. Banner ads and 'pop ups'

These are small advertisements which appear on your screen automatically. You can consider buying banner advertising on sites that you consider can generate some business for you. In fact, there are sites where you can place a banner without any charge, providing you display their banner as well. I list some banner advertising sites below:

. Banner Exchange at: http://www.bannerexchange.com

Find out how you can enter into an exchange of banners on your site and some other sites. It is a free service.

. Banner Women at: http://www.bannerwomen.com/

As you can gather by its name, it focuses on women's sites. If you have any products for women, consider placing your banner ads on this site.

. Four Corners Effective Banners at:
http://www.whitepalm.com/fourcorners/
It is a free design service. So, go for it!

. Electronic Commerce

Contact the Electronic Commerce Association at: **http://www.eca.org.uk/**

You can get advice and help at this site, and benefit from their experience in this specialised field.

. Further suggestion

If you are a small business, you can get a great deal of advice concerning the Internet marketing, developing business connections and the like from the free service of the

Internet Small Business Consortium at: http:// isbc.com

Now, you have some practical sources of information on promoting your business on the Net. When you contact some of the sites, you will learn more about them and what to do to achieve your aims.

. Maintaining your Web site

Once your pages have been uploaded on the server of your ISP, some search systems will have registered your site and you can hope to get visitors. The next stage is to achieve your objectives on the Net.

All systems require some regular maintenance. From the feedback which you will receive from your visitors, you can lean a lot about your Web site. It may be that there are some areas which need to be considered again. It is expected that most readers of this book are either small business owners, managers or individuals who fall within the definition of students in this book, and thus their Web sites are small. Therefore, there is no need to buy any Web management tools. Such tools are rather costly and unnecessary for your present requirements. Web Management tools are for large sites.

Since you have designed your own Web site and you know it well, you should be able to learn more about it by experience and be able to maintain it to the desired level of efficiency. It is suggested that you in the simplest format that suits you keep the following information:

. visitors' negative comments on your Web site

. visitors' suggestions, if any, on your site and its contents

. technical problems such as links disappeared - check them on a regular basis.

. record number of visitors to your Web site. It is an important factor in the rating popularity of the Web contest.

It is highly likely that your ISP firm will include Hit counter, guest book , Perl script for logging visitors to your Web site and access to the server logs. If not, shop around until you find an ISP who include these facilities. These facilities can assist you in knowing which pages get the most hits and which are least popular. Furthermore, such information can help you decide if it is big enough for your requirements or not. You may soon require more space. Thus, a record of visitors is important for the evaluation of your Web site success.

If you have such a record, you should be able to take an appropriate action accordingly, when it is convenient. It does not mean that you leave problems unsolved for a long time as you have no time for solving Web site problems during your business hours. Since the Web site is part of your business, it is desirable that it receives regular attention to up-date it. Some problems, such as the links are missing in your pages will require prompt attention. It may be that one of your pages needs to be updated. If you leave it too late, it will not please your prospective clients/visitors.

On a regular basis, say, monthly, analyse objectively your record of the feedback received. It may be that you have to take some actions to remedy the situation. It will help your business if your site is always up-to-date in terms of its contents. If for some reasons, you decide to move your site to another ISP firm, make sure that you leave a referral page in place for some time. It is a good strategy.

Glossary

Address - the easiest way to describe as the electronic equivalent of a postal address.

ASCII (or Ascii) - acronym for American Standard Code for Information Interchange. It has been widely used since it was introduced in 1963. It has 128 different character values in the range 0-127.

ASCII text file - It does not have any special characters, such as **boldfaced** text.

Attributes - associated values which extends an HTML basic tag. For instance: TYPE ="text/css" is an attribute in the basic tag <STYLE>. It specifies that you are using HTML 4.0 version. eg.

<STYLE TYPE ="text/css">

Browse - It is an act of searching or looking at the screen when you are on the Internet.

Container - It is a component that can be used to contain another component in a graphical user interface. See Frames.

Domain (Domain name) - It is that part of the Internet address which identifies the computer where the address is located. It can be the computer of your ISP or your your chosen name followed by one of the domain names endings allocated to your country. For instance: sales@ MyName.co.uk
In this case, the required country code is .co.uk - the domain name ending.

Download - When you copy files from the network or any other computer on to your own computer it is known as download. When you are copying files this way, then you are down loading files on to your computer.

E-Commerce - Well, if you start selling your goods or services on-line, you will be involved in E-Commerce.

FAQ - It stands for Frequently Asked Questions. On the Net many service providers, such as *newsgroups* have this facility . It is usually on a particular topic.

File Format - The way in which information in a file is encoded is called file format. There are many file formats. See GIF file.

Frameset - It is a set of more than one frame. A frameset by itself contains no information. It requires content. The content of a frame is an HTML document. The browser window can be divided into a number of frames, each containing its own separate information. This is then a frame. A typical set of frames has an index frame, which has navigation links, the top, where you can have your company logo, or banner, and body frame for the text.

Freeware - Software packages can be obtained free of charge from the Internet or through some Internet magazines. See also Shareware.

Front page - this is the first page which appears on your site when someone visits it. See Home page.

FTP - You cannot upload files by means of the browser. Thus you have to do so by means of a program which uses the File Transfer Protocol. Also note that there are FTP sites which are also on the Net.

GIF file - This is an image file. For instance, ADRLogo.gif in which ADR company logo is stored. The file extension is **.gif**. GIF format is most commonly used for viewing images on the World Wide Web.

Graphical user interface - The components such as buttons, text fields and the like help the user to interact with the computer by using the mouse or the keyboard. For short GUI is often used.

Hits - It is a record of the number of visitors to your site. It is very useful for an evaluation of your site.

Home page - It is the index page (index.html file) of an individual or a business on the Internet. Here links to relevant pages are stored. It may also have links stored to some other related sites.

Host or host - It is a computer at the Internet Service Provider which is primarily for the purpose of offering a service to users commercially. If you are a big company, you can have your own host computer.

HotBOT - One of the popular search engines at: **htp:// www.hotbot.com**

HTML - Or html. Acronym for HypertextMarkup Language. In this language, you have learnt to develop your Web pages or document.

HTTP - Acronym for Hypertext Transfer Protocol. The application protocol with the speed necessary for distributing Web pages. It is the first thing you write when you describe a Web address. The format is **http://**

Internet - Broadly speaking, it is a network of computer networks across the world. see diagram in Chapter 1.

Internet Explorer - It is one of the World Wide Web browsers on the market. This book has used it (aol version 5) for viewing HTML document locally. This piece of software from Microsoft is good for this purpose.

Internet Service Provider (ISP) - A business enterprise specialising in providing internet access across the Web. Many ISPs provide a variety of other related services, such as developing a Web site for a client. In the UK, there is a trade organisation called Internet Services Providers in the UK. Some ISPs firms are members of this organisation. Contact them at: **http://www.ispa.org.uk**

ISDN - Integrated Services Digital Network. It is high a speed telephone network. It carries data between computers, much faster and safer than the ordinary telephone system. In the UK, for the high speed data transfer, BT offer two such services:

　　　　HomeHighway for home Internet users, and 　　**BusinessHighway** for businesses.

Links - (or hyperlinks) - a link is highlighted text or an image that can connect you to another site, or another page on the same site or on the same computer locally. Links appear in different colours in accordance with their status(eg. visited link...) and are underlined. Without links in your HTML documents, your documents would just be another display system and no internet communication would take place.

Lycos - A popular search engine at: **http// www.lycos.com**

Mailing List - A group of people with similar interests communicate with each other by E-mail through a central E-mail. There are a large number of such mailing lists across the Web. Surely, you will be able to find many such lists of interest to yourself. You can start your own mailing list. For instance, make a list of all your customers and send them information from your own computer system,. In this case, you are the owner of the list and you control it centrally (it is a traditional list).

Meta information /tag - This information is needed so that a visiting search engine can recognise your site. It does not appear in your pages when pages are viewed by visitors. It actually describes your site and is thus invisible to users.

Netscape - the company's two products namely Navigator and the recent product Communicator , are very popular browsers.

Newsgroups - There are many thousands of international discussion groups on the Internet. They form a special area on the Net and are sometimes known as **usenet**.

Nominet UK - it is the Registry for all **.uk** Internet Domain Names. It is equivalent to DVLA for driving licences. It maintains the database of **.uk** registered Internet names. It is not a governing body, but provides a public service for the **.uk**.

Pixel - A pixel is the smallest fine-grained mosaic which makes up the screen display. There are different sizes of monitors. The standard VGA display is 640x 480 pixels. If you invest freely, you can get a super VGA. It is 800 pixels wide by 600 pixels high.

PoP - It stands for point of presence. If your ISP firm does not PoP or the local-dial telephone number, your telephone bill can be pretty high. Therefore, prior to entering a legally binding contract find out about it first. You will find that larger ISPs have local numbers throughout the UK. It is better to look around for a better ISP.

Protocol - It is a legal agreement between parties that exchange information between computer systems. It governs the rules and procedures for data communication between two computers. The World Wide Web uses a number of protocols. HTTP is the most common. FTP is also used for transferring FTP type files.

Search engine - it is an indexing site. It tracks down useful interesting information from other sites. A visitor can search for sites that mention particular words. There are Meta search engines as well. They are so powerful that instead of using one search engine at a time, they can start a search by using a number of search engines simultaneously. You can get a list of meta search engines at:

http://www.yahoo.com/computers_and_internet/internet/world_wide_web/searching_the_web/all _in_one_search_pages

Shareware - Software packages or programs which you can load from the Internet or get them with a magazine, and where a small charge is required are called shareware.

Standard RGB Values - The standard colours are red, green and blue. All other colours are specified by giving the percentage of red, green and blue.

Tag - it is an HTML element. <P> for example is a basic paragraph tag. Within the tag, you can include some attributes. Most HTML tags are in pairs. The closing tag is written as </P>. It has a forward slash in front of the tag name. For instance: <HTML>.......</HTML> . You can use upper or lower case letters within the angle brackets.

TCP/IP - Transmission Control Protocol/Internet Protocol. It is a communication system which transfers information between computers

Text area - It is one of the user interface components in the GUI system. It allows you to enter more than one line of text. See Forms.

Text editor - HTML documents are prepared by using a text editor, such as **WordPad**. It is a kind of word processor.

Text Field - It is a user interface component. It can allow you to enter only one line of text.

Usenet - Seen **newsgroups**.

Upload - Your HTML pages are stored on your computer hard disc. These files must be transferred to your ISP server. Once they are on your ISP's server, they constitute your Web site. The server is regarded as at a higher level than your own computer. This is the reason for calling the transfer of your files to the server as upload. When you are copying your pages on to the server then you are uploading your files on to your ISP's computer system

URL - An abbreviation for Uniform(or universal)Resource Locator. It is the address system which is used to specify the location of a document in the WWW. For instance: **http://www.you.com**

Web page - it means a single page that appears on your screen when you are connected to a site.

Web rings - these are Web sites, mainly for consumers.

Web server - a computer which has a special software for holding Web pages and passing them to another Web server over the Internet, which in turn passes to the computer visiting the site where Web pages are stored. For instance, if you are searching using your PC, you have to communicate with the site where Web pages are kept via the Web server of your ISP firm.

Web site - A Web site consists of Web pages. It is just like this book, but on -line. A collection of whatever you wish to communicate to the world.

W W W - Interconnected networks of computer networks make up WWW. See Chapter 1.

Yahoo! - It is an internet directory and search engine. It is a very popular site in the world.

Some features of HTML 4. 0 implemented in this book

Markup tags

Tag	Meaning
<A>...</A>	Anchor tag for creating a link to another document or another location.
<ADDRESS>...</ADDRESS>	For including address in the document. It displays the address in in an **italic**.
<B>...</B>	It renders text in **bold**
<BASE>...</BASE>	Use to change the path/base of URL to the relative position of another page.
<BIG>...</BIG>	Displays character which is 2 points bigger than the normal size.
<BODY>...</BODY>	Within these tags is the body of the document. The body part contains the actual content of the document.
 	It breaks the line without stopping the flow of the text to the next line.
<BUTTON>...</BUTTON>	Creates an element called button. It is used in forms.
<CAPTION>...</CAPTION>	It is used in a table to create a caption.
<CENTER>...</CENTER>	It aligns the element in the centre of the browser window.
<CITE>...</CITE>	It is for citation and renders it in italic font.
<CODE>...</CODE>	HTML or programming code. Renders it in a fixed-width.
<COL>...</COL>	Sets a column in a table
<DD>...</DD>	For defining data for each list item.
<DT>...</DT>	for defining each list item.

Tag	Meaning
<EM>...</EM>	Text formatting. Renders text in **italic** with regular emphasis.
<FIELDSET>...</FIELDSET>	It is a form design tag. It makes a group of fields.
<FONT>...</FONT>	Use it to change the font size and style.
<FORM>...</FORM>	It creates form for data input by the user.
<FRAME>...</FRAME>	Frameset container. It identifies the file/URL location.
<FRAMESET>...</FRAMESET>	Its purpose is to close the frameset container.
<HEAD>...</HEAD>	It is one of the two parts of any HTML document. In this section, general information is given such as background colour.
<H1>...</H2>,<H2>...</H2>, <H3>...</H3>,<H4>...</H4> <H5>...</H5> ,<H6>...</H6>	Text headlines. Altogether six levels. Widely implemented in documents.
<HTML>...<HTML>	When HTML files first appeared on the Web, it was used to distinguish an HTML document from other types of documents. Tradition still goes on.
<I>...</I>	Text in *italic.*
<IMG>	It creates a link to an external image. So, the document will display an image.
<INPUT>...</INPUT>	It collects and saves the data entered by the user for further processing.
<LEGEND>...</LEGEND>	It is used for alignment with <FIELDSET> for a form.
<L1>...</L1>	It refers to a list item (it is L and I not L and one).
<LINK>...</.LINK>	It defines the relationship between pages on a site.
<META>	Information known as Meta information is passed to the HTTP or an external program on the server.

Tag	Meaning
`<OL>...</OL>`	Creates ordered list with `<LI>` for individual items.
`<OPTION>...</OPTION>`	Allows selection in a form with the `<SELECT>` tag. Use it with pull-down menus and scrollboxes for multiple choices.
`<P>...</P>`	Makes a paragraph. `</P>` not always needed.
`<SELECT>...</SELECT>`	For making a selection from multiple choices on a form.
`<SMALL>...</SMALL>`	It generates text which is 2 points smaller than the normal text. See `<BIG>` which is just the opposite.
`<STRONG>...</STRONG>`	Text formatting with strong emphasis on a bold font.
`<STYLE>...<STYLE>`	It defines the style sheet. It has been used over and over again in this book.
`<TABLE>...</TABLE>`	It marks the beginning and end of a table.
`<TD>...</TD>`	It is for data entry in a cell of a table. It creates columns as you enter data in a cell.
`<TEXTAREA>...</TEXTAREA>`	Creates a field in which text can be entered on a form
`<TFOOT>...</TFOOT>`	It creates the foot/bottom part of a table.
`<TH>...</TH>`	It is for setting table heading information.
`<THEAD>...</THEAD>`	It creates the header section of a table.
`<TITLE>....</TITLE>`	Every document must have a title. You need this tag for displaying the title of a page.
`<TR>...</TR>`	Marks the beginning and end of a row of a table.
`<U>...</U>`	It underlines the text within.
`<UL>...</UL>`	It creates an unordered list

Attributes

Attribute	Meaning
ACTION	Form handler. It is a pointer to the script/server.
ALIGN	Formatting of the table cells. Use it with <TH> and <TD>
ALINK	Use to select the colour of the active link.
ALT	It specifies the text which should be shown if the graphics image cannot be displayed.
BACKGROUND	Use to define the colour for the background of a page.
BGCOLOR	It sets the background colour of a page with the <BODY> tag.
BORDER	It sets border width. Use with <TABLE> to make an attractive box.
CELLPADDING	It sets the distance in pixels between the cell contents and borders. A feature of table design.
CELLSPACING	It sets the distance in Pixels between cells of a table.
CHECKED	Use with radio buttons and Checkboxes on a form. One can set the element as checked, but the user can change its status.
COLOR	Defines the colour in either name or a pair of hexadecimal numbers.
COLS	It is one of the two <FRAMESET> attributes. It sets the size/relative size of a column in a frame. It divides the window vertically.

Attribute	Meaning
COLSPAN	The number of cells a column spans is given as <TD COLSPAN =3>. It creates a cell which is three columns wide.
CONTENT	It is used with the <META....> tag. Under content, there should be some concise text to identify the aim or the nature of the site.
FRAME	Use to divide the browser window into different areas.
FRAMEBORDER	Use to set the frame border. It can be either visible or hidden. Choose which one is required at a time.
HEIGHT	Use to set or override the height of an element.
HERF	It signifies a hyperlink. It is used with the anchor tag.
LINK	It is used to set the colour of the link not yet visited.
MARGINWIDTH	It is used to control the margin of text or graphics image in a frame. Its value is given in pixels.
METHOD	It is used to submit the data given by the user on a form. It is used within the<FORM...> tag. Its value is POST in almost all case.
MULTIPLE	Use it if multiple selections are allowed on a form.
NAME	Use with the anchor tag. It signifies a particular marked place in a document.
NORESIZE	It implies that a frame cannot be resized. In fact, it is not so. You can.
ROWS	It divides the browser window horizontally. It is the opposite of COLS attribute used with frames.
ROW.SPAN	It is used to set the number of rows a cell spans in a table. It merges rows.

Attribute	Meaning
SCROLLING	It sets scrolling on or off. It is set within the <FRAME> tag.
SELECTED	It is pre-selected for the user in order to encourage the user to accept your selection. The user can still change it.
SIZE	Its purpose is to let you define the size of an element. You can use it with t<FONT>tag to set the size of font.
SPAN	It is used to make a group of some columns in a table.
SRC	It is used with <FRAME> tag in order to link external resources to the page.
START	It is useful when it is required to begin a list at a particular number in an ordered list
STYLE	It is used with <P> tag in order to set the style of the text within the paragraph.
TARGET	Use it within the <BASE> tag to name the frame where the hyperlink page will be sent.
TEXT	Use it on form to specify the type of user input as text and also to set its size. It is implemented within the <INPUT> tag of form design.
TYPE	It is used within <INPUT> tag for setting the text type.
VALIGN	It controls vertical alignment within a cell. See Tables.
VALUE	Use it to give a value to an element. For instance: <option value = man>Manchester as in form application.
VLINK	It is used with hyperlink in order to set the colour of a visited link.
WIDTH	Use it to set the width of margin in a frame application.

Editors & Validators

Since the foundation of this book is based on the idea of learning by experience, designing your own Web pages and testing them locally by using the Internet Explorer or the Netscape Navigator tools, I did not include any HTML editors in this book. There are a large number of editors and validation of HTML documents software packages on the Internet. Some are shareware. The list grows every day. There are a number of Document Type Definition **(DTD)** software packages available on the Internet which are designed to check that the HTML document is correct for a specified HTML standard. Since this book uses HTML 4.0 standard, the relevant DTD software for validating documents is HTML 4.0 standard (W3C). You have to include in your document **<!DOCTYPE>** tag which identifies this standard. The HTML syntax for this DTD is: <!DOCTYPE HTML PUBLIC"-//W3C//DTD HTML 4.0//EN">.

Your document can be rendered without this tag successfully. However, if you decide to use any of the many HTML validation services, in that case, you have to include this tag as the validation service needs this information. It should be noted that all validation packages are not free. Indeed, some of them are free for a limited number of documents to be validated. After that you must pay.

• Can you validate your site with some local tools ?

Definitely yes. You can get from the Yahoo site an HTML validation tool. **How ?** Go to Yahoo site at the following address in order to obtain a tool of your choice:
http://www.yahoo.com/Computers_and_Internet/Information_and_Documentation/
                Data_formats/HTML/Validation_and_checkers

In fact, Yahoo listed 77 such Web pages with their full URL for obtaining further information etc.

• CSE HTML Validator

This is a program which you can run on your computer on a Windows 95/98 systems. The current version Professional version -v4.05 can be downloaded from their site at: http://www.htmlvalidator.com/

The download takes 12 minutes and 4 seconds. It is 242 MB in size. You can evaluate 50 files free of charge. After this number, you must purchase it from their site. It is easy to use. Note that when you are trying to get used to it by running some files, it counts them as evaluated. So, the number 50 files evaluated can be soon reached. Be careful, you do not waste these numbers without benefiting from the free trial period.

• Microsoft's FrontPage

This is another popular page publishing software. In addition to the Web design software itself, it can enable the user to try out the Web site prior to its public viewing. It works in the same way as you have already uploaded to your ISP's Web server. It is possible that your ISP has installed it on their system. In this case, it can be made available for uploading your files on to your ISP system.

References

<u>Some members of the Internet Services Providers Association UK</u>

You can obtain a full list of their members from the press and public section of ISPAs Web site. It is a trade organisation, and its members must observe a laid down code of conduct. ISPA has a complaint Department to whom you can write if you face any difficulties concerning the services provided by any of its current members. I list below some of its members: -

Provider	Location	Category	Web site	E-mail
. ATLAS Internet Ltd	London	Medium	www.atlas.co.uk	info@atlas.co.uk
. BT PLC	London	Corporate	www.btinternet.com	sales@ btinternet.com
. Cable and Wireless	London	Corporate	www.cwcom.net	sales@ mcmail.com
. Cerbernet	London	Small	www.cerbernet.co.uk	sales@cerbernet.co.uk
. Global Internet	London	Large	www.global.net.uk	info@global.net.uk
. INERNET UK	warwickshire	Small	www.internet.uk.net	saels @internet.uk.net
. Kewill ElectricMail Ltd	Cambridge	Medium	www.elmail.c.uk	sales@elmail.co.uk
. Level 3 Communications, Inc	London	Large	www.level3.com	Maria.Farnon@level3.co
. LineOne	London	Large	www.lineone.net	
. PLANET OnLINE Ltd	Leeds	Large	www.theplanet.net	sales @theplanet.co.uk
. Power Internet Ltd	Milton Keynes	Medium	www.powernet.co.uk	sales@powernet.co.uk
. Telinco PLC	Cheshire	Large	www.telinco.net	sales@telinco.net

For an upto-date current list, contact ISPA at: 020 7233 7234 Web site: http://www.ispa.org.uk

E

E-commerce 4, 246,264
Editors 275
Electronic Commerce 262
Embedded style sheets
90,92,98,100
Email addresses 10
Email Promote 260
Euro-Business 260

F

FAQ (see Frequently
Asked Questions)
19,261,264
Feedback from forms 231
Field grouping 241
Fieldset 229,243
File 175 (address)
File format 264
Font tag 58
Font colour tag 85
Font properties 105
Font sizes 58
Footer 134, 138
Form tag 226
Four Corners
Effective Banners 262
Frameborder 196
Framebordercolor 196
Frames 180
Frameset 181,265
FreeLinks 258
Freeware 14,265
Frequently Asked
Questions (see FAQ)
Front Page 265
FrontPage 275
FTP (File Transfer
Protocol) 4,17,175,257

G

GB Internet Marketing
260
GIF file 149,207,265
Global Trade Centre 261
Glossary list 62, 77
Gopher 17,175,176
Gopher root directory,178
Graphical user interface
(GUI) 265
Graphical Web browser 12
Guest book/Guestbook
263

H

Headline tags 33
hex pairs 82
 hexadecimal 82
Hit counter 263
Hits 265
HTML - Hypertext
Markup Language
12,16,20,265
Home Based Business
Marketing 260
Home page 147,154,156
Host 265
HotBot 17,265
HREF tag 150
HTML standard 4
16
hyperlinks see Links
Http (HTTP)
13,16,17,175,266
Http servers 257
https 175

I

IMG 197
In-line style sheet 103
Input tag 227
Internet 3,11,266
Internet Explorer (IE)
14,15,19,29,39,266
Internet Assigned Agency
5
Internet Engineering Task
Force 5
Internet Pages 261
Internet Protocol (IP)7,8
16
Internet Small Business
262
Internet Society (The) 5
Ipswitch Web site 257
ISDN 7,8, 266
ISPA 6,276
ISPs -Internet Service
Providers 5,6,7,9,10,15,
263

J

JapanYellow pages 261
JPG (or HPEG) 149
Javasoft 175

K-L

LAN (Local Area
Network) 1,2